## Socialist Enterprise

In Britain we live in an upside-down economy, in which our needs are sacrificed every day to the "needs" of the economic system itself. But for years the system has failed to deliver, and the Thatcher experiment has made the crisis much, much worse. We now face the prospect of a "third world Britain" before the end of the century unless something is done to halt the slide.

*Socialist Enterprise* plots a bold alternative course for the economy, building on the experiences of trade union and labour movements over the last decade. Escape from economic catastrophe, the authors argue, will require more than just changes in the way the economy is managed from the top. There must also be a fundamental redistribution of economic power in our society — not only between employers and workers, but in favour of all those whose needs the economic system ought to meet.

In the past, socialists have been accused of concentrating on policies for the distribution of wealth, rather than on its production. This book shows that socialists do have detailed, practical policies for producing our way out of the economic crisis — solutions based not on "the logic" of market forces, but on giving the economy back to the people.

# SOCIALIST ENTERPRISE

## RECLAIMING THE ECONOMY

by
Diana Gilhespy
Ken Jones
Tony Manwaring
Henry Neuburger
Adam Sharples

Foreword by Larry Whitty

New*Socialist*/SPOKESMAN

Nottingham : Atlantic Highlands

First published in 1986 by:
Spokesman
Bertrand Russell House
Gamble Street
Nottingham, England
Tel. 0602 708318

and 171 First Avenue, Atlantic Highlands,
New Jersey 07716, USA

ISBN 0-85124-460-2 Hardcase
ISBN 0-85124-470-X Paperback

Typeset, printed and bound by the Russell Press Ltd,
Nottingham (Tel. 0602 784505)

Cover design: Phil Bicker and Stephen Pope
Photograph: Mick Smee

# CONTENTS

# FOREWORD

## Larry Whitty

The credibility of Labour's economic and industrial policies will be a major factor in determining whether Labour wins power; and the success of those policies will be vital in ensuring that we maintain power. Labour will require more than one term in office if we are to fully overcome the underlying causes of Britain's long-term decline.

There is, therefore, an urgent need to develop an economic strategy for the next decade. One which, in giving effect to our commitment to create over one million jobs in two years, recognises the emerging economic and political constraints we face. One which begins as we mean to go on, laying the basis for sustained recovery by ensuring that the long-term needs of the British people guide major decisions in our economy.

Much will be achieved by reversing the immediate impact of Conservative economic mismanagement. But this will not be enough on its own, so steep is our decline as an industrial nation. Expansion, led by public investment in services and capital projects, must be matched by policies for modernising our industries.

Industrial recovery will require more than public finance. Past experience underlines the futility of throwing money at the problems of decline without ensuring that it is effectively used. The growing significance of non-price competitiveness, and of technological innovation in the product and production process alike, demand that strategies are developed for key industries and services which are then carried through in the decisions of major enterprises. This is made all the more urgent as British firms are sold off and run down such that "British industry" now barely exists. An industrial strategy which ignores where economic power lies cannot hope to succeed.

As the authors of this book argue, Labour must lay the basis for a socialist capacity for enterprise. For too long, socialism has been seen as having little to say on how wealth can be created — only how it can be distributed. Yet socialism is rooted in an analysis of production and its impact on society. *Socialist Enterprise* is to be welcomed for affirming and updating that tradition.

# PREFACE

Our aim in this book is to set out a socialist strategy for economic and industrial recovery in Britain. In so doing we build on arguments developed in a previous book, the *Alternative Economic Strategy*, which shared many of the same authors.

*Socialist Enterprise* reflects our concern that the Alternative Economy Strategy (AES) has been least developed in the areas of planning and industrial democracy, and that in the past it has focused to too great an extent on a demand management approach to economic expansion. This is something of an historical accident: it is only the deflationary policies of governments in recent times — not only in Britain but also in many other industrial countries — which has led advocates of the AES to emphasise demand side policies in this way. There can be no doubt that demand policies have been the dominant *short-term* factor in the economic performance of Britain and other major countries, and we reject the new school of right wing economic thinking which treats "supply side" factors as all-important. Equally, socialists have always recognised that if society is to be fundamentally changed, this will require changes in the area of production: a socialist economic strategy will only succeed if it tackles long-term, as well as short-term, problems of under performance. We try in this book, therefore, to develop closely integrated policies for expansion and industrial recovery.

The themes of this book also reflect other growing, and in many ways more far-reaching, concerns. Perhaps the most important is the question of how 'the economy' should be defined. Traditionally, we think of the economy in terms of paid work, and in particular paid manual work carried out in large manufacturing plants. But this definition inevitably excludes the specific needs of women, whose responsibility for caring for children and other dependants must be taken into account in policies for paid work. This narrow definition of the economy also excludes issues concerning the environment and the quality of life, both at work and outside it. Finally, it has meant that the importance of the internal organisation of the state has been largely ignored: yet for many people, the economic policies with the greatest impact on their lives are those determining the efficiency and responsiveness of services provided by national and local government. For all these reasons, a broader view of the economy is needed — one which touches on all aspects of people's lives, in the three sectors of industry, the state and the *unpaid* sector. We try to reflect this in what follows. But the strategy we put forward reflects, above all, our conviction that industrial recovery and social advance will only be possible on the basis of an extension of *democracy* in all spheres of society. In seeking to reclaim the economy for people's needs, socialism and democracy must be inextricably linked.

We would like to pay special thanks to Eileen Davenport and Peter Totterdill for their help in drafting the case study on textiles and clothing; Judy Wajcman, for her contributions to the section on workers co-ops; John Mawson, for making available his extensive research into the initiatives of Labour local authorities; David Elliot, for his insights into the problems of tripartism; Mike Lloyd for his comments on nationalised industries; John Carr, for his insights into contract compliance; Titus Alexander, for his help in drafting the discussion on popular planning; and Roy Green and Sandy Hunt for their comments on various sections. However, responsibility for the final form of the book is ours alone.

Finally, we are indebted to Michelle Beard, Amanda Bebber, Kim Blackman, Janet Edwards, Ursula Keaney and Arlene Ryan who typed the manuscript; and to Ken Fleet and Tony Simpson of *Spokesman* for their support.

**Diana Gilhespy**
**Ken Jones**
**Tony Manwaring**
**Henry Neuburger**
**Adam Sharples**

**September 1986, London**

**CHAPTER 1**

# Introduction

At times we could be forgiven for thinking that Britain's economic problems are incurable. After all, the search for cures has been going on for decades — and yet we are still plagued by mass unemployment, industrial decline and social deprivation. Indeed these problems have been getting much worse, not better, in recent years.

In what follows, it is argued that there *is* a way of halting and reversing Britain's slide into Third World status. But much more is required than changes in economic policy alone. The underlying theme of this book is that there will never be a sustained economic recovery in Britain unless we first achieve a fundamental *redistribution of power* over the way economic decisions are made — and that new forms of democratic, socialist enterprise hold out the best hope for the future.

This theme will be illustrated in many different ways. For example, the development of our economy has been frustrated in the past by the excessive power of multinational and monopoly firms, and of short-term financial interests concentrated in the City of London. *Within industry*, meanwhile, there has never been a democratic sharing of power between management and workers, with the result that much needed modernisation has consistently been neglected. Nor has the power of government ever been mobilised in support of a *long-term strategy* for economic growth: indeed in recent times it has actually been used to make a planned approach to tackling our problems more difficult.

Our argument, in summary, is that none of those who have actually had the power to influence our economy have ever had the will or the ability to use it in the interests of the British people as a whole. In our upside down society, people's needs are constantly sacrificed to what we are told are the needs of the economic system itself.

As socialists we believe that these established centres of power over our economy must be challenged and displaced. We see this as being desirable in its own right, as part of a wider process of making our society more democratic. *But we also believe that it holds the key to economic revival.* Many of the failings of the British economy could be overcome through greater democratic control of economic organisation. The problem at the moment is that it is not our economy — even though it may be our work that sustains it. We believe that greater democracy, so far from being incompatible with economic recovery, is a vital precondition for it. As we shall seek to show, there are many different ways of increasing democracy in the economy: we need to look beyond the traditional reliance on action by the national state, and give a much bigger role to other measures, such as extended collective bargaining by trade unions and greater powers for local communities.

We must also make it clear from the outset that we are not simply seeking an economic revival in the conventional sense of more jobs and greater personal wealth. We believe that a genuinely fairer distribution of economic power in our society would also go hand in hand with a far-reaching redefinition of economic need. It would include, for example, the need for a healthy environment and for greater control over the type and design of goods and services. It also includes the need for a redistribution of power, income and wealth between sexes, races and regions. The extension of democracy must not be confined in the conventional way to 'industry', but is just as vital in other areas, such as in the public services and in the home. Local communities will not be able to shape their own futures, women will not enjoy equality with men, and consumers will not influence the quality or design of products and services, unless they have the power to influence key economic decisions.

### The nature of economic power

At first sight it may seem that we are simply stating the obvious — that a nation's economic performance is a reflection of good or bad economic decisions. It is certainly not unusual for the whole of Britain's economic ills to be laid at the door of a single institution or group of people, whose negligence is alleged to have brought us to our present condition. Favoured examples in recent decades have included incompetent managers, lazy workers, feckless (or alternatively, work-grabbing) immigrants, negligent governments and, perhaps most frequently of all, malicious trade union leaders.

Our own thesis, however, is rather different. Part of what we are saying is that those who have had a degree of influence over the economy have been either unable or unwilling, for one reason or another, to use it constructively. But we are also saying that, as things stand, no single institution or group has the power to promote an effective long-term plan for the British economy. What we propose is political and social change, leading to the enfranchisement of all those whose needs the economy should be meeting. Combined with this, we believe that a collective approach at all levels will prove to be a necessary part of the solution to our economic problems. We advocate, in short, policies of *socialist enterprise* as the way out of Britain's economic impasse.

It may be worth expanding on what we mean by 'economic power'. One theory says that, in a market economy such as ours, power rests with the consumer. The consumer takes decisions about whether to buy particular goods and services ; if the price is too high or perhaps the quality too low, and if a better alternative is available, there is always the right to choose. The 'signals' sent back by the consumer's decisions then determine what is produced and at what price. Because the consumer is assumed to be in the best position to judge what is in his or her own interests, the whole economy under such a system is in turn taken to be directed towards the maximum satisfaction of needs. The advocates of the market economy also claim for it a further advantage, namely that economic power is effectively diffused among millions of individual consumers : the chances of socialist interference in the economic and social system are diminished accordingly. Political liberty and economic liberalism, it is said, are mutually reinforcing.

We believe that this is not a realistic picture of where economic power lies in our society. Even at the simplest level, it is clear that the *power* to consume depends on an individual's income or wealth. The poor exercise less economic power than the rich. Exactly who is poor, and who is rich, is principally a question of power over economic resources. But this is not an academic question. On the contrary, it raises the most fundamental of all social and political issues. Under the market economy theory, such issues are ignored.

The theory also has the convenient advantage, from the point of view of those who actually wield economic power, that the true nature and source of this power is obscured. If your plant closes because of some identifiable decision, such as the withdrawal of a government subsidy, you know whom to blame and how to start fighting it. If your pay is limited by a government-imposed ceiling, that too creates the conditions for political opposition. But if your job or your pay are suddenly threatened by a loss of export orders following a rise in the value of sterling, the enemy is invisible. In these circumstances an attack on the economically weakest classes or groups can always be presented as being a matter of natural necessity — the logical outcome of the workings of market forces.

The concept of the all-powerful consumer turns out to be a very abstract one in practice. It does not refer to any individual consumer; your decisions or mine, taken in isolation, count for nothing in the market. 'Consumer preference' is merely the incidental outcome of millions of unco-ordinated decisions. It is also intrinsically limited. It amounts to either the negative decision not to buy, or else the decision simply to endorse what somebody else has already decided to design and produce. And both types of decision are exercised within the narrow range of goods and services which happen to have been made available.

A moment's reflection is enough to realise, therefore, that most of the key decisions in our economy are not taken by consumers at all — either individually or in the aggregate. The really important decisions are taken by large companies and financial institutions — for example, decisions about what to produce, where to produce it, and where to invest. Yet there is very little, if any, democratic control over these organisations and no way of ensuring that their decisions reflect the best interests of the community. Even elected governments, which take important decisions about taxes and spending, do so largely behind a wall of official secrecy designed to limit genuinely open and democratic debate.

It is these centres of power on which we shall be concentrating particular attention in this book. In historical terms, we believe that the almost unique combination of influences on the British economy goes most of the way to explaining its relatively bad performance since at least 1951. For the future, we believe that a socialist economy and a socialist society require that these powerful influences be curtailed and if possible harnessed behind an overall plan for recovery.

An integral part of redistributing economic power must also be certain changes in basic economic goals and priorities. Much greater importance needs to be attached to activities, for example care for dependants, which at present are not recognised as being economically valuable, in part because they are not paid for and do not appear to form part of the 'market' economy. Many of the goods and services provided in this way — usually by women — are vital to human existence, but are officially not regarded as economic activities at all. The only time this work seems to be given any value is when for some reason it is not done, in which event a 'social problem' invariably arises, suddenly involving economic costs. Of course at the root of all this is another issue to do with economic power — this time the economic power of men as against women. As socialists we believe in a much fairer redistribution of this power — bringing with it not only greater social justice but also a better use of the human resources available to our economy.

## Economic power in Britain

In Chapter 2 we take a detailed look at the structure of the British economy today, and try to identify how power is distributed within it. This analysis suggests that no single institution or group has the solution to Britain's economic problems in its hands. Here we shall give an outline picture only, using one or two examples.

Corporate strategy in this country has been shaped to an extraordinary extent by the dominant position of the City — itself an historical legacy from the time when we were the world's leading industrial nation, with a vast income from imperial investments and trade. To this day the decisions of the major financial institutions in the City routinely fail to match the needs of industry in the UK, as opposed to following short-term profits, wherever and however they can be made. Finance has not been made available to industry on the right terms and conditions. Financial institutions often lack the expertise to evaluate proposals for industrial investment — as opposed, for example, to investment in property or shares — and have insisted that loans be short-term. Established companies with large assets have been favoured compared to smaller companies in newer industries.

The nature of the Stock Market has also made it easier for companies to grow by taking over other companies, rather than through direct industrial investment. They are able to print their own money — company shares — in order to finance these acquisitions. But corporate expansion through merger has very little to do with meeting the basic industrial needs of the economy. In the merger boom of the 1960's, stimulated to a large degree by the government's Industrial Reorganization Corporation, three-quarters of mergers were horizontal across different industries, leading to the creation of unwieldy conglomerates rather than industrial rationalisation. As a result the task of raising the efficiency of industry was further neglected, and in particular we now have a situation where, despite the high degree of industrial concentration in the UK, the average size of plants is smaller than that of our competitors, and still falling. There is little indication that the merger boom of the mid-1980's will turn out to have been any more beneficial to the long-term interests of the economy.

The power of the City is a particularly interesting illustration of our central thesis. There is no reason to suppose that the decisions taken inside the City have ever been irrational, at any rate in the strict sense of not being motivated by the desire to make profits. What is questionable, however, is whether the disproportionate influence of finance capital, and its isolation from industrial capital, are healthy from the point of view of the national economic interest. This excessive concentration of power is a major reason why economic 'revivals' in this country so often seem to find their main expression in either a property boom, a period of merger mania, or a flood of investment capital overseas.

The balance of power inside British industry, between management and unions, presents another interesting case. It is our view that, until the early 1980's, the British working class was able to establish a defensive position of considerable strength in its conflict with employers. The result was a stalemate which worked consistently against the interests of national economic development, although of course the precise degree of influence is impossible to assess with any accuracy. The stalemate could have been broken in any one of a number of different ways. Managers could have recognised the fact of strong trade union organisation, and set about harnessing it behind shared goals. But for most of the post-war period, and with very few exceptions, the employing classes pursued a policy of containment rather than co-operation. Discouraged by trade union power, they avoided the risks of conflict which are always thrown up by economic change, and failed to direct new investment towards expanding capacity or modernising production techniques.

Trade unions exercised a power during this period which they were only rarely given an opportunity, either at corporate or national level, to exercise constructively. And when they were, their inability to influence major decisions left them unable to resolve the conflicts in which they became enmeshed. One result, paradoxically, is that the trade union movement has been made one of the chief scapegoats for the country's economic failure. A brutal attack on it now forms the centrepiece of the Thatcherite experiment. In a curious sense we share the Thatcherite analysis, which attaches such a high degree of importance to resolving the stalemate between the two sides of industry. We differ radically, however, in our suggested solution. As socialists we believe that social progress requires that *greater*, not less, recognition should be afforded to the aspirations of the organised working class. We also hold that this is a vital precondition for any genuine, sustainable economic recovery.

These examples should be enough to indicate that Britain's industrial decline cannot be explained in purely abstract terms — we also have to look closely at the actual structure of economic power, and at the way in which economic decisions are taken. In Britain, the role of a handful of major companies has been crucial — less than 200 of them account for three-quarters of UK exports, and corporate strategy has responded to the particular opportunities and constraints of the UK economy.

The structure of market opportunities facing British firms has tended to discourage investment in innovation-based industries in which rapid product development is vital for competitive success. In the 1930's British industry was dominated by coal, textiles and metal-based activities: rather than respond to the new markets in chemicals and engineering, British firms were able to retreat to safe, Empire markets (the legacy of which is reflected in UK multinationals' production discussed in Chapter 2). The nature of the domestic market, meanwhile, offered a further disincentive to industrial change. The volumes needed to justify new investment could not be achieved. On the one hand, inequalities in income meant that in motor cycles, for example, the greatest demand was for craft bikes. On the other hand, for example in shipbuilding, the fragmented industrial structure led to a supplying industry made up of 'jobbing shipyards' able to meet the occasional needs of small shipowning families but unable to make the transition to large capacity supertankers.

To this history must be added some of the factors described above — the overseas orientation of the City, the encouragement given by the Stock Market to growth through merger, and the balance of class power in industry. As a result British firms have failed to develop the *strategic* response necessary to provide the market volume, finance and production organisation which are preconditions for sustained innovation and growth. Nor has government policy — Labour or Conservative — addressed the fundamental factors which condition corporate behaviour: the concern with overall demand and indicative planning has, by and large, left corporate strategy untouched. The contrast with Germany and Japan, for example, could not be more marked: government there has intervened directly in industrial reorganisation, and the links between industrial and finance capital have been far stronger.

## The Thatcherite experiment

At the core of the Thatcherite programme has been an economic experiment explicitly designed to reverse decades of decline. This experiment is a complex phenomenon, but it can usefully be summarised as an attempt to restore the discipline of market forces to the British economy. This can be illustrated in many different ways.

Perhaps the most dramatic demonstration has been in the labour market, where there has been a concerted attempt to ensure that wages are determined purely by the supply of, and demand for, labour. This has involved deliberately forcing unemployment to record levels; workers' fear of losing their jobs, and the willingness of the unemployed to take jobs at lower wages, have undermined the ability of trade unions to organise collectively in support of improvements in wages or conditions. At the same time, unemployment benefit has been cut in order to put even greater pressure on unemployed people to find work. And of course there has been a wholesale attack on trade unions themselves, with a battery of legal restrictions on the ability to take effective industrial action. Finally, fair wages legislation has been decisively weakened, to remove vital protections for the low paid, so that the market-determined rate of wages is not prevented from falling to its 'correct' economic level.

Government policy has been directed towards strengthening market forces in many other areas. Subsidies to industry and the regions have been slashed on the grounds that they weaken the competitive pressures of the market and perpetuate an 'artificial' state of affairs — only outcomes produced by the untrammelled operation of the market are regarded as 'real' or worthy of being sustained in the long run. Nationalised industries, including many such as transport which have a major social as well as economic role to play, have been forced to operate on a strictly commercial basis. In other cases whole businesses have been auctioned off to private sector buyers, apparently on the basis that private ownership *necessarily* means greater efficiency — even in cases such as British Telecom where the mechanism normally supposed to bring this about (competition) is almost completely absent. Finally, local authorities have been compelled to offer public services to private firms on a tender basis — acceptance of the lowest bid being assumed to be in the best interests of the local community.

In terms of national economic policy, the same philosophy can be seen at work. The underlying principle appears to be that all government activity is undesirable, except for the most rudimentary functions such as safeguarding the value of the currency. The ultimate objective is an economy in which the government spends nothing except the inescapable minimum, for example defence spending to ensure national security, and raises no more in revenue than is absolutely necessary to finance it. Spending and tax-raising beyond these levels are not merely an unwarranted extension of the role of the state, but are both positively harmful to the country's optimum economic performance. This appears to hold in the long run almost regardless of the level of fiscal deflation, interest rates or exchange rate which may be required to sustain it. We saw this most vividly during the first, and purest, phase of the experiment between 1979 and 1981, when national income dropped by 4 per cent and manufacturing output by 14 per cent.

Britain is by no means unique in recent years in having suffered a government driven by a free market view of how the world works. But few other governments have carried the experiment so far, or conducted it with such open class hatred or blindness to the human consequences. Whether Britain is the most suitable patient for such an experiment is another question. As we have already suggested, Britain is unusual in the extent to which the forces operating on its economy are not naturally directed towards the overall good. Unleashing pure market forces upon it has therefore had a number of disastrous, but in our view largely predictable, results. The main one has been that those who started by being the most economically powerful groups have on the whole prospered and expanded their influence still further, while those who are weakest in economic terms have paid a sometimes dreadful price. Contrary to the predictions of the theory, the national economic and social interest has been gravely damaged.

Thatcherism has, in particular, supported and accelerated the long term shift in power from industrial capital to finance capital. It is now the City, more than any other focus of power, which rules Britain. The City passes final judgement on the economic policies of the government, and the government must strive at all times to maintain the City's 'confidence' that the regime is sufficiently monetarist, that public spending is being controlled sufficiently tightly, and that deflationary pressures are not about to be relaxed. It is the City which provides the finance for everything from the government's massive privatisation programme to cosmetic schemes for inner city regeneration. In return for this massive accretion of power, the City has given nothing — no shift whatsover in its own priorities, which in any case the Thatcher Government has never even sought. The result for Britain has been disaster — a vast transfer of investment

capital overseas and a self-indulgent wave of corporate mergers
— but no serious attempt to apply the vast resources at the City's
command to the pressing needs, short and long term, of the UK
economy.

### Third world Britain?

Under the Thatcher experiment, Britain's underlying economic
decline has continued and gathered pace. Only North Sea oil
revenues now disguise its true extent. Without them it would be
impossible to sustain the living standards which the working
population currently enjoys. Britain's present levels of
employment, industrial activity and public services are all being
paid for on borrowed time.

It is worth emphasising how disastrous Tory economic policies
have been for Britain in purely *economic* terms. The Tory Party has
never succeeded in cultivating an image of compassion or
concern for social justice: but at least, so the convention goes, it
can be relied on to promote 'sound' economic policies and
generally do the things that are in the interests of business
growth. The Labour Party, by contrast, seems to have acquired a
reputation for economic mismanagement. The really remarkable
achievement of the Thatcher Governments has been to find a set
of policies which, while designed to make 'economic efficiency'
the overriding objective in almost every sphere of our lives, has
actually had the effect of making our economy *less efficient* — as
well as having all the more predictable results such as a huge
increase in social deprivation, inequality, injustice and division.
As a result we are now in a situation where socialist economic and
industrial policies offer the only serious hope not only of healing
deep social divisions but also of reconstructing a viable and
efficient economy.

Employment levels in manufacturing, construction and the
public services plummeted after 1979. The international
economic climate worsened, it is true, following the oil price rises
of that year. All the major Western countries have faced increased
unemployment during this period. But in Britain's case,
government policies have played an almost uniquely important
part in *creating* a fall in national output and an increase in
unemployment. By pursuing exceptionally high interest rates as
part of the attempt to reduce money supply growth and inflation,
and then letting the market determine the level of the exchange
rate, the Tory Government precipitated a massive crisis in the
manufacturing sector in the period 1979-1981 — especially among
companies which were relatively dependent on export markets
or which had recently expanded investment or stocks in

anticipation of sales growth. Meanwhile attempts to reduce public spending and borrowing resulted in a further deflationary effect: there was a particularly severe impact on employment as capital projects and welfare services were sacrificed to pay for the escalating costs of increasing unemployment — not merely a vicious circle but an insane one.

If we look at another traditional measure of economic success or failure, the balance of payments, we see a similar story. Since 1982, a surplus on manufactured goods has been replaced by large annual deficits — the first such deficits since the Industrial Revolution. Imports and import penetration have risen sharply in virtually every sector of manufacturing. These imports have, of course, been paid for out of oil revenues. But declining oil revenues will no longer be able to offset the growing manufacturing trade deficit in the late 1980's and 1990's.

The price of British goods is of course only one factor in their competitiveness. At least equally significant is their design, quality and reliability, whether they are delivered on time, and the after-sales service — their 'non-price' competitiveness. All the serious evidence suggests that in these areas British goods have become, and will go on becoming, less competitive. We are not adopting the latest innovations in product design and production processes as quickly or extensively as our competitors. Investment fell catastrophically after 1979: indeed, between 1979 and 1982 investment in British manufacturing was insufficient to make up for the normal wear and tear of existing plant and machinery. Half of Britain's factories do not use microelectronics in their production processes, and have no plans to do so in the future.

Lack of investment is only one factor in all this. How effectively investment is used is just as important. Britain has simply failed to apply developments in science and technology to economic production, to train its workforce in the skills of the future, or to organise production efficiently. In this context, the Thatcherite obsession with trade union controls is at best directed towards an irrelevance, and at worst leads to policies which deepen the underlying crisis.

*Research and development (R&D)* policy is crucial. There is no shortage of new ideas and inventions in this country. Over half of the post-war world's most significant inventions have come from Britain — an extraordinary record which by now ought to have made us one of the most wealthy economies in the developed world. But Britain spends less on industrial R&D, and more on defence R&D, than almost all its major competitors. Tory Government policies have made this situation even worse, with cuts in funds for the Research Councils and in specific industrial innovation schemes. Nor have government cuts been made up by increased spending by private companies. Two-fifths of British companies have no strategy for innovation and the use of new technology. Large British firms have followed the government and actually cut their research and development budgets during the recession.

Companies cannot take advantage of new investment because Britain has one of the most *poorly trained* workforces in the developed world. The percentage of the British workforce with recognised qualifications is no more than half that in the USA, Japan and West Germany. But since 1979 Britain has been busily cutting back spending on higher education (with 'technological' universities and polytechnics suffering particularly badly); abolishing Industrial Training Boards; and letting unprecedented numbers of young school-leavers and graduates vegetate in the dole queues. One result of this, for example, is that Britain's engineering industries are now taking on only half the 13,000 apprentices a year that they actually need.

The quality of our *industrial management* is also vital. Japan's success derives in large measure from the way it organises its production processes. This does not simply mean making people work harder. For example, major improvements in costs can be achieved by making sure that parts arrive on time and that stocks are kept at the minimum necessary level. At least £4,000 million would be freed from Britain's stock and work in progress for reinvestment if stock management were as good as in the USA or West Germany, according to one estimate. But almost three-quarters of British engineering concerns do not even have access to a computer.

**Britain's technological weakness**
For the foreseeable future, economic success — indeed economic survival — will depend on keeping in the forefront of developments in the new technologies. But our ability to do this will depend, in turn, on our willingness to confront a number of important questions about economic *power*. Britain will not benefit from the new technologies if the course of events is left to be dictated by foreign multinationals and the City, in the name of 'market forces'. It is therefore particularly instructive to examine briefly the record of the Tory Government in this area.

Ironically enough, the Tories have put much effort into projecting themselves as the Party of new technology and modernisation. There seems to be a genuinely held belief that the latest techniques will be introduced much more quickly and extensively in a climate of unconstrained market forces, free of all government interference. But the reality is disturbingly different.

A 'technological gap' is opening up between Britain and Europe, and — even more alarming — between Europe on the one hand and the USA and Japan on the other. Britain's annual trade deficit in information technology products can be measured in billions of pounds. And the European Community has also begun to record large deficits. US and Japanese companies completely dominate world manufacture of microchips.

This technological gap is largely the result of the increasing power of a limited number of US companies. A report by the British computer firm, ICL, has complained of 'growing technological imperialism' by the USA: "The US appears intent on controlling trade in high technology, either directly or indirectly, and recognises control of information technology in particular as a means of power over others." (*Observer*, 29 January 1984).

Many British firms believe that control over strategic goods is now an established instrument of US commercial policy. This control is exercised in three ways, says ICL: by restricting imports of technologies; by preventing exports to the US by non-US companies; and by pressing other countries to open their markets through the General Agreement on Tariffs and Trade. Any British computer company that uses even a single US microchip may need a US licence for export. Under the extra-territorial practices of US law, the Commerce Department can control both shipments from the US, and also the re-export of US technology. This applies to hardware, software and the know-how of US engineers.

The activities of the United States in this field are a classic illustration of how effective a country can be when the powers of the government and major corporations are co-ordinated together behind a more or less explicit strategy. Britain, by contrast, represents a classic example of how a country can be increasingly left behind by developments in the world economy, for lack of any attempt to co-ordinate its resources. The bitter irony of the situation lies in the Tory Government's belief that its own policies are moulded in the image of the 'free market' US economy.

### Socialist goals for the 1990's

We have argued so far that a major redistribution of economic power will be crucial to reversing Britain's economic decline, and that trying to hand control of the economy over to 'market forces' has had disastrous effects in recent years — making a concerted approach to Britain's problems even more difficult. What is the socialist alternative to all this, and what sort of objectives do socialists set themselves for our economy and society in the 1990's?

A socialist economic strategy must combine two objectives:

*First*, it must reflect people's immediate concerns about jobs, services and incomes. It must build up their confidence and their sense of collective strength, by showing that expansion *is* possible, that it can be sustained, and that it can be paid for. In other words, it must achieve a break from the profound sense of pessimism and defeatism which underlies support for Thatcherite policies. It must show that it is possible for us to take control as a nation of our economic destiny.

*Second*, it must confront longer-term issues, in two closely related ways. On the one hand, it must do more than simply offer people a slightly better version of the society we already have: it must also hold out a positive vision of a better future and a different kind of society. And on the other hand, our strategy must face up to the changes in economic power which are needed if recovery is to be sustainable and based on genuine popular involvement.

A socialist strategy should therefore embody the following principles:

• The enlargement of democratic control over the decisions that affect people's lives, through the extension of individual and trade union rights.

• The right to paid work for those who want it, and the right to continuing retraining and education.

• The promotion of social and economic equality, including that between women and men — at work, at home, and in access to paid work.

• The encouragement of personal creativity and human relationships, allied to a strengthening of collective values.

• The recognition of the social and environmental impact of economic decisions, and the development of healthy working conditions.

We shall say something further here about the first three of these objectives in particular.

**Progress through democratic control**

People must be given greater control over the decisions that affect their lives: that is the major theme of this book. Increasing democratic control, we argue, is inseparable from achieving a more efficient use of economic resources. Key economic decisions, currently taken by large private companies and institutions behind a veil of 'market forces', must be brought out into the open wherever possible and taken in a much more democratic way.

There is more involved in this than passing Acts of Parliament, although these will of course have a crucial role at every stage. Legislation can often be undone at a stroke with a change in government: but measures which devolve power and establish independent areas of initiative are far harder to reverse. This very principle underlies the Tory Government's own privatisation programme, with its attempt (usually very ineffective) to ensure the widest possible spread of share ownership. Another example is Labour's own Health and Safety at Work Act, which greatly enlarged the role of local stewards — this measure has survived largely unscathed despite the hostility of both employers and the subsequent governments.

The need for greater democracy will not be confined to decisions which are currently in private hands. The next Labour Government will need to attach much greater importance than any of its predecessors to the issue of democracy in the various public sectors. That means, for example, seeking to make public corporations much more responsive to workers and consumers alike. And it means much greater decentralisation of control over public services such as housing and social services. It also means making the major annual decisions about public spending more open — so that governments are forced to confront the real extent of social need, and the justification for Treasury limits is constantly challenged.

There is no single formula for extending democratic control. In very few areas, if any, can we expect to achieve some kind of 'pure' democratic model. Modern society is highly complex, and the time people are willing to devote to participating in democratic processes is finite. So we too must recognise limits on the extent to which it will be possible to extend democratic systems. But it is not difficult to imagine many areas of our lives today where important decisions are taken in private or in secret, and where people would welcome much greater consultation and power. Under cover of being the world's oldest democracy (a very dubious claim in itself) Britain in recent years has increasingly been exposed as one of the most secretive and least genuinely democratic of Western countries. If we can do something about that, we believe that our country will benefit in a whole range of different ways — not just through greater freedom in its own right, but through better economic performance, more responsive public services, and a greatly enhanced sense of collective purpose.

## The politics of work

The politics of work — both waged and unwaged — will become more urgent in the 1990's. The right to paid jobs for those who want them will remain a basic socialist objective, because paid work will still be the main source of most people's income, and because it will continue to underpin personal independence and self respect in our society.

A socialist economic strategy must combine the right to work with the right to *fulfilling* work, at home and in paid work. Microtechnology could enable more control over work to be devolved to the individual worker. The design of jobs should therefore become a matter of much greater social concern and discussion.

At the same time the demand to reduce working hours for individuals will also become more urgent for two main reasons. First, in order to provide more jobs at a time when over 5 million want paid work but cannot find it. Second, in order that responsibility for domestic labour, and in particular childcare, can be shared more equally between men and women.

## Extending equality

Extending equality is inseparable from promoting greater democratic control over economic resources. The concentration of wealth in this country confers power over the organisation of the economy and over the lives of other people. At the other end of the scale, poverty and dependence on means tested benefits reduce the control people have over their own lives.

Inequality in our society has increased in manifold ways under the Tories. Inequality between North and South; between the inner cities and the suburbs; between men and women; between black and white; between young and old; between those in paid work and those who are not: all these divisions have widened dramatically in recent years.

A key socialist objective must be, as always, to ensure that our economy is not run simply for the benefit of those who already enjoy a comfortable existence — whether those be in a minority or majority. The economic resources of a country are held in common and should be developed for the common good — not merely 'natural' resources such as North Sea oil, but all the human resources of accumulated knowledge and skills passed from one generation to the next.

## Planning for socialism

A socialist economic strategy must recognise the need for change — indeed that is what socialism has always stood for. For some reason in recent years we seem to have become identified with a static view of the world, the result perhaps of too much uncritical defence of nationalised industries, the welfare state and paternalistic local authority services — not to mention the problems caused by offering support, correctly, to trade unionists involved in major defensive battles. But socialism is nothing if it is not about looking forward to a better society, in which the benefits of scientific and technological progress will be enjoyed by all people. So we must welcome the far-reaching developments which are now taking place all over the world in production technologies and in new products and services. All we insist upon is that these changes should be introduced under social control, for the benefit of everyone — rather than in an uncontrolled way, for the benefit of the few. That means, as we have argued, a redistribution of economic power in our society away from a privileged minority of organisations and groups. And it may also mean that the way in which our lives are organised, and the kinds of technologies that are employed, will be different — so providing the basis for a more democratic economy.

In the chapters which follow we develop a socialist vision of how this might be done:

● *Economic Power in Britain* (Chapter 2) examines the present day structure of the British economy, and the way in which power is distributed within it. This is a vital first step in working out a practical strategy for recovery based on greater democratic control over the economy.

● *Planning Now* (Chapter 3) looks at the lessons of attempts to extend social control, through workers' plans, co-operative production, and the exciting range of initiatives launched by Labour local authorities. These lessons, we argue, both highlight the need for a national strategy of recovery and also force us to rethink how that strategy can work.

● *The Right to Paid Work* (Chapter 4) sets out the case for expansionary measures to restore the right to paid work. We argue that policies for growth must be fully integrated with policies for reorganising the economy within our overall strategy — reflation on its own will not be enough, but it forms the necessary framework for the achievement of our longer-term objectives.

● How to reverse inequalities in economic power by extending different forms of social control in the three main sectors of the economy is the core of this book: *Increasing democracy in the private sector, the state and the unpaid sector* are the themes of Chapters 5-8. We argue for a flexible approach, guided by certain broad democratic principles. In particular we see the need for people themselves to become more involved in taking key economic decisions and in defining the objectives of the economic system — in short, for a new approach based on democratic, socialist enterprise.

• Through case studies on *telecommunications, motors,* and *textiles* (Chapters 9-11) we show how our strategy for socialist enterprise could work in detail. These sectors raise the issues of public ownership and the structure of public industries, multinational producers, local and co-operative enterprise and the promotion of women's equality.

• The concluding chapter (Chapter 12) draws together the lessons of earlier chapters and points to some of the broader political implications of our strategy.

CHAPTER 2

# Economic Power In Britain

Economic decisions shape the lives of every one of us — decisions affecting whether we work, and if so, when and where; whether we are paid for it, and if so, how much; what we are able to buy, and what services we are entitled to. But all these vitally important decisions are not usually taken by us. They are taken by other people — people in positions of economic power. How exactly is this power distributed?

Unfortunately, answering this question is not as straightforward as it might seem. To start with, there is no standard unit of measurement for economic power. And power, even more so than personal wealth, often prefers not to advertise. To complicate matters further, the position is constantly changing — in recent years, in particular, Tory policies have prompted marked shifts in power within the economy.

In this chapter we try various ways of building up a picture of the main concentrations of economic power in Britain today. The picture is inevitably far from complete. Nonetheless, the results are, to some extent, unexpected — and make it necessary to consider revising traditional socialist approaches. The various indicators of economic power which are available to us highlight the growing power of the finance and retailing sectors; the importance of a few major industrial companies, mainly multinationals, concentrated in a few sectors; the number of sectors where, by contrast, few companies are dominant; the growing weakness of the British economy in relation to both Europe and the rest of the world; and finally, the significance of the state — both as employer and as purchaser.

**Sectors of work**
We begin by looking at where people work. Admittedly, this is not an infallible guide to where economic power lies. Many major industrial, financial and retailing companies are actually employing fewer and fewer people. The City's power, to take another example, is not based on the number of people it

employs, but rather on its position at the crossroads of the international financial flows — something deriving from Britain's imperial past. With these important qualifications in mind, we can, nonetheless, draw valuable lessons from the pattern of work in Britain today, and from recent trends within it. Table 1 categorises work according to the following broad sectors:

• *Private companies* make up the largest single sector, employing about half of the working age population. They employ waged workers and make profits from the sale of goods and services.

• *Unwaged workers*, overwhelmingly women, are almost as important in terms of numbers at work. They produce services within the home which are consumed directly by other members of the household. About two-fifths of these unwaged workers also work in other sectors of the economy.

• *Central or local government* is the third largest sector in terms of employment. Services such as education or health are produced by waged workers but made available free or at a standard charge. About one-sixth of the working age population are employed in this way.

• *The self-employed* are the next largest group: they are not waged, but sell their services for profit. In many cases they themselves employ a small number of people.

• *Nationalised industries* are the smallest sector in terms of employment. They produce goods for sale, with any profits accruing to the state.

In addition, of course, one in twelve of the population of working age were registered as *unemployed* in 1982 (the date of the other Table 1 figures).

These categories help us to highlight some important points.

*First*, they emphasise the relative significance of domestic work as an economic activity. More people are 'employed' in this sector than in manufacturing, distribution, public or private services. And within this sector, it is men by and large who wield economic power: women do the work, while men (and children) benefit from the results. Even if we take childcare alone, this is more important a factor in the division of labour than anything else. Not only are millions of women directly engaged in it; but women's role in providing childcare also has an impact on their ability to take employment elsewhere. About 40 per cent of the women doing paid work do so on a part-time basis, while for men part-time working is the exception rather than the rule.

*Second*, if we take a closer look at the figures in Table 1, we see the relatively diminished role of manufacturing. Only about one in three of those employed in producing commodities (goods and services for sale) is engaged in manufacturing — about the same number of people in total as in public services. Socialist economic strategies have traditionally sought to challenge the economic power of the largest manufacturing firms, and there was a time in the early post-war period when the centre of economic power could be said to lie with these firms. But, while their power is significant, new centres of economic power have also developed. The production of goods and services requires the ownership of factories and offices; the employment of workers; access to finance; control over technology; a system for getting the materials needed for production; and a system for distributing the final product. At one time these elements of production were centralised in the major manufacturing companies. They are now more widely dispersed, both between the public and private sectors and between industrial, commercial and financial companies within the private sector.

This second point is underlined by Table 2, which uses three indicators of economic power: employment, turnover and capital. Table 2 shows that:

• Many of the major *employers* are in the *public sector* — the National Health Service, the Civil Service and the Armed Forces are the top employers. Public utilities and local councils are also major employers, and banks and private services figure prominently.

• The largest companies in terms of *turnover* and *capital employed* are the multinational oil producers, BP and Shell; the Electricity Council; and BAT, another multinational. By these criteria, British Coal and British Gas (in the public sector) and BT, GEC, ICI, the Imperial Group and Unilever also exercise considerable economic power.

The prominence of the public sector in our list is striking. Any government can exert considerable influence, simply through public corporations and services, on the lives of millions of people. The rise in the economic role of the public sector should have meant greater democratic control over the economy. But in practice it has meant greater power for bureaucracies.

**Monopoly power?**
A simpler indicator of economic power is provided by the domination by particular companies of their sector. Many of the manufacturing companies we identify in Table 2 can exercise monopoly or near-monopoly power within the UK market. However, the domination of manufacturing industries by the top five companies in those industries is very uneven. This is shown in Table 3. There are a few highly concentrated sectors like car manufacture and oil refining, but high concentration is by no

means universal. In many industries — pharmaceuticals, industrial plant, process machinery, plastics and clothing — the top five companies are responsible for a third or less of output. Market dominance must also be seen in the light of international trade and competition: Table 3 does not take account of this.

Market dominance is therefore important, but its impact can be overstated, especially for particular sectors. These qualifications would be less important if the market dominance of major manufacturing companies was rising through time. But this has not been the case. It remained fairly constant throughout the 1970's, as Table 4 shows. Moreover, manufacturing companies are now less coherent as organisations because distribution and finance tend to be carried out elsewhere, and this also reduces their economic power. For example, our analysis of clothing and textiles (see Chapter 11) shows how the traditional pattern of large and powerful textiles companies controlling — but not owning — small clothing manufacturers, retailers and wholesalers has given way to control by the large retailing chains.

### The rise of commerce

The retail sector and the finance sector have taken over many of the functions once carried out by large manufacturing companies. The retail sector is beginning to rival the power of the manufacturing sector, by acquiring control over the information and distribution systems which were previously under the control of manufacturing companies. The rise of major retailers is reflected in their increasing market domination, shown in Table 5, at a time when that of the major manufacturers stood still. The most recent merger boom has also brought about further concentration of economic power within the retail sector in particular.

The continued growth of the finance sector is also highly significant in terms of the distribution of economic power. Industrial companies in this country have behaved as independent and usually competitive organisations, even though they have sometimes acted in alliance. But the finance sector is far more centralised, and serves as an organising focus of class power. The growth of the finance sector reflects the decreasing ability of manufacturing companies to finance investment from their own retained profits. In the era of manufacturing dominance, manufacturing companies used to finance their relatively limited investments from their substantial profits. Since then, the underlying trend in profitability has been downwards, while the costs of new investment have increased (especially because of higher inflation). As a result, manufacturing and commercial companies have increasingly come to rely on banks for new finance, both for working capital and for fixed investment needs. This often takes the form of short-term finance through overdrafts or leasing arrangements whereby companies hire equipment owned by banks. The effect of the latter is to concentrate the control of a large amount of equipment, at least in principle, in the hands of the banks.

These developments have left the banks with considerable power over industry and commerce. But the banks have not developed the same sense of responsibility shown by their German and Japanese counterparts, who have been the source of finance for their industries for much longer. The form in which British banks provide their finance does not encourage them to take a long-term view of the companies and industries in which they are involved. Recently banks have been forced by the economic recession to become more directly involved, but even when acting collectively, as in the case of the Stone Platt engineering company, they have overwhelmingly taken a short-term view.

There have also been changes in the ultimate source of finance, as witnessed by the rise of the pension funds. Thirty years ago, rich individuals were the main source of outside finance for industry. But now pension funds have taken over. Some people argue that this has somehow dispersed the ownership of property, in a way which has also increased democratic control. In practice, however, the members of a pension fund have no control over the way in which it is operated, and have no legal rights to challenge its investment policies. The rise of pension funds has simply concentrated even more economic power in the hands of the City institutions which operate and 'advise' the pension funds. It has also had the effect of providing them with greater political power: when it comes to defending the rights of property there are 13 million members of pension funds, many of them trade unionists, who can be made to feel they have a stake in the free enterprise economy.

### Britain in the world economy
Any strategy for the British economy must recognise that we are closely tied into the world economy. This is not wholly, or even mainly, a question of the importance to Britain of international trade. Of far greater significance is the dominant role played by multinational companies whose objective has been to make Britain a good base for their international operations, rather than to build up Britain's own industries. The result is that production

in Britain is closely integrated into multinationals' production in overseas plants. Britain's economy is weakened as a result because key aspects of the production process — in particular design and manufacture — are often located abroad. Britain's international orientation, both as a home and as a source country for foreign investment, is shown in Table 5. Most of the large companies operating in Britain have relatively little commitment to actually producing here. These companies are of three types: British based companies with large overseas operations, which either control the production of raw materials or which are concerned with manufacturing; or foreign manufacturing multinationals for whom Britain is now seldom the most important base.

Britain's industrial pre-eminence in the nineteenth century was based on the empire. Many of the largest British based multinationals are still 'imperial'. Their power originated, and indeed is still largely based, on controlling the production of raw materials in the Third World, and the transportation, processing and distribution of them in industrial countries. Of the top ten private multinationals in terms of capital employed listed in Table 2, seven are of this kind — BAT, Lonrho, BP, Shell, Imperial, RTZ and Unilever; while only three — ICI, GEC, and GKN — are manufacturing companies. For imperial multinationals of this kind, producing in Britain is only a small part of a long chain.

During the 1950's, when Britain was still the most prosperous economy in Europe, much effort was devoted to removing restrictions on the international movement of capital and easing the tax treatment of multinational companies. These two factors together helped to make Britain the main European base for US multinationals. It was during this period that the largest of them became based in Britain — for example,Esso, GM, Ford, IBM and ITT. By the end of 1961, 60 per cent of US manufacturing capital in Europe was in Britain. For all industry, the share was 45 per cent.

After the formation of the EEC at the end of the 1950's, the emphasis of US multinational investment switched sharply to the six EEC nations. The US share in British manufacturing capacity dropped to 30 per cent (27 per cent for all industries). Joining the EEC did nothing to reverse the relative decline of US investment in Britain. Only the advent of North Sea oil has had any noticeable effect.

UK based multinationals, meanwhile, shifted their attention from the relics of the empire, first to the EEC and then to North America. The most important result of British membership of the EEC has therefore been the international integration of production in particular areas of manufacturing such as motors and aerospace. Trade with EEC countries has also grown, but this reflects a trend which pre-dated Britain joining the EEC.

## The changing balance of economic power
In examining the distribution of economic power in Britain, we have to be aware that the picture is constantly changing. In the post-war period, the dominant manufacturing and raw material producing companies were quite happy with Keynesian economic policies — that is, government policies which ensured 'that total spending power in the economy was always adequate to maintain full employment. These policies encouraged production and the development of productive capacity, and individual companies could gain from them. It was only when they threatened to bring about a shift in economic power that these policies came under attack.

Keynesian policies meant increased power in the long run for trade unions, for the state, and — on an international scale — for the oil producing countries.

*Trade unions* gained because full (or nearly full) employment policies increased their bargaining strength — gains which were consolidated under the employment protection legislation of the 1974-79 Labour Government. Taking the period from the war until 1979, unionisation advanced in virtually all sectors, as is shown in Table 6. (Unionisation is and always has been strongest in the public sector which contains half of the unionised workforce. The dramatic decline of the manufacturing sector since 1979 has further reinforced this. It has been these *sectoral* shifts rather than any general decline in the role of unions which has been the main factor in the fall in union membership.)

*The state* also increased its economic power during the post-war boom. The duty of the state to intervene in the economy was accepted, and the growth of the welfare state meant an increase in direct employment and spending on a range of public services.

Third, the *oil producing countries* ultimately gained from Keynesian demand management, which ensured sustained, high economic demand on a world scale. At any rate, they were the one group of raw material supplying countries which was able to organise itself effectively and exploit the power the economic climate gave them.

The 1980's have seen a concerted reaction, not so much against Keynesian policies themselves, as against these growing shifts in economic power which the policies entailed. A feature of this reaction, symbolised by the economic policies of Thatcher and Reagan, has been that Keynesian policies have been formally overthrown in favour of a 'monetarist' approach, according to which the obligations of government are limited to ensuring sound money and an economic climate favourable to free enterprise, and no longer extend to guaranteeing full employment. But in reality both the US and British Governments have continued to run budget deficits — spending more than current income — and indeed the US deficit has risen to unprecedented levels (albeit through excessive defence spending). Much more important, arguably, than these changes in economic doctrine have been the related attacks on trade unionism, in this country through deliberate mass unemployment and punitive legislation, and on the boundaries of the state, through wholesale privatisation and 'deregulation'. It is these shifts in economic power which form the real agenda of the New Right.

Another important development in the post-war period has of course been the creation and expansion of the EEC. Many British socialists have always dismissed the EEC as a vehicle for progressive economic and political change — and with some justification, since the EEC was set up to promote the free movement of capital across national boundaries. This, in turn, has increased the flexibility with which employers can respond to any challenge from workers or governments at a national level. Any attempt to bring trade under some sort of non-market control will threaten this freedom of manoeuvre, and will meet with their strong resistance. Moreover, the rise of finance capital and of international companies has led to the development of Euromarkets. These are financial markets which operate largely outside the jurisdiction of any one country. They reduce the control which individual states have over their own finance by making them vulnerable to international movements of capital and corporate funds.

On the other side of the balance sheet, the EEC represents one of the few institutions which seeks to challenge the power of multinationals at a multinational level. This is a potential which a future Labour Government, in conjunction with the British and European trade union movements, could and should exploit. Many of the EEC's initiatives on corporate policy — such as on industrial democracy and health and safety — have also been moderately progressive and have been opposed by most multinationals, in particular through their mouthpiece, the British Government. The Gaullist fear of Britain as a Trojan horse for America in the EEC has been justified in this particular area.

## The legacy of ten years' Tory rule
The radical policies of the 1979 and 1983 Tory Governments have

meant that the slow decline in the power of manufacturing capital has turned into a rout. The growth of the state as employer has been halted. The rise in trade union membership has been reversed. The international orientation of British capital has increased, as has its concentration as a result of a new merger boom. The power and resources of capital have been increased while those of workers have been diminished.

Where will all these changes leave our economy by the 1990's? By then we shall be left with a still substantial public sector, but one whose scope for initiatives will have been severely limited and whose morale will be very low. We will have a trade union movement, much depleted in numbers, which will have been fighting largely defensive struggles for ten years. We will by then have a private industry which will have expanded mainly in the areas it has 'acquired' from the public sector. In many of those areas it will have a low paid and heavily exploited workforce. In its traditional areas it will be suffering badly from the underinvestment in equipment and training which has occurred throughout the 1980's.

In a period of rapid technological change this will make Britain extremely vulnerable. British industry will be largely owned by companies with better production facilities overseas. This will even be the case in industries such as financial services in which we now have a lead. Britain's 'Third World' economy will have largely lost the ability to re-equip itself and will be dependent on imported technologies.

Divisions based on wealth and skills will be exacerbated by divisions between the information 'rich' and poor, partly the result of the privatisation of BT, described in Chapter 9. These developments underpin the growth of a 'two-tier' labour market, with an elite few enjoying well-paid, qualified employment, while for others (especially women and black people) work is likely to be poorly paid and often part-time. Such patterns will be compounded by profound changes in where people work, in particular the growth of smaller workplaces in the service sector and the shift away from urban and industrial centres.

As the oil begins to run out, Britain will have few special resources of skills, equipment or raw materials to offer. Worst of all, its ability to take control of its own economic affairs will have been seriously weakened. The need for a strategy to restore economic self-determination will be more urgent than ever.

## Conclusions

The balance of power in the economy can and does change over time — between manufacturing firms and the retail and finance sectors, between households and companies, between different companies and between companies and government. But however these relations change, in our society it is those with corporate or financial power who initiate strategic economic decisions, while workers or their organisations react to events. They can sometimes shape key decisions by resistance. They can make proposals and demands. But it is normally the employer who controls the access to information and relations between the company or organisation and other parts of the economy.

Much the same considerations apply to non-waged workers in the home (Chapter 8). Their ability to shape decisions affecting their lives depends on their access to finance, information and the freedom to organise. This will, in their case, come largely from outside the family in the form of paid employment in one of the other sectors, or from support services like childcare provided by the public sector. Because a significant proportion of such workers also work in the waged sector, there is an interaction between the two. The ability of women with household responsibilities to organise in their waged workplaces will depend on their position in the home, and vice versa. The state will also play a key role, both as direct employer of about half of the waged married women and as a provider of services.

Our strategy for economic recovery is based on socialist enterprise — on working people themselves having the rights and resources they need to take key economic decisions, at work and in their communities. The analysis of the British economy we have outlined suggests that this cannot be achieved simply by relying on the traditional remedies of nationalisation and 'planning agreements' with key manufacturing companies:

*First*, large companies and organisations of all kinds employ only a relatively small part of the working age population. Table 2 accounts for only one sixth, and of those only half are in private companies. The addition of the next hundred largest organisations would only add another fifteenth of the working age population. Nationalisation and old style planning agreements would therefore do little directly to increase the economic power of three quarters of the people of working age.

*Second*, almost no private companies in this country have ever employed more than 200,000 people. Only BT does so now. And yet there are six public organisations which employ more than that, as Table 2 shows. It is hardly surprising that nationalisation has come to be associated with centralisation and bureaucracy. Despite this, the Left has paid almost no attention to the problems of the *internal* organisation of the public sector: next time round, these mistakes must not be repeated. Experience shows that greater democracy is not an automatic consequence of industrial planning and public ownership. We therefore need to find structures in which people can develop and exercise their own power, rather than merely changing the name of the employers who exercise it.

*Third,* the growing importance of finance capital and the major retailers in the economy indicates the vulnerability of manufacturing companies, and highlights centres of economic power other than manufacturing. Taking existing manufacturing companies into public ownership will not in itself be the answer to Britain's increasingly desperate economic problems. We need to pay much greater attention than in the past to areas outside manufacturing. This includes the finance and distribution sectors in particular — which, as we discuss further in Chapter 6, will be much more important in the future in any strategy to extend democratic control over the economy.

## Table 1: Employment in different sectors in 1982
*All figures in thousands*

| | Total | Women | | Men | |
|---|---|---|---|---|---|
| | | *Full-time* | *Part-time* | *Full-time* | *Part-time* |
| Private employees | 13,154 | 3,065 | 1,940 | 7,684 | 465 |
| Public corporations | 1,759 | 247 | 63 | 1,426 | 23 |
| Self-employed | 2,100 | 300 | — | 1,800 | — |
| Sub-total: commodity production | 17,013 | 3,612 | 2,003 | 10,910 | 488 |
| (of which: manufacturing) | (5,612 ) | (1,249 ) | (365) | (3,934) | (64) |
| Unpaid domestic work | 12,300 | 7,800 | 4,300 | — | — |
| (of which: childcare:) | (6,800) | (4,100) | (2,700) | — | — |
| Public services | 5,016 | 1,659 | 1,526 | 1,590 | ·241 |
| Unemployed | 2,700 | 700 | — | 2,000 | — |
| Adjustment* | −4,300 | — | −4,300 | — | — |
| Total | 32,529 | 13,771 | 3,529 | 14,500 | 729 |

* Adjustment to allow for estimated double counting of women who do unpaid work in the home as well as paid work outside.

Sources: National Income Blue Book 1983, General Household Survey 1982.

## Table 2: Organisations listed by indicators of economic power: 1984

| Employer | Industry | Employment | Turnover £bn | Capital £bn |
|---|---|---|---|---|
| National Health Service | Health | 1,250,000 | | |
| Civil Service | Administration | 666,000 | | |
| Armed Forces | Military | 328,000 | | |
| British Coal | Coal | 282,000 | 4.7 | 4.0 |
| British Telecom | Telecomms | 246,000 | 5.7 | 8.4 |
| British Rail | Railways | 220,000 | 2.8 | 1.3 |
| Post Office | Postal services | 205,000 | 2.5 | 1.3 |
| GEC* | Electrical | 189,000 | 4.2 | 2.1 |
| BAT* | Tobacco/retail | 178,000 | 11.3(3) | 4.6 |
| Lonrho* | Diverse | 150,000 | 2.6 | 0.8 |
| Electricity Council | Elec. supply | 147,000 | 8.4 | 32.6(1) |
| BP* | Oil | 145,000 | 34.6(1) | 17.3(2) |
| Shell | Oil | N/A | 21.9(2) | 12.0(3) |
| Grand Metropolitan | Hotels/leisure | 129,000 | 3.9 | 2.3 |
| ICI* | Chemicals | 124,000 | 7.4 | 5.4 |
| British Steel | Steel | 112,000 | 3.4 | 2.6 |
| Strathclyde Council | Local authority | 108,000 | | |
| British Gas | Gas supply | 106,000 | 5.2 | 11.0 |
| BL* | Motors | 105,000 | 3.1 | 1.3 |
| Imperial Group | Tobacco/food | 101,000 | 4.6 | 1.1 |
| Thorn EMI* | Electrical | 98,000 | 2.4 | 0.9 |
| Inner London Ed. Auth. | Education | 88,000 | | |
| British Aerospace | Aircraft | 79,000 | 2.0 | 0.9 |
| Nat. West Bank | Banking | 77,000 | | |
| Barclays Bank | Banking | 75,000 | | |
| George Weston | Food | 73,000 | 2.9 | 0.8 |
| Courtaulds | Textiles | 73,000 | 1.9 | 0.7 |
| Lucas* | Engineering | 72,000 | 1.2 | 0.6 |
| GKN* | Engineering | 72,000 | 1.9 | 1.0 |
| RTZ* | Mining/metals | 70,000 | 3.7 | 5.2 |
| Ford | Motors | 69,000 | 3.3 | 2.1 |
| Midland Bank | Banking | 69,000 | | |
| Unilever | Food/diverse | 69,000 | 5.5 | 2.4 |
| Bass | Brewing | 69,000 | 1.9 | 1.4 |
| Boots | Retailing/drugs | 69,000 | 1.7 | 0.7 |
| Trust House Forte | Hotels | 60,000 | 0.9 | 0.8 |
| Dunlop | Rubber | 59,000 | 1.5 | 0.8 |
| London Transport | Transport | 58,000 | 0.5 | 1.7 |
| Reed International* | Paper | 57,000 | 1.7 | 0.7 |
| GUS | Retailing | 56,000 | 1.7 | 0.7 |
| National Bus Co. | Transport | 52,000 | 0.7 | 0.3 |
| Lloyds Bank | Banking | 52,000 | | |

| Employer | Industry | Employment | Turnover £bn | Capital £bn |
|---|---|---|---|---|
| Lancashire Council | Local authority | 52,000 | | |
| Sainsbury's | Retailing | 52,000 | 2.2 | 0.5 |
| Woolworths | Retailing | 52,000 | 1.1 | 0.7 |
| Sears Holdings | Retailing | 51,000 | 1.6 | 0.9 |
| BET | Electrical | 50,000 | 0.9 | 0.6 |
| BICC* | Cables | 50,000 | 1.7 | 0.5 |
| Tesco | Retailing | 50,000 | 2.0 | 0.3 |
| Metal Box* | Metal manu-facture | 49,000 | 1.2 | 0.6 |
| Marks & Spencer | Retailing | 48,000 | 2.5 | 1.3 |
| British Airways | Transport | 48,000 | 2.2 | 0.8 |
| Essex Council | Local authority | 48,000 | | |
| Hampshire Council | Local authority | 48,000 | | |
| Hawker Siddeley | Engineering | 47,000 | 1.4 | 0.9 |
| Rank Hovis* | Food | 47,000 | 1.6 | 0.4 |
| Kent Council | Local authority | 45,000 | | |
| Coats Patons | Textiles | 45,000 | 0.9 | 0.5 |
| Rolls Royce | Engineering | 45,000 | 1.5 | 0.4 |
| Hanson Trust* | Diverse | 44,000 | 1.2 | 0.5 |
| Plessey* | Electronics | 44,000 | 1.0 | 0.4 |
| Thomas Tilling* | Diverse | 43,000 | 2.3 | 1.0 |
| Pilkington | Glass | 40,000 | 1.0 | 1.3 |
| United Biscuits* | Food | 40,000 | 1.2 | 0.4 |

*These are multinational producers — the figures shown are for their worldwide operations.

Rankings of top three are shown in brackets.

Sources: Times 1000 Companies 1984 edition; Joint Manpower Watch; Annual Abstract of Statistics; Extel.

## Table 3: Concentration ratios for sectors of manufacturing industry: 1980

| Industry | Net output | Concentration ratio* | | |
|---|---|---|---|---|
| | £billion | Employment | Output | Investment |
| Cars | 2.4 | 91 | 91 | 95 |
| Oil | 2.1 | 68 | 77 | 76 |
| Bread | 1.1 | 63 | 65 | 51 |
| Beer | 1.1 | 54 | 60 | 45 |
| Rubber | 1.0 | 54 | 59 | 63 |
| Basic electrical equipment | 1.2 | 48 | 51 | 51 |
| Telecom equipment | 1.3 | 49 | 49 | 39 |
| Car parts | 1.2 | 37 | 40 | 50 |
| Pharmaceuticals | 1.4 | 32 | 36 | 37 |
| Special chems/ fertilisers | 1.0 | 32 | 36 | 37 |
| Industrial plant | 1.4 | 21 | 20 | 15 |
| Hand tools | 1.9 | 16 | 19 | 15 |
| Process machinery | 1.1 | 21 | 16 | 12 |
| Mining machinery | 3.0 | 15 | 14 | 14 |
| Furniture | 1.1 | 11 | 12 | 18 |
| Plastics | 1.6 | 12 | 12 | 12 |
| Clothing | 1.5 | 13 | 12 | 10 |

* Percentages attributable to the largest five companies in those sectors with a net output of more than £1 billion.

Source: Census of Production 1980

# Table 4: Concentration in manufacturing and retailing

|  | Concentration ratio* | |
|---|---|---|
|  | *Manufacturing* <br> *(Top 100 companies)* | *Retailing* <br> *(Top 20 companies)* |
| 1935 | 24 | |
| 1949 | 22 | |
| 1953 | 27 | |
| 1958 | 32 | |
| 1963 | 37 | |
| 1968 | 41 | |
| 1970 | 40 | |
| 1971 | 40 | |
| 1972 | 41 | |
| 1973 | 42 | |
| 1974 | 42 | |
| 1975 | 42 | |
| 1976 | 42 | 13.8 |
| 1977 | 41 | |
| 1978 | 41 | |
| 1979 | 42 | |
| 1980 | 41 | 16.1 |

*Share of top companies in net output or turnover (per cent)

Sources: Business Monitors PA 1002 and SDA 25

## Table 5: Distribution of US direct investment

| | Share of the stock of US investment in: | | | |
| | UK | | Europe | |
| | Manufacturing | Total | Manufacturing | Total |
|---|---|---|---|---|
| 1950 | 14.2 | 7.2 | 24.3 | 14.7 |
| 1955 | 14.6 | 7.4 | 25.5 | 15.5 |
| 1960 | 19.6 | 10.2 | 34.4 | 21.6 |
| 1965 | 17.1 | 10.4 | 39.9 | 28.4 |
| 1970 | 15.4 | 10.4 | 42.5 | 31.4 |
| 1975 | 13.5 | 11.2 | 46.5 | 39.8 |
| 1980 | 15.6 | 13.2 | 50.8 | 44.8 |
| 1982 | 14.3 | 13.7 | 48.7 | 45.1 |

All figures are percentages.
Source: British Business (various numbers)

## Table 6: Trade union membership

| | Thousands | | | |
| | Public | Manufacturing | Construction | Farming & Private Services |
|---|---|---|---|---|
| 1948 | 3,279 | 3,720 | 835 | 665 |
| | (71) | (51) | (36) | (14) |
| 1968 | 3,661 | 4,138 | 603 | 768 |
| | (66) | (50) | (29) | (13) |
| 1973 | 4,244 | 4,726 | 545 | 894 |
| | (73) | (60) | (29) | (14) |
| 1979 | 5,199 | 5,157 | 605 | 1,215 |
| | (82) | (70) | (34) | (17) |
| 1982 | 5,003 | 3,747 | 463 | 1,122 |
| | (82) | (65) | (31) | (16) |

Notes:
Figures in parentheses are trade union densities — the proportion of those employed in a sector who are members of a union.
The classifications are based on Bain and do not correspond to the classifications used in other tables. In particular, no distinction is made between public services and nationalised industries. Road and sea transport are omitted.
Up to 1979 the data come from: G. Bain 'Union Growth in Britain', *British Journal of Industrial Relations*, 1983. Subsequent figures are consistent projections based on the annual article on trade union membership in the DE Gazette. This includes an implicit allocation of the membership of unions which the DE do not themselves allocate to industries.

CHAPTER 3

# Planning Now

Even in the midst of economic recession, it is possible to find examples of greater democratic control being exerted over the economy. Workers' plans, workers' co-ops and the interventions of Labour local authorities have all shown in different ways that private interest is not the only criterion by which to make economic decisions. They have also become increasingly important as signposts towards a new industrial and economic strategy. In this chapter, we discuss their potential and their limitations. Such interventions do not provide any easy answers: a national strategy cannot simply be made up of thousands of local initiatives. But we must learn the lessons of these local initiatives at a national level, and harness their full potential within the context of an effective national strategy.

## WORKERS' PLANS

In recent years workers' plans have become an increasingly important influence on the industrial policies put forward by socialists. These plans have, typically, been produced by working people threatened with redundancy and closure, in an effort to show how their jobs and plants can be saved. They have challenged corporate strategies by questioning the existing product range and the existing system of production. They have therefore gone beyond the routine challenge to management decisions over wages and conditions. We shall argue from this that workers' plans must not be considered in isolation, but should instead form a crucial part of our wider efforts to extend industrial democracy.

Many workers' plans have succeeded in winning popular support and in stimulating collective action. They have done this by outlining practical solutions to immediate problems, unlike national strategies which all too often appear abstract and remote. They have shown how the skills and imagination of working people are currently wasted, and how the criterion of private profit ignores social considerations. By raising the issue of 'production for social need' — a term which has become widely used in the light of the Lucas plan — they have also challenged current priorities in public spending and in the uses to which new technology is put.

Workers' plans have also been significant in organisational terms. British trade unions have tended to organise at shop floor and plant level, while British companies have developed through merger into multi-plant organisations. As a result, unions often do not have the right structure to confront corporate decisions over closures and redundancies. Workers' plans have helped stimulate the growth of joint union combine committees which bring together shop stewards from different unions and plants.

## Two Examples:
### I. Lucas Aerospace

The alternative corporate plan drawn up the Joint Shop Stewards Committee of Lucas Aerospace is the most notable example of a workers' plan. The *Financial Times* described the plan as "one of the most radical alternative plans ever drawn up by workers for their company". The *Engineer* hailed it as "a twentieth century version of the industrial revolution".

The Joint Shop Stewards Committee brought together 13,000 staff and shop-floor workers in 17 factories, thus enabling them to develop a united response. The plan analysed the likely impact on Lucas Aerospace of developments in the world aerospace industry; identified the unmet needs and new markets to which the company's resources could be directed; and described the products, processes and training programme which would be involved. The proposed products fell into six broad categories: medical equipment, alternative energy sources, transport systems, braking systems, oceanics and telechiric (or remote control) equipment.

The plan was never implemented, even though important factors helped its development. It was drawn up by highly skilled workers: aerospace is almost unique in combining a high proportion of design, scientific and technical workers with many skilled manual workers. The workers were also used to versatile, small-batch production. The Lucas stewards could draw on the tradition of alternative production in the industry, which switches between military and civil production. Lucas Aerospace's main customers were the government, or government-owned companies: planned production of a kind was therefore already accepted and the workers had only to question *how* it should be done. Finally, the Committee benefited from the informal recognition given by Lucas.

The plan was frustrated, however, by internal divisions and by the lack of support from the official trade union movement and the Labour Government. There were important organisational divisions within the Combine Committee and the members were not always kept adequately informed. The experience emphasised how difficult it is to sustain the collective strength needed to translate a workers' plan into reality, and how important it is for local action to be backed up at national level. Sadly, this support was not forthcoming.

Labour's industry ministers refused to discuss the plan, arguing that the company was considering it. Ministers were advised by civil servants who were in close contact with Lucas management; indeed the Permanent Secretary, Sir Anthony Part, left the Department to become a director of Lucas Industries. The plan was not discussed within the framework of the Government's 'industrial strategy' (Chapter 5) because, it was claimed, Lucas Aerospace did not fit into any of the strategy's 39 sectors.

The Confederation of Shipbuilding and Engineering Unions (the 'Confed')was slow to support the combine, largely due to the tension between the combine and AUEW-TASS. Eventually it did establish a committee, with representatives from each major union and site, which drew up a report on Lucas' corporate strategy. This was backed up by both political pressure and industrial sanctions, such as a refusal to allow work to be transferred between plants. The Confed then met the Government and Lucas. The report was barely used and few of its demands were met, apart from vague promises to consider the viability of some of the proposed products. When the Conservative Government replaced Labour, the plan was ignored and its principal architects eventually dismissed. The Chairman of Lucas had said to the Government in 1976: "You cannot plan Lucas". As it turned out, he was right.

## II. United Biscuits

In June 1983, United Biscuits, Britain's largest biscuit manufacturer, announced plans to close its Liverpool factory with the loss of 2,000 jobs. The unions were given enough time after the announcement to prepare a 157 page plan with the help of a management consultancy. The plan showed how to keep the plant open by diversifying into new products with a reduced workforce. It claimed that £6.5 million a year could be saved along with 1,100 of the 2,000 jobs. These savings would be made by cutting the wage bill and cutting the acreage of the site by a third, turning losses into annual profits of £5.5 million. A £1 million investment programme was proposed in new products such as fresh sandwiches, salads and oven-fresh pizzas, to create 160 new jobs and an extra £1.3 million a year profit.

The plan was described by the *Financial Times* as "an imaginative and detailed response" that "breaks new ground for the union movement": "its acceptance would go some way to establishing a new, constructive pattern in trade union campaigns against closures" (17 November 1983). United Biscuits Chairman, Sir Hector Laing, described it as a "superb job, with a great deal going for it" (*Guardian*, 30 November 1983). But the plan was still rejected. The company 'shifted the goalposts', the union claimed, by arguing first that the Liverpool plant was not profitable, then the biscuit division and finally the whole group. This convinced the unions that short-term savings were not the real reason for closure, but rather long-term plans to concentrate on fewer sites and use new technology to gain economies of scale. The rejection of the plan was a reminder that rational argument alone does not guarantee success.

**Production for social need**
Workers' plans have increasingly become associated with the idea of 'production for social need' — that is, making socially useful products in which there may be no commercial profit. In practice, however, they have largely been about restoring the viability of plants and products. Indeed, the Lucas stewards argued for the production of heat pumps on the grounds that this would meet social needs *and* be profitable.

Given the practical constraints, it would be surprising if workers' plans had not concentrated on profitability. This is what enabled workers' plans at Ramparts Engineering and Leyland Wallcoverings, for example, to succeed in reducing job losses, and save around 50 jobs in each case.

In most cases, however, firms have rejected the proposals for new products made in workers' plans. Sometimes the products concerned have not been profitable while on other occasions potentially profitable ideas have been rejected because of incompetent managers and directors. There may also be political reasons why firms feel bound to reject workers' plans, however well thought out they may be.

If products are unprofitable, their manufacture will need a public subsidy of some kind. The same applies if they are only profitable once social costs and benefits are taken into account. Moreover, many of the products in the Lucas plan, for example, were for purchase by the public sector. Government support is therefore important in many different ways.

The need for financial or commercial support is not the only reason for government intervention. Products may be *potentially* profitable but still rejected. Indeed, the failure of British capitalism could be said to be the failure to identify and meet new markets. The government may therefore need to intervene far more directly in the development and manufacture of new products itself.

In some cases, a new product may not be sufficiently profitable compared to the company's existing range. This applies to companies like Lucas, which rely heavily on military contracts and can share in the excess profits reaped by defence contractors. Companies may not wish to commit resources to new markets, requiring the development of new expertise. This is especially likely at a time of intense competition during a world recession.

Products may also be rejected because of political conflicts within the enterprise. To cede the prerogative over major decisions of corporate strategy could undermine management power at all levels. Many new issues could then become the subject of collective bargaining. Lucas Industries' Chairman, Sir Bernard Scott, remarked two months after the initial rejection of the workers' proposals: "The managing director's job is to operate our corporate plan in a ruthless fashion. The plan is sacrosanct".

If products are profitable but firms still fail to respond, there is little that government intervention can do directly. The government cannot make all the decisions which must be taken within the enterprise. But even in these cases it can help by creating some of the necessary conditions for the development of workers' plans. In particular, government action is needed to reduce unemployment (thereby shifting bargaining power towards working people) and to establish the rights and resources workers need to challenge companies' economic power.

### Conclusions
Workers' plans have played a valuable role in challenging the legitimacy of corporate decisions. By showing that threatened plants can have a future, they have helped to raise morale and provide a focus for collective action, even though they are typically the product of skilled workers or 'outsiders'. But there are few examples of the proposals in workers' plans being adopted. This is perhaps not surprising, given the hostile economic and political climate created by Tory Government policies — the new emphasis on aggressive management and the

fear of risk-taking generated by recession and mass unemployment. In order to flourish, workers' plans need to be backed up by economic power — through the support of government (both at national and local level) and through an extension of industrial democracy.

## WORKERS' CO-OPS

Workers' co-ops are often held up as a pure form of industrial democracy. The ideal model of co-ops is one in which working people, given training and the experience of self-management, can extend their control over the workplace to strategic decisions made in the enterprise. They are owned and controlled by worker members on a one-member, one-vote basis, and not by shareholders or the state. Profitability is not the overriding objective because it is enough that the co-operative covers its costs and funds future investment.

The actual experience of workers' co-ops, however, sometimes conflicts with this ideal. Some have failed to survive or have only kept going at the expense of workers' own pay and conditions. In such cases, the experience of defeat or of self-exploitation can actually undermine support for socialist solutions.

### The politics of co-ops

Different types of co-ops give rise to different experiences for the workers involved, and we must be sensitive to the distinction between co-ops established through voluntary conversion; 'middle class' co-ops; the worker co-ops of the 1970's; and the more successful co-ops, established with local authority backing, in the 1980's.

The Industrial Common Ownership Movement was established by Scott Bader in 1958 with the aim of starting new enterprises and placing existing companies under common ownership. A Quaker and Christian Socialist, Bader handed over his successful chemical firm to the workforce in 1951. Other private companies have followed Bader's lead. These firms have been commercially successful, an achievement which should not be underestimated. Although they have the legal status of a co-op, their management structure has often remained unchanged. Under the present constitution at Scott Bader, Godric Bader, son of the founder, is company Chairman for life, and retains considerable power. Unions play little part in determining pay and conditions. The system can best be described as one of benevolent paternalism: more an extensive system of *participation* in management than worker self-management. Although *not* typical of ICOM co-ops, this should act as a warning to those who judge co-ops by name alone.

Many very small companies have been set up as co-ops from scratch. In the 1970's many people were attracted to the idea of co-ops, and over 200 sprang up as a result. Many of the people involved were middle-class, well educated, under 35 and few had children. Typical ventures were left printers, bookshops, wholefoods suppliers, and builders' collectives. Most are struggling financially, operating in labour-intensive sectors where the profit margin is low. They are heavily dependent on funds from local authorities, ICOF (the Movement's funding branch) and on members' own savings. In general, unions have played no part in their establishment and running. They often survive through low pay, unpaid overtime, and poor working conditions often close to sweated labour. An impressive degree of workers' control is practised — with equal pay, job rotation, and sharing of responsibility for running the firm. The members often have personal access to professional help and other resources. Their youth and backgound mean that questions of pay and job security are less important to them.

Some co-ops arose out of factory occupations during the 1970's. After a period of closures and redundancies, workers were searching for more effective means of defending their right to work than the traditional strike. The first example was at Fakenham. These were small-scale initiatives until the advent of the 1974 Labour Government. The Government, with Tony Benn as the Secretary of State for Industry, financed the formation of three workers' co-ops, at Meriden, Scottish Daily News, and Kirkby Manufacturing and Engineering — all resulting from occupations sparked off by the threat of closure.

In economic terms these co-ops have been failures. Heavily undercapitalised and in a bad market position, they were handicapped from the start. Co-op ownership could not reverse the decline of firms which capitalists had failed to run at a profit. As a result, they were forced to choose between reducing wages and accepting the very redundancies they sought to avert. Meriden only managed to prolong its life because the workforce accepted redundancies and the reintroduction of wage differentials. Such fundamental compromises have reduced workers' control to little more than a formality.

In no case does there seem to have been any strong initial feelings in favour of the co-operative principle. Most of the workers were not asserting their right to self-management. They were willing to negotiate about *any* proposals to save their jobs. Had it been possible to persuade new capitalists to move in, the workers would have agreed. Working people often have neither the confidence, skills nor financial resources to want to take on the risks involved in ownership. Faced with financial pressure, many co-ops have had to turn to middle-class managers to bail them out.

The most impressive phase in the growth of co-ops has been the most recent: there are now thirty times more workers' co-ops than in the mid 1970's. Co-ops have had a better record of survival than other small businesses, reflecting the greater commitment of their members. This growth clearly reflects the increase in unemployment, which has forced many to look at new ways of working. The most important factor, however, has been the support provided by Labour local authorities. The range of new co-ops is extremely varied: for example, City Limits, London's successful weekly listings magazine; Pallion Business Services in Sunderland, set up and run by a group of physically handicapped people, provides office and business services; MONS, a Sheffield-based engineering co-op, has developed and produced a de-humidifier.

The *kind* of support Labour councils provide has been sensitive to the particular problems co-ops face. Above all, advice and management help is provided through over 70 local co-operative development agencies, reflecting co-ops' need for assistance on starting up, product development, marketing, training and legal questions. In addition, investment finance is given through enterprise boards, the development agencies themselves, and new revolving loan funds: £7 million was given in 1985-86 alone. Co-ops are also being helped with premises, planning applications, and in liaising with local trade unions.

**The lessons of Fakenham, Kirkby and other co-ops**
The history of Fakenham Enterprises is described in fascinating detail by Judy Wajcman in her book, *Women in Control*. It was the first entirely female co-op to be set up after a series of factory occupations in the early 1970's. It was established in Norfolk, in 1972, after an 18-week work-in. Before the occupation, Fakenham was a satellite factory of a Norwich shoe firm. It employed 45 women, mainly as shoe-machinists. It was particularly vulnerable because it was doing only one part of the production process, machining, with the rest carried out by the parent company. Reflecting the decline of the British footwear industry, the company was to be closed because it was not profitable.

Of the 45 women, 12 responded by occupying the factory, making skirts and handbags which they sold in the local market. The work-in and the co-op were both prompted by the pressure to keep a job. They would have been quite happy if the former owners had been persuaded to reverse the closure or new owners persuaded to move in. As well as bearing a heavy domestic work load, the women had always had to do paid work. Their wages formed a necessary part of the family income, without which many would have fallen into poverty. Most had often experienced redundancy before, and so felt that if Fakenham closed they might never get another job. Forming a co-op was their last resort.

During the work-in, work was organised collectively and income was shared. Individual articles were made by one person instead of being split up, as before the occupation. The new system led to an improvement in the 'atmosphere' at work. But anxiety about the firm's viability came to dominate daily experience, so that radical changes in work practices did not neccessarily lead to radical changes in their *ideas* about work and politics.

In economic terms, the co-op was an unmitigated failure. It was set up with hopelessly inadequate finance (from the Scott Bader Commonwealth). Unable to develop its own product, it had to rely on labour-only contracts. Fakenham Enterprises was not unusual in this respect. Co-ops often rely on sub-contracting from larger firms in low-paid sweated trades, like the clothing industry, where many of the jobs are traditionally 'women's jobs'. One contractor treated the women as a collection of homeworkers. He gradually got the women totally dependent on his work and took more and more control of the enterprise. By 1977, Fakenham Enterprises was no longer a self-managed factory.

Fakenham was also under pressure from *within*, from the new recruits to the co-op. Most of the women who joined after its formation worked part-time, from 9 am to 3.30 pm. Responsibility for school-age children prevented them working the long hours needed during the occupation; or later, to rescue the co-op from collapse. For them, the main appeal was the unusually convenient hours, which fitted in with the school day.

The experience of Fakenham Enterprises should caution those on the Left who have recently discovered co-ops, and see them as an instant solution. At the very least, advocates of co-ops must say why they expect co-ops to prosper at a time when so many capitalist businesses are failing. The undoubted commitment of co-operators is an enormous asset, but it does not by itself guarantee the efficient organisation of production, or adequate product development and marketing. A study of seven Welsh co-ops, carried out by the Ruskin Trade Union Research Unit and commissioned by the Wales TUC, found that the most pressing problems facing co-ops were raising enough start-up capital, finding secure premises, developing marketing skills and obtaining advice of sufficient calibre. These lessons are now being taken into account by Labour local authorities — which helps to explain their relative success in supporting co-ops.

The relationship between co-ops and trade unions is also crucial. The fear that co-ops will undermine wage levels is one explanation for British unions' antipathy to co-ops, but this fear is often unfounded. Co-ops have, moreover, benefited from support given by the local union officials; for example, the Wales TUC has helped set up the Wales TUC Co-operative Development and Training Centre, whilst in Liverpool print unions have backed Printers Inc. and Parados Graphics. Over 55 per cent of all co-ops are unionised, compared to 10 per cent of small businesses.

Kirkby showed vividly the problems encountered by shop stewards in coping with responsibility for enterprise strategy. Tony Eccles, in his compelling account of Kirkby's history, *Under New Management*, concludes that the co-op could have survived with competent management. It did have products which would sell, but adopted a policy of under-pricing, starving the co-op of funds for new product development. It did not fail simply because of sabotage from banks, civil servants and politicians. Indeed, Eccles argues that the National Westminster Bank showed political flair in providing overdraft facilities. After initial hostility during Tony Benn's period as Minister, civil servants in the Department of Industry were sympathetic. But they, the National Enterprise Board, the Co-operative Development Agency and junior ministers all failed to offer the *positive* support the co-op needed. Even the *Daily Telegraph* was forced to conclude: "what has happened at Kirkby…does prove that co-operatives which look to Whitehall to finance them are just asking for trouble" (22 September 1978).

The decisive reason for the failure of Kirkby was the dominance of leading shop stewards, and their inability to reconcile their traditional union role with their new role as directors of the co-op. As one steward remarked: "we're used to fighting the management. It is hard for us and our members to realise that we are the management". The importance of management skills was neglected. Given an insistence on a single channel of representation, with stewards acting as directors, the failure of senior stewards to accept any responsibility for competent management proved debilitating. Instead of day to day involvement in management, they sought to save the co-op through major political interventions.

The role played by the stewards prevented the other co-operators gaining in self-confidence and skills, and this proved crucial. Eccles argues: "The skills which are required to promote solidarity in the face of management initiatives may be quite inappropriate once the initiative all rests with the employees. A shop-floor culture which is collective, oral, reactive and which deduces from experience is quite different to a managing culture which is individualistic and takes initiatives based on analysis".

The experience of Kirkby does not lend support to the conclusion that workers' control must inevitably conflict with economic efficiency. The problem was not that consensus undermined output, but that the failure to produce undermined the commitment of the co-operators, and created tensions which made consensus impossible. In these circumstances, it was a major achievement that Kirkby survived for four years.

**Conclusions**

The experience at Fakenham and Kirkby should not disguise the fact that many co-ops have weathered the recession better than small businesses. Co-ops *have* extended the control that many people have over their working lives and created new jobs, often for women, racial minorities and others who are denied them.

It is clear, as the success of the support provided by Labour councils underlines, that co-ops cannot be developed from above, especially in large or medium sized firms which have failed as private enterprises. Management skills and self-confidence can only be gained through a learning process, with financial, technical and managerial assistance. The problems are especially acute in medium sized firms where shop stewards and co-operators have to cope with new responsibilities. In co-ops which are not sensitive to these problems, the experience will ultimately prove demoralising. The assumption that people will want to form co-ops and extend control over their working lives, all too easily neglects the difficulties faced by working people. Co-operative development should be an *option* available to working people, who should decide for themselves whether they have the resources to succeed.

# LABOUR LOCAL AUTHORITY INITIATIVES

Labour authorities at the GLC, West Midlands, Lancashire, Sheffield and Leeds have in recent years launched a range of economic initiatives to create jobs and rebuild local industry. These have been based on socialist principles of equality of opportunity, co-operation, democratic involvement in investment decisions, and in the planned production of goods and services. Other Labour authorities, including Merseyside and West Yorkshire Metropolitan Counties, and London boroughs such as Hackney and Haringey, are now following their example.

The initiatives were developed in the face of rising unemployment and public expenditure cutbacks. Local elections after 1979 brought to power, or strengthened the position of, a new brand of local Labour party committed to a more active form of local socialism.

In developing new local economic policies, Labour politicians formed alliances with other groups — trade unionists, trades councils, academics, the voluntary sector, the co-operative movement, women's groups, and organisations representing the ethnic minorities and the unemployed. Through various formal and informal discussions, ideas were translated into manifestos for local elections.

These developments reflected trends in the Labour movement stretching back over the previous decade: in particular, the widespread reaction to previous Labour Governments' bureaucratic, technocratic and centralist approach to economic planning.

### The characteristics of the local initiatives
The initiatives of Labour authorities have been based on a rejection not only of the policies of the Conservative Government, but also many of the assumptions on which the policies of past Labour Governments have been based.

They have rejected, *first*, competitive promotion, with local authorities vying with each other for an ever diminishing pool of mobile industry. Instead, the emphasis has been on an *indigenous* based strategy, which builds on the skills, knowledge and expertise of local business, the workforce and the community.

*Second*, they have rejected a 'generalised' approach to wealth creation through provision of land and buildings and the idea that this will automatically revitalise the local economy. Instead, land and bulidings are seen as part of a *package* that includes all potential forms of assistance, the combination depending on the circumstances. Initiatives are set in the wider context of trends in the local economy and beyond, informed by detailed research that enables authorities to anticipate, rather than just react to, events. Within this policy framework, initiatives are *targeted* on particular sectors, firms, areas and social groups.

*Third*, the 'arms length' relationship with the private sector has been rejected. Instead, the authorities have, for the most part, sought to *intervene* directly in the decision making of private firms. They have used the leverage of financial and other assistance to secure public *accountability* to wider economic and social goals. This has been done by providing aid in the form of equity or loan capital, negotiating planning and investment agreements, and linking public contracts to local authority objectives.

*Fourth,* they have rejected attempts to regenerate the local economy through small firms alone. In the West Midlands it would take 100 years of small firms policy to replace the jobs lost at BL alone. There is *no* evidence that the new jobs created in small firms can offset the job loss in large firms in the manufacturing sector. Instead, in London and the West Midlands, efforts have been concentrated on medium sized or large locally based firms, on which many small firms depend, because they have a greater impact on employment and their wages and conditions are better. Firms have been singled out in industries with a scale of production that can be influenced by local authority intervention, and which benefit other firms in the local economy.

*Fifth,* the division between economic and social policy has been rejected. Production has been assisted if it is both consistent with wider social objectives and can provide long-term profits. Economic departments have tackled welfare rights, low pay and equal opportunities.

And *sixth,* many authorities have rejected a technocratic approach to planning. Instead, they have tried to open up local government so that it can support popular initiatives. (These experiments in popular planning are discussed in Chapter 7).

### Technological change
In London, five technology networks (Technets) sponsored by the Greater London Enterprise Board, are bringing together community and workplace groups with academics. The networks will seek to identify products which embody socially useful applications of new technology. Each network will have one or more buildings near the campus of the associated academic institution, with a shop front. The centres will be run by a committee including representative community groups, academic bodies, local boroughs, trades councils and other trade union bodies. They will have enterprise support units to produce and market those products which can be developed to prototype stage in their workshops. Each centre will contribute to a product bank of innovations patented by the networks.

The West Midlands County Council, Lanchester Polytechnic and the Lucas Aerospace Shop Stewards Committee have established the Unit for the Development of Alternative Products, to support initiatives such as the Bitteswell Employment Alliance, which was formed by redundant British Aerospace workers. In Sheffield, joint companies have been established with the education institutions to facilitate the transfer of new technology to local firms. One of the first examples of Sheffield's developing strategy was the support given to a group of machine tool workers following the closure of their factory by Elliots. The Council's Employment Department made available a nursery unit rent free, together with loans and grants to buy basic machine tool equipment, and help in developing a business plan. Support has been provided to a local co-op to develop a new product for tackling the problem of dampness in council housing.

**Training**
New technology policy is linked to training. This is shown in the work of the Leeds Industry and Estates Department, established in October 1982. The Department set up the Leeds Group on Industry and Employment to bring together groups concerned with economic and employment questions, which prepared a report on new technology in Leeds. Within three months the Department prepared a policy for new technology development in the city targeted on new firms, small firms and co-operatives. This also dealt with the problems of disadvantaged groups in the labour market, particularly women and young blacks, and their need for training. Stress has been placed on improving the prospects of individuals in the job market; a high technology orientation, to prepare people for the jobs of the future; strong links between the training centres and local communities; and providing a variety of schemes and projects funded from different sources on one or adjacent sites. The Department has also tried to make sure that the Youth Training Schemes in which the city council is involved, either as managing agent or direct sponsor, are fully monitored with the trade unions.

Four training centres run by local community management committees have now been established with two further schemes in the final stage of preparation. The Harehills 'ITEC' acts as a training centre for unemployed young people and as a support for product and business development in information technology. The East Leeds Women's Workshop runs courses for women in electronics, computing, joinery and carpentry, with a high proportion coming from ethnic minorities. The Sweet Street

High Technology Centre provides courses on basic electronics, advance electronics and field service engineering, exclusively for women.
In London, the GLC established the Greater London Training Board, with a budget of £4 million in 1983-84, supporting some 2,300 apprenticeship and adult training places. In the West Midlands nearly 3,000 training places are available on various initiatives as part of a programme to maintain and develop basic skills for local industry, and to retrain, with particular emphasis on the needs of disadvantaged groups.

**Integrating social and economic policy**
Social measures have been integrated with economic and industrial initiatives. Training programmes in the West Midlands form part of a wider community strategy, which involves measures to increase the take up of welfare benefits, attack illegal low pay, provide work opportunities and counselling for the unemployed, and to assist voluntary groups. An independent West Midlands Low Pay Unit has been set up, funded by the County Council. The Unit publicises the role of the Wages Councils and encourages workers to ensure that they receive the legal level of pay. It dealt with 35,000 enquiries in its first six months.
The Council has also been concerned about the issue of poverty. Its research has shown that over 70 per cent of the county's unemployed receive means-tested supplementary benefits. Some 126,000 claimants in the county are missing out on about £15 million a year in supplementary benefits. The Council has launched a series of welfare benefits campaigns, which have increased take up by £2 million at a cost of only £10,000. These steps are important not only for social reasons, but also because they raise spending in the local economy.
Unemployed workers' centres have been set up in Birmingham, Coventry and Sandwell. The Birmingham Trade Union Resource Centre has been established and the Coventry Workshop supported, to back union campaigns against closure. The Economic Development Unit has a trade union liaison officer and several officers have been involved in campaigns with shop stewards from BL, Dunlop and Lucas. A 'Jobs at Risk' information pack is available for workers whose company is in difficulty or about to close down.
In Leeds, the City Council has a trade union liaison officer who has worked with trade unionists in the clothing industry. In Sheffield, the Department's Research and Resource Unit worked with the steel unions to produce a report showing how the steel

industry can be saved, and has been heavily involved in campaigns over the proposed 'Phoenix III' merger. In London, the GLC funded childcare projects, which we describe in Chapter 7. The GLC's Industrial Development Unit set up an Early Warning System to help workers identify signs that point towards closures and redundancies. The Project Development Unit funded over a dozen trade union resource centres. The Hackney Trades Council Support Unit, jointly funded by the GLC and Hackney Council, monitors local industry and assisted local tenants and direct labour workers to develop a plan for repairs and maintenance on council estates. The GLC Popular Planning Unit helped people in North Woolwich to oppose the Urban Development Corporation's proposal to build an airport in the area. The GLC also helped Kodak workers in Britain, France, Belgium, and Ireland, who have been resisting the multinational's plans to run down its operations in Europe.

**Enterprise boards**
One of the most significant steps taken by Labour authorities has been to establish new institutions — enterprise boards — to rebuild the local economy. These boards have enabled the authorities to bypass central government capital controls, to act speedily in mobilising private sector funds, to develop a focus of public sector expertise in economic development, and to have the legal right to take major equity stakes in private companies. Co-operative Development Agencies have also been set up; these are discussed elsewhere in this chapter, and in Chapter 6. The enterprise boards are all limited companies. They include:
• The *Greater London Enterprise Board*, which became operational in March 1983. The Board was given a full range of functions so that it can tailor assistance — training, new technology, property, marketing, finance and management — to the needs of specific projects. It has about 70 staff and in 1983-84 was allocated a total of £32 million, of which £18 million was available for projects and investments. The allocation for 1984-85 was also £32 million.
• The *West Midlands Enterprise Board* was established early in 1982 with initial finance of £3.5 million. By the summer of 1984 it had received grants from West Midlands County Council totalling £8.4 million. The Board has a small staff, reflecting its narrower focus on investment. The County's Economic Development Unit handled other areas of economic development activity and was brought in to provide additional support where appropriate.
• The *West Yorkshire Enterprise Board* became operational at the

end of 1982. It was set up to avoid central government capital controls at a time when much of the area had lost assisted area status. It was launched with a grant of £5.6 million in the financial year 1982-83 and a further £6 million for 1983-84.

• *Lancashire Enterprises Limited* was established in March 1982 with an initial capital of £2.7 million and subsequent grants of £4 million in 1983-84 and £4.5 million in 1984-85. Unlike the others, it acts as the sole agency for the County's economic development initiatives. It can function as a merchant bank, an estate agent, a development agency, a management consultant, or an institutional investor. It has about 20 staff, and divisions concerned with property, training, co-operatives and investment.

### Objectives and criteria for investment

The objectives and investment criteria of the Boards differ widely. In West Yorkshire and the West Midlands, the Boards have restricted their role to providing share capital for small and medium sized unquoted companies — something which the private capital markets consistently fail to do. The aim is mainly to secure viable long-term investment and jobs, thereby ensuring socially acceptable employment practices and a restricted range of other objectives. They possess the expertise to negotiate with various agencies to put together investment packages which companies and their advisors cannot arrange themselves.

The West Midlands Board has invested in local unquoted manufacturing companies through the provision of long-term equity and loan finance. The objective is to secure a sound and profitable long-term investment for the county whilst at the same time spreading the risk. The Board aims to provide no more than 50 per cent of the new finance. By early 1984 investments had already brought forth an additional £24 million with a leverage of £4 of private sector money for every £1 made available by the County. Other funds have come from a £2.5 million grant from the County and money from the London Transport pension fund and five London Borough pension funds.

The West Yorkshire Board combines equity and loan finance, ideally in a ratio of 20:80, with higher risk ventures receiving a greater proportion of equity. The Board maximises the use of its funds by raising as much money as possible from private sources and only using its own for topping up. Stakes of greater than 30 per cent are rarely taken.

In both the West Midlands and West Yorkshire considerable advice is given to help companies develop a detailed business plan. Consultancy surveys have also been undertaken in the

West Midlands into traditional metal manufacturing companies in the Black Country, and firms in growth sectors. These have revealed an absence of business planning and marketing skills, poor financial gearing, and a failure to introduce new technology. A County Council Business Development Team located within the Economic Development Unit has been set up to provide consultancy support.

Those Boards which have restricted themselves largely to a financial role have found that it is more difficult to exploit their relationship with firms fully by mobilising other forms of support, such as land and premises. This also makes it more difficult to adopt a sectoral approach.

The Lancashire Board uses the profits generated to support non-commercial employment initiatives, such as training. It concentrates investments on small to medium sized companies with 30-500 employees. Most investments fall in the range of £50,000 — £100,000. The Board normally takes a 26 per cent shareholding in a company but this can be extended to 50 per cent.

The London Board not only seeks to make commercially viable investments, but also to achieve wider social objectives through public sector investment, by analysing the wider costs and benefits of a particular project. The GLC's annual funding agreement with the Board was weighted towards projects with wider social benefits.

### Enterprise planning

Enterprise planning is the means by which wider social objectives are pursued. The London Board writes into its equity or loan agreement conditions regarding health and safety, trade union recognition, low pay, purchasing policy and so on. The Board works with the company and its workers on the development of a business plan, to secure maximum worker involvement on a continuing basis. It is necessary to proceed at a different pace in different companies. The starting point is collective bargaining and trade union recognition. Greater participation may mean sharing knowledge about the business, leading to direct worker involvement in developing corporate plans and seats on the board, or alternatively a workers' co-operative. Through enterprise planning, the Board also provides finance, premises and specialist business advisory services. It has secured equal opportunities clauses in agreements with firms and developed training programmes.

In the West Midlands, Lancashire and West Yorkshire, enterprise planning enables Board representatives to be appointed on to company boards, and thereby assume control. Less emphasis has been placed on wider social objectives, or on trade union involvement than in London, partly because of the reticence of local unions.

## Wider objectives
West Yorkshire has not related investment to sectoral objectives, on the grounds that this might unbalance the portfolio, thereby putting overall returns at risk. Nor have the Lancashire Board's investments been guided by any detailed sectoral criteria. However, it has intervened to pull together the town's fragmented fishing industry into a distribution centre, and to persuade Icelandic trawlers to sell catches at Fleetwood. It has taken a shareholding in Fish Ancillary Equipment Limited, and invested in fish merchant and processing companies.

In the West Midlands and London, interventions have been related to sectoral work and, in the case of London, to both the GLC's overall economic strategy and its social objectives. For example, a sector statement on the West Midlands Foundry sector led to a conference of companies, unions, manufacturers' associations, the engineering training board and industry research associations. An export marketing scheme was then set up.

## Local enterprise boards
The London Board jointly funds and runs local enterprise boards in Hackney and Haringey. Although they are independent they operate within the Board's policy framework. They will play a complementary role, with smaller companies.

## Enterprise boards assessed
Lancashire Enterprises expressed a common sentiment amongst the Boards when it summed up its role: 'on (our) own (we) cannot regenerate the whole of the county's severely eroded industrial base. Given the economic context in which we function, we can only serve as a *model* of what can be done if the finance and, more importantly, the will is there.'

Despite the view often expressed that the private sector would not accept 'onerous' conditions in return for public investment, it is clear that it is finding the terms of public accountability no more rigorous than those demanded by the banks and financial institutions. The Boards' requirements have not discouraged companies coming forward. They are levering private investment in a ratio of between 1:1 and 1:3.

The notion that only lame duck firms are involved is refuted by the rigorous financial evaluations that are undertaken, the large number of propositions which are turned down — in Lancashire, 19 out of 20 requests are rejected — and by the Boards' trading profits. There were a number of early failures, mainly due to political pressures and inexperience — the West Midlands has had three — but the Boards have learned from experience. They all have failure rates well below the 30 per cent considered acceptable by ICFC, the major private sector finance agency. The provision of equity and long-term development capital is inevitably risky and it is generally recognised that the Boards' commercial appraisal is often more demanding (and constructive) than that of most private sector financial institutions.

**The local authority as employer and purchaser**
Many local authorities have explicitly decided not to set up an enterprise board. Sheffield, for example, operates at a city, rather than a county level, so there are less resources for investment. Nor, as a Metropolitan District, does the city manage the pension fund of its employees. Moreover, councillors did not want to risk losing policy control over decision making. And they believed that they could do what they wanted to anyway, including taking minority stakes in companies, without having to set up an enterprise board.

Sheffield's Employment Department argues that any intervention must be public sector led. This is interesting given the limited resources at the disposal of most Labour local authorities. The Department began in 1981 by giving priority to financial assistance for private firms. Only 66 loans were given in response to 500 applications. Work now concentrates on co-operatives and equal opportunities initiatives, and on joint ventures with the private sector. However, doubts exist about giving more support to general private sector schemes, because other sources of finance are available, and because the private sector failed to come forward with many acceptable proposals. These doubts were heightened when a major investment, Wincotts, went into receivership.

Instead, Sheffield City Council has tried to exploit the *direct* leverage that local authorities have in the local economy, as indicated in Chapter 2. The Council employs nearly 32,000, about a quarter of all paid employment in the city, making it five times larger than the largest industrial employer, BSC. It therefore has a major impact on the labour market through its employment, training and recruitment practices. The Council has an annual budget of £240 million, spending approximately £80 million on purchases, £20 million of this being spent in Sheffield and providing orders for no fewer than 900 local firms. The City Council's capital and revenue spending of £84 million on construction and related activity accounts for three quarters of all investment in the local construction industry.

The Council's Equal Opportunities Panel, for example, increased the number of young women applying for apprentice training in the works department. The Economic and Public Sector Panel, established in July 1983, helped set up the Local Government Campaign Working Party, which includes councillors, representatives from trade unions and other organisations in the city to defend jobs and services. The panel has also helped promote municipal enterprise, such as a municipal security service based on an expansion of the parks patrol, and a horticultural project, so that the City Council can produce in-house the £250,000 of shrubs and trees it buys each year. The panel has also developed a contracts compliance policy, by preparing a list of 850 firms which supply all the departments. The list will be reviewed every two years and a working party of councillors has been set up to consider appeals from companies.

**The GLC: equal opportunities and contract compliance**
Until its abolition in March 1986, the GLC placed great emphasis on tackling the inequalities faced by women and ethnic minorities in the labour market. In 1981 the GLC agreed a revised and strengthened policy for its 20,000 employees. The policy was monitored by an Equal Opportunities Monitoring Group which included nominees from all GLC unions, senior management and council members. The Group also produced a Code of Practice on equal opportunities which covered every aspect of the GLC's employment procedures and dealt with special needs, such as those of people with domestic responsibilities and of people with disabilities. An Equal Opportunities Unit was established in September 1982 which advised the Personnel Department on equal opportunities. Two workplace day nurseries were opened for GLC employees. The Council also approved the principle that job-sharing should be available to all existing and potential employees. A charter on part-time work was prepared to allow improvements in promotion and career opportunities for part-time workers. One of the most innovatory GLC departments, the London Fire Brigade, set up a separate equal opportunities section.

As well as trying to set its own house in order, the GLC used its intervention through the Enterprise Board to promote equal opportunities. Firms that wanted assistance were expected to meet the GLC's equal opportunities requirements. Several women's co-operatives were funded, including Lambeth Toys, a co-op of Asian and West Indian women; Letterbox Library, a book club run by single parent women; and Matrix, an architects' co-op that works with housing co-ops and community groups. Training projects to improve the position of women include the Haringey Women's Training and Education Centre and the Women's Motor Mechanics Workshop.

To support ethnic minority businesses the Board has funded an Afro-Caribbean Bank and specialist advisory and consultancy services. Special training measures have also been supported, such as the Tower Hamlets Training Forum, which provides specialist training for the clothing industry and includes many female trainees from the Bengali Community.

The most effective means of promoting equal opportunities, however, may be through contract compliance, the implications of which for national policy are discussed in Chapter 6. The GLC had a purchasing power of £500 million a year. Its purchasing policy was modelled on the United States system of Federal Contract Compliance — widely regarded as one of the most significant steps in advancing equality at work for women and ethnic minorities in the United States.

The GLC set up a contracts compliance unit in March 1983, after extensive consultation with the Equal Opportunities Commission, the Commission for Racial Equality, trade unions and employers' associations. The Council held an approved list of over 4,000 contractors and 16,000 suppliers from whom tenders were invited for the supply of goods and services. A Code of Practice required contractors to pay fair wages and comply with the Council's health and safety policy; to employ their workers directly; to be members of a trade association; to comply with the Sex Discrimination and Race Relations Acts; and to provide a breakdown of their workforce, indicating the numbers of women and ethnic minority workers in various occupational categories and information about selection, recruitment and advertising of jobs.

Because of the scale and nature of problems within the London building industry, an Equal Opportunities Unit for construction was set up. The Unit focused on all companies with which the GLC spent over £100,000 in 1982-83 — about 100. A number of legal obstacles had to be overcome. The Unit did not require firms to be unionised, because this would have contravened the 1982 Employment Act, but rather that no action be taken by employers to deter contacts by employees with trade unions. Employers generally kept to fair wages clauses, partly because this policy has been pursued since the establishment of the London County Council's supplies department in 1909. The 1980 Competition Act demands that there is full competition between firms hoping to be awarded local authority contracts, but this was overcome by requiring compliance before the point of contract.

## Conclusions

The lessons of the economic initiatives taken by Labour local authorities are far-reaching, both for the role of local initiatives within a national strategy and for national strategy itself. These initiatives show what can be achieved by using local knowledge and resources to deal with specific local economic problems. But the limited scale of what is being achieved must also be recognised, in terms of reducing unemployment and rebuilding industry. On a national scale, only a handful of jobs and firms have been saved and created. These achievements are examples of what can be achieved. But without a sympathetic national government, even these gains could be overwhelmed by the effects of deflation and rate-capping.

The lack of a supportive national policy has been the single most important factor limiting the success of local initiatives. We cannot, however, conclude that they would have achieved all their objectives even given such support. First, the lack of clarity in objectives has sometimes been a major obstacle. Local economic initiatives have tried to combine saving jobs, strengthening the local economy and various social objectives. The pursuit of social objectives often imposes extra costs. From the perspective of the national economy these costs may be offset by other benefits, such as savings on unemployment benefit. These savings cannot, however, be taken into account at local level. Second, many local authority interventions have resulted from *reactions* to events. They have not, therefore, been fully informed by sector strategies. As a result, sector strategies have sometimes proved incoherent and unworkable. On the other hand, it is impossible to conclude in the light of recent experience that only the absence of national support has held local initiatives back. Clearly, both national *and* local policy alike must be developed if either is to succeed.

Even having taken these limitations into account, however, it must be recognised that local initiatives have highlighted major inadequacies in existing regional policy (see Chapter 6). Their lessons for national policy go far beyond a call to devolve resources, and promote indigenous growth. In their relationship with the private sector, local initiatives have shown the importance of intervening directly, using a package of measures to support firms and extend accountability. By involving the local workforce and community, and integrating economic and social goals, they have, in some cases, shown an alternative to technocratic intervention. And, in their recognition of the impact of the public sector, as employer and purchaser, they have highlighted the potential power — and responsibility — of national government. What we must now decide is which decisions should be taken at what level, because there is an inherent limit to what can be achieved locally.

## PLANNING NOW: THE LESSONS

Current attempts to bring economic decision making under democratic control have important lessons for national policy. Workers' plans have highlighted the wasted skills of working people and the potential for developing new products. But the fact that few have been implemented points to the limits of even more imaginative forms of collective bargaining in a hostile economic and political environment. Workers' co-ops have shown that working people can extend control over production within their enterprise. But the tension between trade unionists as representatives and as managers underlines the problems that will be encountered in extending industrial democracy, in private and public enterprise. And, in many cases, co-ops are kept going by the self-exploitation of their members. The initiatives of Labour local authorities provide exciting models of what can be achieved through intervention that combines a package of measures with accountability, and the recognition of wider social objectives. But, on their own, these initiatives will barely dent the rise in unemployment. Their future, moreover, is at risk as resources are taken away by a hostile government.

Local initiatives must be backed by the power of national government if they are to achieve their full potential. As the powers and resources of local government are being undermined by the Conservative Government, the significance of national government as a focus for action increases.

By far the major reason why state power at a national level is important is that it heavily determines the economic environment within which each enterprise has to operate. It has a major influence on the level of demand, the exchange rate, the availability of credit, interest rates and levels of taxation and subsidy — all of which have a substantial impact. In recent years those levers have been operated so as to create a slump, sending firms out of business and creating mass unemployment. The potential for resisting this at a local level is strictly limited.

Local successes cannot simply be generalised. Particular groups of workers often gain at the expense of others. Many of the struggles which were most publicised in the late 1970's — for example at Gardner's, Lee Jeans or Staffa — were at least in part about the *transfer* of jobs: in the case of Gardner's from sub-contractors to the main plant; with Lee Jeans between Scotland and Northern Ireland; and with Staffa between London and Plymouth. This does not diminish these struggles but they can have little or no impact on *overall* employment since this is primarily determined by the overall demand in the economy. Similarly a co-operative could create jobs by providing goods and services at present provided by other companies so that no net new jobs are created.

The importance of national economic power should not mean that its limitations are forgotten. Britain is closely integrated into, and therefore vulnerable to developments in, international production and trading. Action should be taken internationally, at a European level, to deal with multinationals in Britain. But this may not be possible. The leverage that national government has, above all through access to the domestic market, is far greater than the leverage of local government or workers at plant level.

Second, the *legislative* power of national government is vital. Local action may be able to blunt the impact of rate-capping, at least for a short time, but it has not been able to overturn it or to delay the abolition of the GLC and metropolitan county councils. And new laws are needed to increase the rights of working people to influence enterprise decisions, the resources available to co-ops and the rights of consumers.

Third, the power of national government can provide a channel, and in many cases the only channel, through which workers can escape the logic of, or gain access to, the market. 'Socially useful' products are often designed for sale to the public sector, as the example of the Sheffield de-humidifier shows. In this case it is the level and allocation of public spending that is at stake. Where products are potentially profitable, they may still need the same kind of government support to bring them to the market as is enjoyed by many private firms, for example through public purchasing or financial assistance for product development.

Finally, it is only at a national level that local initiatives can be co-ordinated, and their claims on resources made consistent with broader economic and social criteria. A national industrial policy must, for the most part, be developed and implemented at a *national* level: it cannot simply be reduced to an aggregation of local initiatives. Many regions may want to attract major motor assembly plants but a national strategy for motor manufacturing and design will have to choose between manufacturers and, therefore, regions. In the case of textiles and clothing, dominated by multinationals in which small firms can also play a vital role, there is scope for considerable local initiative within the framework of a national strategy. Both sectors are discussed in our case studies (Chapters 10 and 11).

The importance of national government is not an argument for saying that legislative power is sufficient on its own — but it is necessary. Without it, local initiatives will be frustrated, and planning now will become increasingly limited in scope and achievement.

CHAPTER 4

# A Right To Paid Work

A minimum condition for taking greater democratic control over
the economy is that we should establish a right to paid work. This
is a vital objective in itself. It implies a right to an independent
income and thus to participate and share in the country's
growing wealth. It also means a right for each person to apply
and develop their abilities and skills and thus make choices about
their own life. A right to paid work will not guarantee any of these
things — many women, for example, are prevented from
fulfilling their potential by their responsibility for the care of
dependants — but it is a necessary beginning.

A right to paid work is also important because the level of
unemployment is a key indicator and regulator of the balance of
power in society. When the Conservative Government was
elected in 1979 it set out on an economic strategy which inevitably
and predictably raised unemployment to levels not experienced
for a generation. Unemployment has played a key part in
undermining trade union bargaining power, depressing wages,
increasing profits, and promoting a profound restructuring of
industry involving widespread redundancies. Unemployment
has bred unemployment.

It is easy to see the slump into mass unemployment as
something inevitable which we are all forced to stand by
helplessly and watch. To individuals, families or firms, the
economy looks fixed and forbidding: beyond individual control
and therefore beyond society's control. It is precisely that feeling
of helplessness — of powerlessness in the face of economic forces
beyond human intervention — that the present Government tries
to encourage.

It is only when we look beyond the fragmented individual
units of the economy and day-to-day transactions of the market
place that we start to see the interconnections and interdependence of economic activity. The way individuals spend
their money will not affect their chances of employment. The way
we collectively spend our money does. Individually we can only

compete for jobs and markets. Collectively, we can create them. Workers acting alone must take the wage on offer. Together they can negotiate over what they are paid.

Nor is unemployment inevitable: despite the world recession, unemployment has remained below 4 per cent in Austria, Japan, Norway, Sweden, and Switzerland. And, while technological change means that no government can rely on manufacturing to recreate the "full employment" of the 1960s, there is considerable scope for expansion in services — both private and public. Moreover, the recent rise in unemployment in Britain is *not* the result of investment in new technologies: Britain has had the fastest rise in unemployment, but has been the *slowest* to invest in new technologies, of the major industrial countries.

More generally, governments can have a substantial impact on the number of jobs available through their influence over the total level of demand in the economy. But it is also important to understand the constraints on government action imposed by the way in which any economy, and particularly the British economy, is tied into the international financial, industrial and trading system.

**How can governments create jobs?**
How can governments influence the chance of finding paid work? The government has enormous powers over the economy. It can push interest rates up or down by setting the level at which it will borrow from the banking system. It can influence the exchange rate by buying and selling on the foreign exchange markets and by influencing expectations of how the value of the currency will change. And most importantly, through its control of taxation and public spending programmes, it can directly influence the level of spending in the economy as a whole.

Moreover, the public sector employs around one in three of the workforce, and through central government, local government and public corporations, produces a substantial part of the goods and services on which we rely. Decisions about the way these economic levers are used are profoundly political. They not only determine the direction of economic activity within the public sector, but set a framework for the activity outside it.

In simple terms, the level of employment is set by the level of production. It is possible to create more jobs without producing anything more, for example by cutting the working hours of those presently employed. But private employers are not going to rush to do this unless pay is cut by a corresponding amount. It is also posible to cut unemployment by taking people out of the workforce without creating any new jobs, or by putting people into 'make work' schemes which add nothing to the useful goods and services the country produces. So, with these qualifications, an increase in employment will not happen without a more rapid increase in the production of goods and services — public and private — in the economy and therefore an increase in economic growth.

## Growth versus Greens

Economic growth as measured by conventional accounting methods is not an accurate indicator of welfare. The 'non-financial' costs of production are not given due weight. Industrial growth has gone hand in hand with pollution, waste and noise, the disruption of communities and the encouragement of acquisitive, materialistic values at the expense of any others. A more democratic economy should involve a much higher value being put on the conditions in which people live and work, and would not degrade or destroy the natural environment. Some argue that this will mean curbing economic growth rather than encouraging it. Is there a conflict, therefore, between "environmental" concerns and the right to paid work?

Part of the answer is that some of the problems for the environment lie in the way existing production is organised, rather than in the growth of production as such. Zero growth would solve no problems if the organisation of production itself were not tackled. One objective should therefore be to ensure that those who have power over production are held accountable for the costs they impose on society, that extra wealth is used to help us meet the cost of controlling pollution and improving the environment, and that new values are built into the organisation of work and the design of products.

Another part of the answer lies in challenging the sovereignty of the market. Market mechanisms can lead firms to produce low quality, disposable goods, or goods with built-in obsolescence, in the attempt to increase sales and profits. Similarly, the depletion of non-renewable resources goes on largely unchecked because market mechanisms do not respond sufficiently quickly to the needs of future generations. Private firms (and often public ones too) try to ignore the impact of their own decisions on the world's resources because they fear that if they do not maintain production they will loose market share.

Some of these problems can be alleviated or overcome by modifying market mechanisms — for example, through taxes on polluters or on over-rapid depletion of resources. Others can be dealt with by government regulation — 'holding the ring' to ensure honest and safe trading. But in other cases, where there is a clear conflict between market outcomes and the public welfare, more direct intervention will be necessary. This may mean in some cases a slower rate of economic 'growth', as it is conventionally defined.

New methods of assessing *social* profitability, reflecting broader costs and benefits, need to be developed. For example, plant closure decisions should consider:

• Whether the units were loss making or simply returning lower profits than could be obtained elsewhere.

• If losses were made, whether they could be reversed.

• Whether the cost of action needed to reverse the losses was less than the cost of closure.

• What sort of public/private package would be needed to maintain production.

This kind of approach could have a powerful impact. It would involve working people at critical moments, and could build up their self-confidence. It would rely on local initiatives, and would necessarily draw out the links between corporate strategy and plant decisions. Such an approach must also be extended beyond closures. Frequently closure of a plant becomes inevitable because its equipment is obsolete. This process must be part of a review which avoids the need for closure in the first place.

Planning inquiries, social audits and environmental impact assessments are all established ways of evaluating the wider impact of economic decisions:

• *Planning inquiries* are the best known, but deficient for our purpose. Their scope has tended to be restricted: alternative means of achieving objectives are often ignored and participation is limited. They are too slow and their procedure too judicial.

• *Social audits* have gained some popularity as a test of enterprise profitability, especially in response to plant closures. They offer a way of tracing the social costs and benefits arising from investment, as well as the impact on resource depletion, local and national employment, and the stress on existing social investment in education, health and other services.

• *Environmental impact assessments* involve examining different ways of reaching goals, and calculating the social, economic and environmental costs and benefits in each case.

We can learn from all of these methods. Above all it is important to realise that the value of any system is determined by the scope for real participation, and by the breadth of consultation. The value of planning inquiries, for example, is limited where there is too little public funding; where access to information is restricted; and where inquiries are sited in remote locations. All too often such inquiries are not a method of decision making but either a rubber-stamping mechanism or a technique for delay by objectors. Finally, the usefulness of such methods is limited because they are mainly relevant to 'one-off' decisions: improved product design and the avoidance of built-in obsolescence, for example, will require *continuous* involvement, perhaps within a framework of legal minimum standards monitored by trade unions and community groups.

**Instruments for expansion**
How can production be expanded? It is worth distinguishing between two circumstances. If most people who want paid work already have it, the only way to get more out of the economy is by people working longer, harder and more efficiently, or by using more capital equipment to help them. On the other hand, if there are massive unused resources of people and equipment — as there are in Britain at the moment — the simplest way to increase production is to bring these wasted resources back into use; to build a bridge between the waste of unemployment and the want of unmet needs.

The simple reason why people who want paid work are unemployed is that the goods and services they could be producing could not be sold. Firms have low order books which they can easily meet with their existing staff. Initially, therefore, the key to increasing production is to increase demand. There are many different ways that a government can do this:

1. *Consumer spending* can be increased by cutting taxes on income or spending to raise 'disposable' income. Lower interest rates encourage purchases on credit, and higher pay (particularly for the lowest paid) will tend to increase spending.

2. *Exports* can be promoted by a lower exchange rate which makes export sales more profitable and competitive. It will also make imports more expensive and so direct spending towards home produced goods.

3. *Investment* in capital equipment is encouraged most effectively by the prospect of growing markets. Cheaper finance from lower interest rates also helps.

4. *Public spending* on services such as health and education, capital projects such as house building, and benefits such as pensions and child benefit provide a simple and effective way of increasing demand.

Using these instruments a government can create the conditions for expanded production and therefore employment. If this is not done, markets will tend to remain static and this will tend to depress investment and innovation and so make the long-term prospects even worse. Attempts at industrial restructuring, and local initiatives to promote employment, will have limited results unless the right framework for expansion can be set at national level.

In the following sections we want to look in more detail at the kind of package that could be effective in Britain in the late 1980's, and at some of the conditions for its success. Three themes that are important to our argument are:

• First, that the detailed design of the package is important. Each economic package embodies definite political choices and priorities, for example as between spending on infrastructure projects and spending to relieve poverty.

• Second, we argue that one of the weaknesses of policy making in Britain has been a lack of co-ordination between the Treasury and government departments responsible for industrial development. The overall regulation of the economy through "macro-economic" policies has to be closely and carefully linked to plans for structural reform of industry.

• Third, there are real constraints on what can be achieved in a single, open economy like Britain. Careful judgements have to be made about where these constraints can be overcome and where we have to live within them.

**A bridge between waste and want**
We have argued that the first step towards democratic control of the economy has to be a plan for mobilising unused resources to meet unmet needs. But what kind of plan? How fast can we move? And who is to pay for it?

Each of the measures available to governments has different advantages and drawbacks. Cuts in VAT, for example, increase spending power and cut prices at the same time. They are a good way of getting more spending without inflation. But their impact on jobs is limited by a large leakage of spending on imports.

Increased public spending, on the other hand, has a three-fold advantage. It feeds directly into domestic jobs and can be targeted at areas where jobs are needed most. And it helps us to meet our social objectives for improved community services. Table 1 below shows the rough cost per job from different kinds of public intervention, measured in terms of additional public borrowing. This is not a wholly satisfactory basis for comparing policy options, but it does illustrate the sizeable advantage of higher public spending as against lower taxes.

Within public spending programmes, there is a choice to be made between services, investment and benefits; and in labour intensive activities there are further choices between increased pay and service provision. But however it is spent, public spending feeds directly through to private spending.

## Table 1: The cost of job creation

The cost in extra public borrowing (in 1984-85 prices) for each person removed from the unemployment count by:

| | £ p.a. |
|---|---|
| *Tax cuts* | |
| Employer's National Insurance contributions | 59,200 |
| VAT | 58,800 |
| Income Tax | 47,000 |
| *Public investment* | |
| Health | 51,000 |
| Roads | 32,700 |
| Average | 26,200 |
| Education | 26,200 |
| Housing | 15,800 |
| *Public services* | |
| Defence | 45,200 |
| Average | 15,300 |
| Health | 10,700 |
| Education/Local government | 10,400 |

Source: Gavyn Davies and David Metcalf, *The Times* 9 April 1985

We have heard so much in recent years from government supporters about how public spending can damage the economy. But it is worth spending a few moments spelling out the real links. Employing more teachers means that public spending goes into pay packets. From there it boosts spending on the whole range of goods and services produced by the private sector so prompting them to increase production and take on more staff. The extra staff taken on, both in the public sector and outside, will pay part of their wages in tax and part of their spending in VAT, so completing the circle and bringing extra revenue back to the government.

The same cycle takes place when the government spends money on benefits and capital projects. The impact of the initial public spending is "multiplied" in the private sector, boosting economic activity and jobs. If the extra spending is paid for out of taxation, its net effect will be much smaller because tax drains spending power out of the economy just as public spending puts it back in. So public spending is most effective in boosting the economy when it is paid for out of savings — money which would not otherwise have been spent. This is what the government is doing when it pays for spending by increasing public borrowing. It is effectively putting people's savings to work in mobilising the country's unused resources. It is not a "quick fix" or a "live now, pay later" philosophy; it is a sensible form of economic management which is essential if the country's resources are to be fully used. Economists call it reflation. It has had a bad press and needs some rehabilitation.

The detailed design of any package to boost the economy must depend on the economic conditions prevailing at the time it is introduced. The government should be looking at the level of employment and the amount of spare capacity in the economy; the level of inflation and prospects for external price increases such as in oil; and the balance of trade. These are some factors which should be taken into account:

1. *Different kinds of spending create different kinds of jobs.* For example, roughly 65 per cent of those working in public services such as health, education and social services are women. Increased spending on these services will create many job opportunities for women. Public investment in infrastructure, on the other hand, tends to concentrate job creation on jobs such as construction which are mostly done by men.

2. *Public spending can have important secondary benefits.* For example, a large expansion of child care facilities would both create thousands of jobs — in practice for women — and help to liberate mothers who would otherwise be trapped in the home, unable to take paid work.

3. *There are strong advantages in targeting spending on areas where jobs are needed most.* For example, a supplementary rate support grant to fund job intensive local council services could be paid selectively according to the level of unemployment within each local authority. Council services are highly labour intensive, and local authorities are often in a very good position to expand services quickly in a way that both creates jobs and meets local needs.

**How quickly can we move?**
The amount which the government borrows each year — currently defined by the public sector borrowing requirement (PSBR) — provides a rough indicator of whether the government is expanding or contracting the economy. A rise in the PSBR usually means that the government is increasing its spending without raising taxes to pay for it — or indicates some injection of spending power into the economy. Since 1979 the Tory

Government has endowed the PSBR with almost mystical significance, as the centrepiece of its "medium term financial strategy". At the start we were told that it was important to cut the PSBR because lower borrowing would mean a smaller increase in money supply and that would bring lower inflation. More recently those money supply targets have been almost completely abandoned as it has become clear that the claimed links do not exist. Nonetheless the PSBR remains at the centre of Tory strategy, largely as a signal to the financial markets that nothing is going to be done to disturb the comfortable climate of high interest rates and dole queue-depressed inflation.

There is broad agreement outside the Conservative Party that some government action to reflate the economy is needed but there are widely divergent views about how fast and how far the government should go. We would argue that the starting point for any discussion on the extent of reflation should be the solid ground of the 'real' economy of people producing goods and services and looking for work, and not the ephemeral 'financial' economy which is the starting point for monetarism. This is not to say that these financial factors are unimportant. They do impose practical contraints on what governments can do, which must be set against the needs of the real economy. But a touchstone for the democratic economy is that it should free policy making from the tyranny of the fragile and elusive "confidence" of the financial markets. In practical terms this means looking at the numbers of jobless, the extent of spare capacity, the need for training, and the speed with which people can be put to work. The level of spending required should flow from this and not be determined by some arbitrary PSBR target.

This is easy to say but harder to do. Once business confidence is lost, capital tends to leave the country, forcing down the exchange rate and pushing up import costs. Interest rates have to go higher to persuade people to lend to the government, adding further to costs. Anticipating a slow-down, business finds it sensible to cut its investment in new capacity and training. The pressures on a government trying to break the straitjacket of economic orthodoxy would be enormous. But a project for economic recovery, while recognising this, must be prepared to take on these pressures and reassert the power of common sense over the arbitrariness of financial power.

## Who pays?
The immediate challenge facing anyone who argues for more public spending is: how to pay for it ? The present Government claims it is a choice between raising taxes which stifle enterprise

or fuelling inflation by printing money. They ignore the third option, which is to sell government debt to the private sector — the pension funds, life insurance companies, building societies, merchant banks, local authorities and other institutions — which are delighted to find a safe home for the funds they manage. It is ironic that borrowing by British Telecom as a public corporation to fund investment in communications was counted as part of the PSBR and so was regarded as a damaging drain on the economy. As a private company BT can underake exactly the same borrowing to fund exactly the same investment and this is presented as a life saving injection into the communications industry of the future. A clear case of the upside-down economy at work.

But if borrowing makes so much sense, why is it seen with such suspicion ? This is difficult to explain. In Japan, one of the most successful economies, public borrowing is far higher than in Britain, and there are many other examples. Part of the suspicion seems to derive from a deeply cautious streak among many people who feel that it is dangerous to get into debt; although borrowing by governments (which can always raise taxes to pay off the debt) is a wholly different matter to borrowing by individuals, the fears of the individual must be projected upwards.


## Push and pull

As policy making became more sophisticated in Britain after the war there remained a strangely crude divorce between policies to pull the economy along through higher demand and policies to push it through cheaper and better organised supply. The Treasury has looked after the macro-economic "demand" side. The "supply" side has received passing attention from the Department of Industry and Trade, and of Energy, with occasional interventions by the Bank of England.

An attempt to link macro and micro policy flowered briefly under the National Plan and the Department of Economic Affairs in the mid-1960's but the overriding priority given to the balance of payments, together with the absence of any effective instruments of intervention, drove this initiative into an early and undeserved grave (Chapter 5).

It cannot be emphasised too strongly that one of the most important conditions for the success of a project for a democratic economy is an effective link between "macro" policies for expansion of the economy and policies of structural intervention in industry and trade. This is the missing link, the absence of which has crippled numerous attempts at economic reform. But what does this mean in practice?

*First*, it means that the government needs to take a view about how it expects and wants the economy to develop over three to five years ahead. It is reasonably straightforward to work out what these projections mean for individual sectors of the economy and that in turn will help individual companies to plan their investment strategies. This kind of forward thinking also helps governments to anticipate what difficulties might arise, for example with shortages of skilled labour or rising demands for imports, and to take early steps to deal with them. If this kind of medium term economic plan is to be effective, it must above all be credible. We cannot rely on it working only if people believe it will work and act accordingly, the approach taken under the National Plan of the 1960's. It must be based on a practical assessment of economic potential backed up by a realistic appraisal of the instruments available to achieve that potential. And this in turn raises questions of economic *power*: will the decisions taken by major industrial and finance companies be consistent with the demands of recovery?

*Second*, the macro-micro link means being prepared to intervene quickly and effectively to steer resources towards delivering the best result. For example, if the initial projections suggest a shortage of teachers or skilled electrical engineers then it will take a minimum of three years to remedy these deficiencies. It is only by looking ahead that the problem can be avoided. Similarly, if rising demand for particular manufactured goods is forecast and existing UK capacity cannot meet that demand then it makes sense to make sure that investment takes place rather than waiting for imports to soar and the resulting trade imbalance to choke off growth.

*Third*, the government should build these economic projections into its own design for a jobs package. For example, it would not make sense to plan a massive programme of rail electrification without making sure that the UK steel and electronics industries were sufficiently geared up to meet the demand. For such links to work, an essential precondition is a much improved flow of information between government departments and between government and companies.

### The limits on expansion

A successful strategy must take into account the limits on growth and intervene where necessary to overcome them. Two of the most important constraints arise from the particular way that

Britain is locked into the international economy through trade
and through international capital movements. A third constraint
is imposed by the threat of rising inflation.

*Trade policy*
Britain's trade is in surplus at the moment: a £3 billion deficit on
manufactured trade is being covered by a larger surplus on oil
trade. Under a government committed to expansion there are
going to be two major problems. Oil production is going to
decline, leaving a gap to be filled. And as more people get back to
work and have more to spend, imports are going to accelerate.
This is not a disaster. Countries can live with trade deficits for
quite a long time. And with an effective exchange control
scheme, capital invested overseas will be returning. This will give
us extra foreign exchange to pay for imports. However, we
cannot afford to let imports and exports get too far out of line. The
pressures we are likely to face on trade will depend heavily on
what is happening in the rest of the world and particularly in
Europe. The French Socialist Government, for example, tried to
boost the economy in 1981 and 1982 at a time when the rest of the
European economy was moving into slump. The result was that
France became an attractive target for other countries' exporters
and a trade deficit amounting to nearly £10,000 million emerged
in 1983. The Government appeared to have no plans ready to
handle this problem, being reluctant to devalue the franc or
consider import controls. The result was that expanison was
abandoned in 1983 in a switch to austerity that has become all too
familiar to socialists.

How can we avoid these problems in Britain? We can begin by
talking to other governments, particularly those that are
politically sympathetic, to try to get some joint action on jobs. If
several countries can expand together then one country's import
problem is the other country's export boom. The problem of trade
imbalances which arises from going it alone will be diminished.

However, we should not pin too much hope on this. A joint
European plan for jobs is an ideal worth working for, but the
chances of finding many socialist governments in power in key
European counties at the same time are small. At the moment
there would be little support from France, Germany or Italy and
we should not pretend that alliances with countries such as
Greece, Sweden and Norway will have any significant impact on
Britain's trade prospects.

If we cannot get a response from other countries, do we have to
learn to live with unemployment? We would argue strongly
against this pessimistic view. The first thing we must do is bring

the pound down to a more competitive level in relation to European currencies. That makes imports dearer and exports easier to sell abroad. But all our experience of Britain's trading patterns suggests that these price adjustments are not going to be enough. Non-price factors and the decisons of multinational firms are increasingly important in determining trade flows. The government must therefore be ready to intervene directly to promote exports and stop imports growing too fast. There are many ways this can be done:

• The government should be hard-headed in its dealings with companies. A big factor behind Britain's import boom is decisions by manufacturers and retailers to buy components and finished goods abroad, as the motor industry in particular shows (Chapter 10).

• The government can make it easier to buy within the UK and more difficult to import by putting buyers in touch with UK producers and setting up administrative barriers for importers. In some cases we can negotiate voluntary restraints on trade such as that which currently applies to the import of Japanese cars to the UK.

• The government should monitor import penetration in a range of sectors and be prepared to impose import penetration ceilings where necessary.

• If the import problem shows any sign of getting out of hand, the government must be prepared to use more radical measures such as an import deposit scheme for all manufactured goods or a general supplementary tariff.

Expanding the economy to create jobs will mean more trade, not less. This should be used as the basis for discussions with other European countries. It would be self-defeating on their part if they were to force Britain back into slump by blocking import regulations, especially if such measures were primarily directed at restricting the growth of imports rather than cutting existing levels. Developing counties will also benefit from expanding UK markets, while import controls will not be directed mainly at their products — in textiles, for example, the import "threat" comes not from developing countries but from Europe (Chapter 11).

*Exchange controls*
In 1979 the controls on capital movements, which had been in place since 1939, were stripped away. The result has been a huge outflow of funds, now running at about £10,000 million a year. A great deal of this money takes the form of investments abroad by pension funds and life assurance companies.

The Labour Party has proposed an imaginative scheme to get

some of this money back. Under this scheme, long-term savings institutions would only get their current tax privileges if they reduce their overseas investments below a fixed percentage of total investments.

This should bring a steady flow of funds back into the country which will help to keep the pound up and pay for growing imports. But these schemes for exchange control will do nothing to stop banks, companies and overseas holders of sterling from moving huge volumes of cash across the exchanges for speculative reasons. This is a problem because the pound is now far more exposed than it was in the "sterling crisis" of 1976. There is a strong chance that the pound could be hit by a wave of speculative selling, resulting at least in part from political motives. To counter this threat, the government must be prepared to ride out storms of this kind and not be panicked into unnecessary changes in policy — in the past the pound has fluctuated far more wildly than in 1976 but this has not started a political crisis. In addition, a future Labour Government will need to take steps to control overseas investment by industrial companies. This should be possible by an extension of the repatriation scheme described above.

*The EEC*
Many will argue that membership of the EEC is incompatible with industrial planning or exchange controls. The Treaty of Rome is, after all, largely designed to promote the free movement of capital across national boundaries.

Practical experience of the actions of member states, however, points to rather different conclusions. Many have been able to introduce policies for industrial reorganisation in sectors such as textiles, both at national and EEC level, which have involved substantial state intervention and finance. British industries such as steel have been particularly hard hit by EEC schemes, but mainly because British governments have wanted them to be: despite EEC backed capacity "reductions" in steel it is only in Britain that capacity has been drastically cut back. Indeed, EEC regulations specifically recognise the right of member states to introduce (temporary) measures to curb imports, if the alternative would be a balance of payments crisis which prevents the implementation of policies for full employment.

We would argue for a two-stage approach. First, the real limitations imposed by EEC membership must be addressed through negotiations. There is a considerable common interest among European states in concerted *industrial* action in sectors such as information technology, which will require massive and sustained investment, and in which Europe (let alone Britain) is falling further and further behind the USA and Japan.

Only if these negotiations failed, and if EEC laws proved to be a binding constraint, would it be necessary to go further and reconsider membership. Obviously many other political factors would be involved in this, and withdrawal would not be a certain outcome — economic and industrial planning might therefore have to adapt to some continuing constraints.

*Inflation*

The most common objection raised against plans to expand the economy is that they will cause accelerating inflation. The monetarists have dressed up the argument in their own theoretical clothing: reflation means more public borrowing, which means a higher 'money supply', which means higher prices. Mrs. Thatcher has a cruder approach. Reflation equals inflation, she declares. More traditional economists point to the pressure from wage claims that must be expected as the economy picks up and the threat of unemployment is lifted. They might also warn about companies taking advantage of growing markets to boost their profits by lifting prices.

Our case is that each of these pressures exists but there is nothing inevitable about inflation rising as the economy grows. We argue that the best way to understand inflation is to see it as a process of *conflict* over the broad distribution of income between profits, wages and tax. Firms raise prices to cover rising costs and keep up, or increase, their profit margins — the share of income going to profits. Workers aim for wage rises which at least cover the rising cost of living and where possible achieve a rising standard of living. The government makes sure that its income from taxes keeps its value.

The system is stable as long as each of these three broad groups is happy with the share it is getting. If the national income is growing at 3 per cent then profits, wages and tax revenue can all increase by 3 per cent without anyone losing their share. But if real national income is cut by, for example, a sudden increase in import prices, or if there is a sharp increase in taxation, or firms move aggressively to increase profits, then conflicts are set up which emerge as inflation. The resulting inflation tends to accelerate faster if each group has the strength to defend its position and advance new claims. If oil prices rise and firms pass on the increase to customers, who in turn pass on the cost by pursuing compensatory wage increases from employers, who in turn pass on the extra wage cost to customers, then the ingredients exist for an inflationary spiral. In the late 1960's and early 1970's, to take another example, skilled workers were faced both with general inflation and high *marginal* tax rates — wage increases higher than the inflation rate were therefore needed to preserve their real incomes.

Is inflation more likely as the economy expands and, if so, how can it be controlled? Reflation can in fact *ease* pressures for inflation. Real national income will rise as resources are brought back into use and firms' costs will fall as productive capacity is used more efficiently. The government can help by cutting taxes on the price of goods and services. The key to controlling inflation lies in anticipating — and, where necessary, regulating — the conflict over distribution which could give rise to inflation.

That certainly means monitoring prices and profits. Companies have increased their profit share substantially in recent years and there should be some scope for this being reduced. It will also mean government discussing with the trade unions a broad framework for wage bargaining — a 'fair wages strategy' — which embodies trade union priorities for redistribution and real wage growth while reconciling these with the income available for economic growth. The needs of different bargaining groups should also be recognised. In particular, new comparability mechanisms will be required in order to reconcile the demands of public sector workers and private sector workers. Agreement will also be needed on how we are to make early progress towards eliminating low pay without setting up a self-defeating "domino" effect throughout the wages structure, and on the role of a statutory minimum wage in this. Nationally imposed pay "norms" have not succeeded in the past and have proved politically disastrous for the labour and trade union movement: there is no question of seeking to repeat the experiment again. But there will still be many issues in this area needing to be resolved at national level as an important part of the planning process.

### Conclusions

We have argued in this chapter that the extent of the likely constraints on economic expansion requires that national policies for growth go hand in hand with action on the "supply" side. The existence of these constraints should not, however, be taken to mean that expansion is impossible or should be abandoned: indeed, industrial recovery, a more equitable division of work within the unpaid sector, and environmental improvement are all likely to be far more difficult to achieve without growth.

Nevertheless, it is vital that any expansion can be *sustained*. Any "dash for growth" followed by "socialist austerity", as has happened in France, would be counter-productive in both economic and political terms. Hence our concentration in the rest of the book on policies for the three main "sectors" of the economy, illustrated by case studies of three industries.

## CHAPTER 5

# Extending Democracy In Industry: The Case For Strategic Planning

### Introduction

A strategy for industrial recovery can only succeed, we argue, if major enterprise decisions are no longer taken on a company by company basis but instead are informed by 'strategic planning' — that is, policies for key industrial sectors and for key processes (such as the use of information technologies). This is how other economies have adapted to new forms of competition based on product innovation and technical change. But this does not mean that foreign models should simply be copied. Industrial structure varies according to different countries' circumstances: in Japan, business conglomerates bring together manufacturing, finance and distribution, and their decisions are shaped by state-guided planning priorities; in the USA, corporate giants co-ordinate networks of decentralised business units; in Italy, co-operative associations provide marketing and financial help for small firms. Nor does it mean that we are advocating planning by the state, acting on its own. To be effective, policies for strategic planning must, we argue, be drawn up and implemented by government, industry, working people through their unions, and local communities.

In Britain, strategic planning will shape enterprise decisions only if the present structure of economic power is changed. *British* industry, as we have argued in Chapter 2, barely exists any longer, as control over key technologies has passed to foreign hands; major British firms are locked into a complex network of multinational decisions; the interests of industry and finance are largely divorced, the City exerting a unique influence; giant retail firms have grown up, with profits dependent on goods and services which can just as well be produced abroad. Further decline is therefore likely unless Britain's long-term interests guide key enterprise decisions. Moreover, we are concerned to promote a wide range of social objectives and to integrate these with our economic strategy. The task is not simply to rebuild the economy but also to reshape it.

Strategic planning should inform key decisions within individual sectors and within individual enterprises. Japan's strength is rooted in the decision to support sectors which rely on new products and technologies — including electronics, petrochemicals, motors and aerospace. Conventional market theory would have led to a very different conclusion: investment in labour-intensive industries. These national priorities guide the provision of finance from the Japan Development Bank and from private banks: decisions on individual projects are taken in the context of the sectoral strategy. Similarly, in Italy, co-operative marketing ventures and financial help from the *consorzi* have strengthened the industries concerned by promoting a complementary product range amongst small firms (guaranteeing, for example, that duplication in the product ranges of local firms is minimised).

Product-led competition means that a response at the enterprise level alone is unlikely to be effective. Continuous flexibility, informed by strategic planning, is needed to identify new product opportunities and respond to them. The rising costs of technological development, the price of failure, and the inherent uncertainty of this new competition, all mean that few individual firms have the resources to go it alone.

Inflexible structures, based on mass producing standard products, are no longer appropriate. To survive, enterprises must instead be flexible in developing and integrating a range of functions: product design and process innovation, marketing, distribution and sales. This does not mean owning the capacity to fulfil each function; rather it means collaboration, with individual operations closely integrated into an overall system. The need for sectoral or process-wide planning is again underlined, as is the scale of the task facing firms in Britain, with their old-fashioned structures still geared to price-led competition.

This chapter discusses how strategic planning can operate at all levels of the economy, integrating enterprise decisions with broader plans. This, we argue, may mean challenging corporate power — using state power at national and local level to do this, combined with the active involvement of working people. New rights should be extended to trade unionists at every level. In discussing the industrial strategy of the last Labour Government, we argue that it is necessary to go beyond planning agreements as they were originally conceived. First, corporate decisions should be influenced through the exercise of commercial leverage. Second, a new institutional framework will be needed to develop and implement sector strategies. Third, there must also be a recognition that specific measures, such as contract compliance, are needed if women are to benefit fully from our strategy.

## LESSONS FROM HOME AND ABROAD

Recent experience in Britain underlines the scale of the task. Attempts at planning have been ineffective because they have not changed key enterprise decisions. Other government policies have had a much greater, and often contradictory, impact. Government powers have not been used to extend collective bargaining, leaving Labour Governments in a weak position in relation to corporate and financial power. Ineffective use has been made of the publicly owned industries.

### The National Plan, 1965-July 1966

While it is unwise to conclude too much from a single example, the experience of Harold Wilson's short-lived National Plan does suggest that *indicative* planning — plans not backed up by sanctions — is unlikely to be effective on its own. Companies were supposed to behave differently simply because the government forecast higher growth. The Plan brought together government spending plans; estimates of what people and private sector firms would buy; industry's expectations of what growth would mean for investment, employment, imports; and so on. But only by expecting export growth to double could a balance of payments crisis be assumed away, and as a result it was difficult to get the Plan taken seriously. It was soon abandoned in the face of short-term macro-economic pressures; in 1966, demand in the economy was cut to reduce imports, and in 1967, under mounting pressure, the Government devalued. This underlines both the need to integrate industrial policy with national economic policy and also the importance of overcoming Treasury power if such integration is to succeed. Finally, and critically, the Plan had no teeth: there was no method to ensure that major firms took any notice of it.

### Labour's industrial policy, 1974-79

"If all this destruction was to build something new, if all this sacrifice was to some better end, then it might be worth it, or at least it would be important to weigh things up. But it's been for nothing." The bitter sense of disappointment with the industrial policy of the last Labour Government is summed up by this comment from a shop steward, made during an inquiry by four trades councils (*State Intervention In Industry*).

The policy was one of 'selective intervention', a pragmatic approach involving government subsidies to modify and sometimes override market decisions. This contrasts with the approach of the current Conservative Government, in which state intervention is seen as sometimes necessary to make the market work better, but always undesirable in principle. Labour's approach was similar to that of the Heath administration : the powers used were based as much on the 1972 Industry Act as on Labour's Industry Act of 1975.

Labour's policy combined selective aid with tripartism. A special meeting of the National Economic Development Council (NEDC) in November 1975 approved the White Paper, *An Approach to Industrial Strategy*. The policy was based on convincing management and unions that it was in their interest to alter their behaviour to achieve a high output/high wage economy. "The main purpose was to get industry to put its own house in order", one senior civil servant commented (Wyn Grant, 1982, p.63).

Detailed measures were expected to emerge from 39 Sector Working Parties (SWPs), covering 40 per cent of manufacturing output, mainly in engineering, textiles and chemicals. These sector strategies had little impact, however. There was no mechanism to ensure their implementation at enterprise level. One study of 35 companies operating in four industries did not find a single investment decision which had been taken because of an SWP recommendation.

Selective aid was provided through a phethora of schemes geared to specific programmes. The micro-electronics support programme, for example, was partly shaped by the discussions of the Electronics Components SWP and other SWPs. But there was little control over the use of the money by firms. Investment decisions were not linked to a sectoral strategy. Moreover the impact of financial assistance was limited because many firms did not know of the incentives available. Money allocated to schemes was often left unspent.

Other aspects of government policy were independent of the industrial strategy. Tax relief to industry, on investment and stock appreciation, dwarfed the money available under aid schemes. The National Enterprise Board (NEB) operated autonomously: the computer company, INMOS, was set up without consultation with the SWP concerned. Above all, the deflation which followed the IMF negotiations signalled the priority given to short-term macro-economic pressures.

Labour's industrial strategy bore little relationship as it turned out to Labour policy in the early 1970's, which envisaged planning agreements and the NEB playing a central role. Stuart Holland's influential *The Socialist Challenge* had argued that a few major corporations, mainly multinationals, dominated the economy. By negotiating planning agreements with these companies on their investment plans, in return for financial assistance, the government could shape the entire economy. The NEB was to have powers to acquire shares, including a majority or a complete holding, in any company. Industrial democracy was to be extended through wide ranging proposals (which were to sink without trace) for the disclosure of information.

Only two planning agreements were concluded, with Chrysler and with the National Coal Board — a far cry from the 100 which Labour Party policy sought. The 1975 White Paper said that agreements had to be voluntary, and that financial help would be given regardless: "There will be no statutory requirement upon a company to conclude an Agreement; not even as a condition for receiving financial assistance. Aid under the Industry Act 1973, including regional development grants, will of course continue to be available for companies not covered by Planning Agreements."

The NEB figured more prominently than planning agreements, but its role bore little relation to the original conception. "No British institution has ever diverged quite as sharply as the NEB from the track which its designers tried to lay down," *Management Today* has remarked. Harold Wilson made this clear in his autobiography: "The role and the power of the NEB were strictly defined; above all, it was to have no marauding role."

The NEB sought to be judged on strictly commercial criteria. "Although funded from public sources, the NEB has to exercise a commercial judgement in the same way as any other business", Lord Ryder, the NEB's first chairman, stated. However, the NEB recognised that "it expected to take a wider view of the national benefits and opportunities that flow from any investment" (The NEB's first Annual Report): this provided the rationale for seeking long-term returns on investment. It took over the ailing Fairey engineering and aviation group in 1977, as part of its strategy for industrial reorganisation, despite strong City opposition. It also made some progress in computers and electronics, by acquiring substantial shareholdings in ICL and Ferranti, and through creating three new companies — INMOS (semiconductor manufacture), NEXOS (office equipment) and INSAC (computer software).

The NEB's ability to take a long-term view was constrained by the 15-20 per cent rate of return it was required to earn. Between

1976 and 1978 it earned over 11 per cent, but this slumped to 5 per cent in 1979. The only exceptions to the target were British Leyland and Rolls Royce, for which 10 per cent was thought adequate. The NEB was also constrained by limited finance, with an initial borrowing limit of only £700 million, raised to £1,000 million in 1978. Moreover, the NEB had been able to invest only £50 million in new acquisitions by 1978: 94 per cent of its loans were taken up by British Leyland and Rolls Royce, both of which required radical restructuring. Finally, it was often prevented from playing an active role because it was not integrated into the development of a broader industrial strategy: for example, KTM, an advanced machine tool company, could have been used to modernise the machine tool industry together with the government owned Alfred Herberts — instead, government help was limited to a financial restructuring.

"The credibility of the NEB as it was constituted was practically nil with us," the secretary of the Parsons joint union committee remarked, looking back at the NEB's involvement. The NEB failed to involve working people or extend industrial democracy. (For example, within six months of taking over Fairey, a subsidiary of it — Tress Engineering — was closed on the recommendation of a consultant's report which neither stewards, union officials nor Northern MPs were allowed to see.) Trade union members of the Board were there as individuals, with no obligation to report back.

### Labour's industrial policy assessed
Labour's industrial policy failed to reverse Britain's decline: in 23 of the sectors covered by the 39 SWPs, imports increased and employment fell. Despite piecemeal interventions by the NEB and a few cases of nationalisation, such as shipbuilding, the policy failed to alter enterprise decisions as part of a broader strategy of sectoral or process-based modernisation. Although the 'watering down' of Labour's policy was partly responsible, this merely reflected the opposition from private centres of economic power with which any progressive strategy must contend. Even if the original policy had been operated fully, it is doubtful if it would have succeeded. Any government must rely on private companies to deliver higher production, in order to win popular support and fulfil electoral promises. This inevitably placed limits on the government's bargaining power. But elements of economic and industrial policy which condition enterprise behaviour were not combined in a coherent package, with the result that the necessary commercial leverage could not be obtained: tripartite discussions, selective aid, tax relief, the

NEB, and macro-economic policy all pulled in different directions.

The close relationships built up by civil servants with companies over many years also constrained the Government; in advising Ministers they were always likely to reflect the view of private companies, narrowing the policy options available. Nor, finally, were the policy objectives coherent. Modernising Britain's outdated industries inevitably leads to some job loss, which it may be impossible to offset by higher output within individual plants or firms. But there was a complete failure to identify new products which could be produced using the skills of those threatened by redundancy, as the fate of the Lucus Aerospace alternative plan sadly demonstrated (see Chapter 3).

## French socialist planning

On coming to power, the Mitterrand administration was committed to reviving industrial planning. It enjoyed advantages which a Labour Government could not rely on. The Socialist Party was wholeheartedly committed to the principle of planning. A planning agency already existed, which dated back to the period of post-war reconstruction (the French Planning Commission : the CGP). Finally, business, the Civil Service and unions all had some commitment to planning, based on long experience.

The scope of industrial planning in France has, however, been limited. The Fourth Plan (1961-66) is commonly seen as the most successful, with industrial growth and public spending targets being met. Even so, the planning was purely indicative. The Mitterrand administration's Ninth Plan (1984-88) laid strong emphasis on a medium-term industrial strategy. Extensive nationalisation was carried out, giving the state direct control over one-third of exports and one quarter of investment. But its pattern owed more to that of previous state subsidies than to plans for industrial recovery. Planning was largely confined to the state sector and even this was limited: 'planning contracts' with nationalised industries were confined to financial control, and did not cover corporate strategies.

As in Britain, private sector companies are eligible for a wide range of state aids. There is no co-ordination of these: companies unable to get money from the Industry Ministry can turn to the Ministry of Finance. The state typically provides aid in the form of loan stock, and has deliberately not taken voting rights. This makes it unlikely that any private companies would negotiate voluntary planning contracts.

A further similarity with Britain has been the failure to

integrate industrial planning with macro-economic policy. In 1982 the French chose to protect the franc, as Labour in 1966 sought to protect sterling; rather than heading off a balance of payments crisis by devaluing, the French Government cut domestic demand, damaging prospects for investment and growth.

## CHANGING ENTERPRISE DECISIONS

Our argument has been that industrial recovery will depend on changing key enterprise decisions, which in turn means challenging private centres of economic and industrial power through a new framework of institutions and rights. The strategy we develop goes beyond planning agreements; we argue for the use of state power to obtain commercial leverage, alongside increased industrial democracy, and extending — and making full use of — the publicly owned industries.

### The Chrysler fiasco

"There is no tangible advantage or carrot to lure a company into bed with the government against its natural inclination to stay at arms length. Planning Agreements look fearsome (deterring most companies from the start) but when you open the door there is nothing there — thereby disappointing those companies that have persevered", wrote Victor Keegan in *The Guardian*, commenting on planning agreements under the last Labour Government.

The failure to achieve planning agreements cannot be explained simply by a lack of political will. The policy was not linked to a broader strategy, so that even if agreements had been negotiated, it is uncertain whether they would have helped industrial recovery. They were not backed up by commercial leverage, and so would have failed to challenge enterprise decision making. They were not linked to trade union involvement, so there was little pressure for them from below. An uncritical assessment of corporate strategy would have been presented to Ministers by civil servants, and there would have been no mechanism to enforce them. Finally, there was a complete failure to recognise, let alone resolve, the tensions which could result from modernisation, with the result that short-term pressures won out over longer-term considerations. The divorce of planning from industrial democracy, for all the difficulties which are involved in their integration, proved crucially debilitating. These problems were vividly demonstrated in the case of the solitary private sector agreement, with Chrysler.

The Chrysler agreement was concluded in December 1975 as part of a rescue package costing over £160 million in grants and loans. The agreement stated that:
"Chrysler (UK)…shall not without prior consent in writing of the Secretary of State, sell, lend, transfer or otherwise dispose of any part of the undertakings of the Chrysler (UK) Group or the assets of the Chrysler (UK) Group", and that, "Chrysler Corporation shall not…take any step or permit any step to be taken which would have the effect that Chrysler Corporation would be the absolute owner of less than 80 per cent …of the equity share capital of Chrysler (UK)".

In September 1978, despite those clauses, Chrysler UK was sold to Peugeot-Citroen of France: Chrysler concluded its deal without telling the British Government. By 1978 Chrysler had received grants and loans of about £80 million. A declaration of intent, signed by the Government and Peugeot, stated only that UK employment would be maintained "to the extent consistent with prevailing economic conditions". The declaration was not legally binding, and a demand for an equity stake by the Government was rejected.

There were short-term gains: some 50,000 jobs, including those indirectly dependent on Chrysler, were preserved and £500 million was added to the balance of payments. But neither the agreement nor the declaration secured the *long-term* future of the Chrysler plants. Employment in Chrysler UK's Talbot operation fell from 31,000 in 1974 to 21,000 in 1976. The loss of jobs has subsequently been matched by a loss of capacity. Peugeot Talbot's Whitley design centre, one of the most advanced in Britain, has recently been transferred to France. The British plants have been largely reduced to assembly operations.

The Chrysler 'rescue' underlines the danger of intervention shaped by short-term political pressures. This danger is even greater when the government lacks a long-term strategy. Political pressures created a dynamic of their own. "The postures adopted for eventual public relations effects began to exert their own chemistry. They began to believe what they were telling each other — that they were all making a major effort to save the company"(*The Sunday Times*, 14th December 1975).

The Chrysler fiasco destroyed the credibility of the Government's industrial strategy at a stroke. Three months before, the Central Policy Review Staff had undertaken a major analysis of the motor industry, which concluded that there was 25 per cent over-capacity: as *The Guardian* commented, "it would be a misuse of public money to throw good money after bad by committing long-term finance to enable a US subsidiary which could not survive on its own, to set up as a second state-owned competitor to the nationalised British Leyland" (10th November 1975). Only one month before, the Government had unveiled its new industrial strategy, emphasising that resources would be concentrated on areas which promised long-term viability. The agreement gave unions only 'consultative' status: "It was a con. The two parties of the establishment were imposing it on the workforce", a Chrysler steward commented. *Chrysler's crisis: the workers' answer*, submitted by a joint union delegation in December 1975, expressed concern about Chrysler's prospects. The investment gap between Chrysler's French and UK subsidiaries was wide and growing; capital and equipment had been shifted overseas; Chrysler's UK design staff effectively worked for French plants. As *The Times* remarked, "in the turbulent history of Rootes Motors, then Chrysler UK, there is a cycle of governments concluding agreements, only to see them changed or varied. That is a recipe for cynicism within the workforce" (11th August 1978).

**British Leyland**
The Labour Government's industrial policy was dominated by the rescue of British Leyland (BL). However unfairly, state intervention, 'lame ducks' and strikes become synonymous, helping to pave the way for the laissez-faire ideology of Thatcherism. The Government was, of course, saddled with perhaps the most spectacular example of private sector failure in British industry. No Government could have been expected to reverse in five years the legacy of twenty. Nevertheless, even the possibility of eventually achieving this was reduced by the failure to link industrial democracy and planning, and the assumption that industrial democracy could be divorced from collective bargaining.

Lord Ryder was appointed to lead an inquiry into the bankrupt company. The Government took over a company abandoned by private capital, with an unattractive model range produced on out-of-date equipment. Perhaps the most important legacy of private ownership was the fragmented structure of plants, brought together in the merger boom in the pursuit of short-term profit. By the early 1970's BL's declared profits concealed massive losses, as a result of unsound accounting practices. Matters were made worse because almost all the notional profits were distributed. Finally, BL lacked an effective dealership network in the USA and Europe, previous dealerships having been broken up in a series of short-term cost-cutting exercises under private ownership. Nor was the government prepared to tackle the thorny problem of fleet sales for business use, which determine the demand in the key large car sector where the greatest unit profits can be made. So, even had the Ryder strategy succeeded, and BL been able to produce an attractive model range, there was no mechanism to ensure the cars could actually be sold.

Ryder's strategy for recovery relied on a £200 million investment programme over eight years, the cost of which was to be recovered through a massive increase in sales. No attempt was made to assess whether these cars could be sold. Nor did the plan face up to the consequences for jobs of higher investment. Instead, Ryder relied on an ill-defined process of industrial democracy — in practice, little more than limited consultation at a national level on BL's planning — to solve the problems of inefficient production. The issue of overstaffing was side-stepped. 'Planned' sales and investment increases were supposed to require extra manpower which would "partly — perhaps mainly — offset any manpower reduction from increased productivity". The question of work standards was also dodged. Fragmented bargaining arrangements remained — there were 56 bargaining units for 30 plants. Ryder proposed one per plant but laid down no timetable for rationalisation.

'Industrial democracy' became an all purpose panacea, but in practice it was simply assumed that co-operation would be forthcoming once management's point of view was explained. The union role was limited because of this, as well as by a lack of resources and expertise. The greatest flaw was that industrial democracy was kept separate from collective bargaining. Hence the paradox: a centralised system of participation superimposed on a fragmented bargaining structure and payments system. The latter determined manning levels and the effort rate in practice, but there was no agreement between management and labour over either. The divorce of local participation forums at plant level from collective bargaining limited the impact both of stewards on the participation process, and also of the agreements themselves reached through participation.

During the Ryder era the company fundamentally failed to face up to the need to rationalise its product range and plants: if planning was to succeed it would have had to learn to cope with decline, in employment if not in output or value-added. Industrial democracy by itself can solve nothing. Ryder recommended that BL should remain a major producer of cars, through rationalisation financed by public money. The 1977 Concept Study proposed four options, differentiated by the volume they set out to achieve, ranging from 1.2 million vehicles to 450,000 each year. The first option was pursued, in line with the 1977 Corporate Plan. It was described as "financially viable, (with) a competitive model range covering all sections of the market, produced in rationalised, modernised facilities and would be capable of prospering under almost any circumstances" (1977 *Concept Plan*: Leyland Cars Joint Management Committee). The Plan represented the triumph of hope over reason.

There were positive lessons, however. The Mini Metro is a product of that period. A market leader, it would not have existed but for state intervention. Union lay representatives were involved in virtually all stages of the introduction of new plant facilities. Manning levels were set in line with major competitors: they emerged from bargaining with the NEB, and were a pre-condition for further finance. Important issues were settled in local participation forums. The Metro line is an important example because it represents *new* investment: increases in process efficiency were linked to investment in new product technology so that no jobs were lost. Of course, the fact of new investment is not a sufficient guarantee that it will be successfully introduced. But the basis for efficient performance was partly established in the Ryder era. The subsequent change in management style under Michael Edwardes, culminating in the scrapping of existing agreements on work practices, exploited the co-operation which had been developed.

The problems encountered at BL were typical of those which will face a future Labour Government. Whole areas of manufacturing have been abandoned by private capital. Massive new investment will be needed. If this investment is to be efficiently used, powerful tensions must be resolved by negotiation. It will not always be possible to guarantee jobs as a result of market growth. BL's 1977 Concept Plan remarked that "all evidence suggests (that) any action of the severity envisaged in (the lower volume options) would generate such reaction in employee relations that it would be counter-productive". Unfortunately, preserving jobs in a frozen industrial structure cannot be the test of a socialist industrial strategy. Such problems can only be resolved through hard bargaining between unions, management and government.

**British Steel**
Steel presented major problems for the Labour Government, as falling demand led to apparent overcapacity. A series of closures of smaller plants was announced, the result of BSC's management's determination to protect their overinvestment in bulk steel making capacity in five large plants during the 1970's. This investment led to high fixed costs, and prices which were set

so high as to cause the loss of market shares. As demand failed to match capacity, BSC was trapped in a vicious circle of decline: excess capacity, uncompetitive prices, high fixed costs and heavy financial losses.

BSC's investment was a result of the Ten Year Development Strategy of the early 1970's. Opinions differed on the capacity required for 1983, with BSC arguing for 43 million tonnes per annum (mtpa), the Joint Study Group (of BSC and DTI officials) 28-36 mtpa and McKinsey's management consultants, 23 mtpa. The then Conservative Government agreed to the upper limits of the 28-36 mtpa range, and this finally emerged as a limit of 36-38 mtpa.

Defenders of the strategy argue that hindsight makes criticism easy — that there was no way of knowing what demand would turn out to be. But BSC continually biased their proposals in favour of a 'big is beautiful' strategy. First, the February 1971 Corporate Plan (which proposed a 43 mtpa capacity) gave no alternative paths of development. Second, when asked to consider the future profits of *alternative* investment options, BSC failed to follow standard investment procedures which would have favoured smaller capacity options. These procedures are used to select which of a number of options will yield the greatest return under varying circumstances. They involve:

• *First*, investment options are ranked according to the future profitability expected from each, the most profitable being selected. BSC considered 12 options of various capacities and plant configurations; however, option 10 — which included the retention of small plants such as Corby within a low capacity strategy — was discarded even though its anticipated profits exceeded options 7 and 12, which favoured higher capacities.

• *Second*, 'sensitivity' of the projected returns to varying assumptions about future demand and so on is assessed, by means of a 'sensitivity analysis'. However, the strategy was not only based on inadequate assumptions — for example, a continual growth rate of 3.5 per cent and an inflation rate of 6 per cent — but the assumptions were only varied by marginal amounts — inflation by only 0.5 per cent either way, export prices by 1 per cent, and no variation at all allowed in operating costs. Even so, the anticipated returns varied by 200 per cent; yet no consideration was given to whether the high expected returns were probable or not.

• *Third*, allowance is then normally made for the risk which is associated with each considered option; the higher the risk, the greater the return which must be expected. But BSC failed to do this. Had they done so, they would have found that smaller

capacity options were the most profitable.
This experience has obvious lessons. Demand can be forecast
and allowance made for various assumptions. But these
techniques will only be used *and acted upon* if decision making is
made the subject of democratic scrutiny. An alliance of BSC
management and the Government Minister favoured high
capacity: the former to save the 'jewel in the crown', Redcar; the
latter to project an image of modernisation. Similar decisions
could easily have been taken by a Labour Government in
consultation with unions, as the motor industry shows. Indeed,
the Labour Government failed to challenge the basic assumptions
underlying BSC's plans. Consultation with those who have an
interest in expansion is not enough: the decision making process
itself must be made public.

**Beyond planning agreements**
The Chrysler and BL examples both underline the need to link
sector strategies with enterprise decisions through the effective
use of state power and industrial democracy. State power, we
argue, can only influence enterprise decisions by exerting
commercial leverage. This leverage can be obtained if the factors
which shape the corporate strategy of particular firms are
identified and are themselves shaped by government policy.
     Such an approach involves going beyond planning
agreements. Voluntary planning agreements offered nothing to
make it worthwhile for firms to negotiate. But compulsory
planning agreements are a contradiction in terms — they assume
that companies can be forced to agree to certain commitments.
They only worked when legal control meant *commercial* control,
as in the case of the British National Oil Corporation, whose
negotiations with oil companies were backed up by control over
access to oil licences. BNOC was also able to succeed by
establishing *new* companies through joint ventures, rather than
having to take over existing companies. Planning agreements,
moreover, were not linked to sector strategies and — as a result —
to giving working people a say over key enterprise decisions.
     It is only within the context of broader sector/process-wide
strategies that enterprise decisions can be evaluated; and it is only
through involvement at the broader level — as well as the
enterprise level — that industrial democracy can be developed. In
the case of Chrysler, a long-term strategy for motors would have
meant the closure of the company's UK plants. Unions
representing Chrysler workers inevitably opposed this: without
an alternative strategy for their industry, there was no possibility
that the long-term economic case for closure would be accepted.

Moreover, whilst the 'Think Tank' report on the motor industry did represent a strategic response, it was not properly drawn up with, or widely debated within, motor industry unions. Finally, it is only at the sectoral level that *positive* responses to particular plant closures can be discussed: shopfloor proposals to move into public transport production, or develop environmentally safer private transport, were never evaluated.

There was a real danger that unions' influence would have been weakened — not strengthened — in the negotiation of planning agreements. Department of Industry civil servants and the management of top firms have long-established links which preclude unions from any effective role. Agreements negotiated by governments and firms could easily have been presented to unions as finished agreements, which 'their' government had endorsed.

### Enterprise planning

Central to our approach is obtaining commercial leverage through packages of support tailored to the needs and opportunities of particular firms — including access to finance and markets, the provision of management consultancy and advice, support for training and research. Assisted firms should, we argue, produce a business plan, negotiated with unions, if such support is to be made available. These plans should include the promotion of equality for women and black workers. Through 'enterprise planning', Labour local authorities have already begun to put this approach into practice (Chapter 3): their initiatives at least demonstrate the principles of the approach, even though their achievements should not be overstated. In particular, the scale of support provided by national government to private firms offers the possibility of substantially greater leverage than can be achieved locally.

Enterprise planning can offer the radical possibility of changing the boundary between the private and public sectors. All financial help to private companies should be tied to specified and enforceable objectives. Wherever possible, assistance should be in the form of equity or loan capital. There will be important exceptions to this: in bargaining with multinationals, a Labour Government may not have the clout to insist that an equity stake is taken, nor will it often want it when ownership would only provide control over one plant in a multinational production process.

For enterprise planning to be effective, industrial democracy must also be developed through the extension of collective bargaining. Only those who work in particular companies can develop the knowledge needed to negotiate business plans. Leaving this to civil servants would not only undermine industrial democracy; experience suggests it would also lead to business plans which closely reflect the assessment of top corporate management. It might also be impractical and unpopular: the massively expanded Civil Service needed to put enterprise planning into effect would, at best, involve considerable co-ordination, and, at worst, would require Ministers to overcome strong opposition; and it would also justifiably create an image of planning as remote and bureaucratic. Finally, those who work in firms not only have the right to influence the decisions which shape their lives; they have an immediate interest — their jobs and income, and those of the communities in which they live.

### Promoting sexual equality
Enterprise planning, together with legislative changes such as the introduction of a statutory minimum wage and contract compliance policies, can help promote the equality of women at work. The negotiation of business plans provides an opportunity for improving the quality of women's working lives as well as the number of jobs available. This requires that women themselves organise through their unions to develop and press their own demands. This, in turn, demands that women are not prevented from so doing by domestic responsibilities. A strategy for equality at work must therefore extend beyond the workplace. And it must challenge the image of the male shopfloor worker and workplace: clerical jobs, which mostly employ women, are likely to be hardest hit by the impact of new technologies, while the largest growth is likely to be in highly skilled professional jobs — where women are held back by lack of training and promotion opportunities — and in services, which are often low paid and non-unionised.

Women and men should have the *opportunity* to share paid work and family care. To achieve this, parents with children under five should have access to education, play and care facilities: at present, only one quarter of children under five can get full-time day care. A statutory duty could be placed on local authorities to provide such care. In addition, care for the elderly, disabled and handicapped should be seen as the responsibility of the whole community. Radical reforms are also needed in education and training so that women are encouraged to widen their skills and pursue 'male' careers.

Positive action programmes can provide a way of setting targets and ensuring they are reached. There should be open advertising for jobs, with job definitions and interview procedures examined for discriminatory elements. Women should be trained during normal working hours in traditionally 'male' skills, especially in the area of new technologies. Part-time workers should receive hourly wage rates and other benefits equivalent to those paid to full-time workers. Homeworkers should be given protection against unfair dismissal; redundancy pay; and expenses for costs incurred in their work. The specific health and safety requirements of women at work should be acknowledged: pregnant women, in particular, require options for different work. Women, through their trade unions, should press for demands which would permit childcare and other domestic responsibilities to be shared: a shorter working day, job sharing and part-time working for all grades, paid time-off for fathers as well as mothers to care for sick dependants, and the establishment of workplace nurseries.

## INDUSTRIAL DEMOCRACY

The experience of industrial democracy in Britain conjures up many images, all of them falling far short of the hopes held by its advocates. Beer and sandwiches at number 10. "I'm all right Jack." Strikes in vital public services. Early morning renditions of company songs in Japanese firms. The case for industrial democracy is, nevertherless, compelling.

Working people have no say over the decisions that determine the success of the firms in which they work. All too often the first they know about the closure of their plant is when they read about it in the local newspaper. Nor are they likely to have a positive influence over the way in which work is organised, much less investment decisions or product development. To the extent that they do have any influence, it is through collective organisation in trade unions. But, in modern economies, where innovation and product quality are vital, so too is the involvement of working people. And in an economy such as Britain, where economic power is so often used purely in the pursuit of short-term gain, such influence is essential.

We argue that industrial democracy can best be developed through the extension of collective bargaining. In this section we assess the proposals for linking industrial democracy with economic planning made by the TUC and the Labour Party. Then we look at the experience of consultation schemes to see whether the scope of collective bargaining can be widened at the enterprise level. If collective bargaining is to be extended to the sector level, a strategy of tripartite bargaining should, we argue, be developed. Achieving this, however, will mean changes in trade union objectives and organisation.

## 'Economic planning and industrial democracy'

The statement *Economic Planning and Industrial Democracy*, published by the TUC and Labour Party, proposes new institutions linking economic planning to industrial democracy. Extending collective bargaining is seen as the key method of achieving this. If planning is to build on the skills and knowledge of working people, and thereby avoid being remote and bureaucratic, it must be based on industrial democracy. If industrial democracy is to win the support of working people it must build on the existing strengths of collective bargaining.

At *company* level, the statement proposes that workers would have new rights to information, consultation and representation:

● *Information rights* would include details of the company's financial position, investment plans, performance figures and manpower plans.

● *Consultation rights* would include a minimum 90 days notice of closures, and an obligation on management to discuss alternative strategies proposed by workers.

● *Representation rights* on subsidiary and main boards would be available to members of Joint Union Committees (JUCs) bringing together all unions within companies.

These rights would be available as unions in particular firms demanded them. A 'trigger mechanism' would operate, with the right to information being readily available, the right to consultation being triggered by a request from one union or the JUC, and the right to representation being dependent on the formation of such a Committee. The aim is to ensure that workers and their representatives are not burdened with responsibilities which undermine their existing role. New rights should only be taken on in the process of extending collective bargaining. This would culminate in unions bargaining over corporate strategy in 'planning committees', composed of management and JUC representatives. In addition, union representatives would be given improved facilities, paid time-off for training and facilities for meetings.

At *sector* level, sectoral strategies would be developed through *sector planning committees* of the 'National Planning Council'. These would bring together individual company plans in a particular sector. Representation would be tripartite, bringing together unions, management and government.

At *national* level, sectoral strategies would be co-ordinated by the *National Planning Council*. This would formulate a five-year macro-economic and industrial plan, drawing on information provided by the government *Department of Planning*. The plan would form an annual national economic assessment, covering the balance between consumption and investment in the public and private sectors, and the share of national income going to profits, wages and the social wage. The Public Expenditure Survey Committee (see Chapter 7), which allocates public spending, would be integrated with the planning process to ensure that the long-term strategy is not undermined by short-term financial considerations.

The statement is less clear on how the extension of collective bargaining fits in with the planning institutions and, in particular, planning agreements. Reconciling these two approaches, through the use of government powers as an *enabling* force, lies at the heart of our strategy.

### Extending collective bargaining: the enterprise level

Past experiments in industrial democracy in state owned industries underline the need to develop industrial democracy by extending collective bargaining, and show that the difficulties involved are not solved by a mere change of ownership. Worker directors in the steel industry, for example, had no duty to report back, were enmeshed within confidentiality rules and became increasingly divorced from their membership. Industrial democracy was unrelated to existing bargaining structures.

Health and safety at work is one example of the extension of collective bargaining. The 1974 Act requires employers to consult trade unions through Health and Safety Committees. Monitoring of standards is mostly carried out by union representatives themselves, not by civil servants.

Does the widespread and increasing use of *consultative methods* raise the possibility of extending workers' influence over issues of corporate strategy? Consultative committees exist in about one-third of workplaces in the private sector, and in almost half in the public sector, according to a recent study. The range of issues commonly discussed is, however, extremely limited. The practical effect of consultation is, for the most part, even more limited. Recent studies have concluded that consultative arrangements are essentially communications exercises for management, which stress the value of consensus and the legitimacy of managerial goals. Management, at all levels, are implacably opposed to the extension of workers' influence and exhibit a high degree of class awareness in expressing this. Participation often works best for management where there are important divisions within the workforce, along lines of skill, sex, race and age.

Corporate structure also works against effective participation. Complex collective bargaining and consultation arrangements have tended to develop, reflecting the geographical dispersion of plants and the elaborate and overlapping structure of enterprise decision making. Firms are organised hierarchically, whereas unions are fragmented across plants, giving management effective power over important decisions above plant level.

The experience of consultation does not therefore point to a shared basis for the extension of collective bargaining. Management and unions have different objectives in seeking to consult. It is for precisely this reason that consultation has been divorced from collective bargaining, and the range of decisions which trade unionists can influence remains limited.

## Extending collective bargaining: the sector level

*Economic Planning and Industrial Democracy* argues that collective bargaining can be extended to the sector level through revamped versions of the tripartite Sector Working Parties of the NEDC. The importance of tripartite bargaining over sectoral strategies has already been discussed. Unions must be involved in strategic planning if industrial democracy is to have any substance: major enterprise decisions are shaped by the sector in which they operate and by developments in key processes in which they compete. BL unions, for example, may negotiate a business plan with the company, the viability of which would be threatened if the government encouraged a Japanese manufacturer to expand; conversely, the sectoral rationale for running down Vauxhall/GM (discussed in Chapter 10) would have had no authority unless Vauxhall unions had been involved in drawing up the strategy.

The advantage of tripartite negotiation is that it gives unions the opportunity to engage in *direct* discussions with management and government, the key decision makers. The use of state power on behalf of working people is not a substitute for their own initiatives: bipartite government-company negotiations can leave working people isolated, their interests defined by the company with which the agreement is being negotiated. Tripartism extends rights to a far greater number of working people than planning agreements can.

In theory, tripartism also enables a consensus to be reached on the changes needed for sectoral reconstruction. But in practice this has not happened. Consensus tends to be reached by dodging controversial issues. As a result, action is limited to matters such as improving statistics and standards. Issues such as company restructuring may give rise to limited discussion but no action, while issues which encroach on collective bargaining or government spending are not even discussed.

Tripartite institutions are further undermined where they do not bring together the decision takers in each sector. Management tend to participate as individuals. Seniority is sacrificed in favour of technical knowledge. Management representatives are usually nominated by trade associations rather than by companies — or by the CBI, the internal structure of which is not geared to sectoral planning. They participate mainly in order to lobby government and unions. Full-time union officials tend to represent their union or the TUC, rather than specific groups of members. On the other hand, regional and lay officials face difficulties in reporting back to members because of internal union structures. Reporting back is further undermined by confidentiality rules and by a lack of adequate staff or resources. For all these reasons union representatives can find it difficult to play an active or initiating role. Unions participate to gain information and lobby government, not for wider or strategic goals. Finally, government representatives play a limited role. There are less of them, they are usually more junior and they tend to attend for short periods only. Thus tripartite committees tend to be seen as self-help rather than policy-making bodies. They might more accurately be described as bipartism plus one.

Management and government get far more out of straightforward bilateral contact. The relationship is partly based on information which the companies would be reluctant to share with their competitors. Trade unions and management, meanwhile, pursue their respective interests through collective bargaining. The SWP is only seen as important if collective bargaining is strong at the company level, because this gives national officials a linking role, or alternatively if collective bargaining is weak at all levels. The SWP is often used to explain management's case for changing working practices, without providing the precondition — namely, the ability to link such changes to long-term investment plans.

Tripartite institutions can sometimes work, however. The Civil Engineering EDC benefited from the membership of a Conservative Government Minister, encouraging senior managers and union officials to attend. The companies drew on a strong trade association, suggesting that the existence of a trade association need not undermine the SWP if the latter has sufficient purpose; indeed, the reverse may be the case. The unions, unusually, came to the Committee with a relatively well worked out position, established in the TUC's Construction Committee. Civil servants from both the Department of Environment and Treasury also attended, the latter fearing the spending implications of decisions taken by the former. The Committee also benefited from the cohesiveness of the parties, and the resolution of potential conflicts in bipartite institutions, such as the Civil Engineering Construction Conciliation Board. Because of all these circumstances, the Committee has dealt with some important issues, such as how to spend a £2.5 million public research budget.

Conflict between firms is the underlying reason for the limits on tripartism's achievements. Companies can agree on the need to increase UK market shares, but not, for example, which company should loose out to gain economies of scale. The Petrochemical Sector Working Party collapsed in January 1983, amid much bitterness, in the face of sweeping rationalisation. It was unable to generate a strategic response of the kind sought by unions because individual companies had their own plans for retrenchment.

On the other hand, certain trends are increasing integration within sectors. Companies are becoming increasingly specialised because of their need to share rising development costs and to achieve economies of scale. As a result, they are collaborating in many sectors, through joint ventures and cross-trading of key components. This collaboration coexists with competition. ESPRIT, the EEC's high technology programme to secure collaboration in information technologies, aims to get companies to work together at the 'precompetitive stage' on research and development.

## From tripartism to tripartite bargaining

Sectoral tripartism, we have argued, lacks the means to resolve the problems it can identify. Its relationship with other planning institutions is therefore crucial. Bipartite negotiations and the actions of the major institutions of intervention should relate to the sectoral strategy agreed through tripartite negotiation. By making assistance conditional upon a business plan negotiated with unions, collective bargaining can also be extended to embrace key issues. In this way, the relationship between tripartite and bipartite action can become reinforcing, and key decision makers will become involved in both.

This strategy can be termed *tripartite bargaining*: it recognises that negotiation will be needed — both bipartite and tripartite — to overcome the phoney consensus of tripartism. Such an approach is more realistic than giving tripartite institutions executive power. Companies are likely to oppose vigorously a system which forces them to divulge corporate strategy to their competitors. Trying to force companies to participate on these terms would create a degree of conflict which could seriously retard both economic recovery and the process of extending industrial democracy. The government would be forced to climb down, in order not to endanger recovery and risk losing popularity.

The possibilities for action at the sectoral level will depend on the industrial structure of specific sectors, and the nature of the decisions themselves. In sectors where public ownership plays an important role, or there is intense competition among fragmented companies (such as foundries), there will be less resistance to sectoral planning. Where there is an oligopolistic structure, sectoral planning is less likely to succeed. Nevertheless, certain decisions could still be reached at a sectoral level. These include the allocation of 'precompetitive' research budgets. Decisions which involve joint ventures could also be discussed at a sectoral level, although followed by bipartite negotiation. Economic Development Committees, which bring together Sector Working Parties, should be chaired by a Minister in order to give them greater status.

The details of economic and industrial policy must be hammered out between unions and a Labour Government *before* entering into tripartite negotiation. The NEDC became ineffective by the end of 1975 because it was there that the TUC was forced to develop policy and lobby the government in the presence (and sometimes with the support) of the CBI. Industrial policies had not already been resolved in the TUC-Labour Party Liaison Committee. The success of a strategy which attempts to tackle deeply rooted power structures depends on building up in advance the commitment of unions and the Party, *at all levels*. Otherwise unions and the government will go into tripartite institutions unprepared and possibly divided, and be forced to make concessions which undermine the whole strategy.

Finally, the extension of collective bargaining poses an immense challenge for trade unions, whose bargaining power has been weakened by recession and anti-union legislation, and whose resources are fully stretched in defending existing rights. Working people often have neither the resources or self-confidence to take responsibility quickly for corporate decisions. The problems encountered in existing consultation arrangements and their implications for extending collective bargaining; the difficulties unions have had in taking on responsibility for management in co-operatives (Chapter 3); a culture which denies the value of manual skills; an education system which limits expectations; a training system (such as it is) which schools for the dole; and a mass media which sanctions corporate power: all these suggest that the process by which the self-confidence of working people can develop will inevitably be uncertain and uneven. Employers will fight to retain existing prerogatives and will not easily share their skills, much less their power, with working people.

The extension of collective bargaining requires a strategic perspective, by government and unions alike, during the first years of a Labour Government, but a tactical concern with wages and conditions will continue to vie with this. Trade unions may not always want the responsibility for corporate decisions. This has been the experience of the West Midlands Enterprise Board in negotiating enterprise plans: trade union representatives on the Board have asked not be held responsible for intervention in the company from which they are drawn. Instead, trade unionists have preferred to concentrate on influencing the overall strategy of the Board.

Union structures will also need to undergo rapid change. Representatives on company boards and sectoral committees should be under a duty to report back. Internal procedures must be developed if extended collective bargaining is not to be seen as bureaucratic and remote. The resources available to union representatives must be massively expanded. This could be provided through a network of 'planning colleges', linked to local academic institutions, rather than the single National Planning College which has been proposed.

## Productive efficiency and the extension of collective bargaining

Involving working people can be a way of boosting productive efficiency. But it cannot be *assumed* that if people feel part of an organisation, they will work harder. The growing importance of new, product-led forms of competition undermines this crude approach. Getting people to work harder cannot guarantee that more sophisticated and reliable goods and services are produced. Instead, product design, research, finance, marketing, distribution and other functions must all be integrated. Nevertheless, the organisation of production remains vital. Japan's industrial success shows some of the tensions that can arise. Japanese firms have perfected the art of organising the production process as a continuous flow, coupled with flexibility to respond to changes in demand; the breaking down of existing job boundaries; and a shift towards preventive maintenance within the skilled grades. Production flexibility is becoming more important because of the pressure to shorten production runs and reduce stock costs, and in order to cover the costs of ever more expensive plant and machinery.

However, Japanese efficiency is not only achieved through the application of production *techniques*. The success of these techniques is rooted in a specific form of social organisation, itself the product of Japanese culture and history. Corporate paternalism was dominant when Taylorist methods of work organisation were brought in, enabling a form of group solidarity to be built up. This solidarity coexists with extreme competition between individuals: promotion is linked to seniority and merit awards, assessed three times each year by the company. Workers are often tied to the firm through company housing, which they buy through a company loan and which can only be repaid after a lifetime's work. Japan's dual labour market is another source of flexibility for the major firms. Health and safety standards are relatively low, especially in sub-contracted firms. Temporary workers are recruited from the ranks of failed 'lifetime' employees, and work side by side though paid different rates for the same work. Sexual divisions are also significant, women being employed in sub-contracted firms on rates which by law can be lower than male wages. Compulsory overtime is worked (annual hours worked in Japan average 2,300 compared to 1,200 in Sweden). Finally, and critically, communist unions were defeated at a time of bitter class conflict following the Second World War.

Japan shows that production techniques cannot be divorced from their social context. Nevertheless, production efficiency in Britain could be greatly increased by harnessing the commitment of working people to better organisation of the production process. The shift from low wage, low value-added to high wage, high value-added production must be linked to better training, investment in new production methods and greater rewards. But there will still be a tension between productive efficiency and the quality of work, which can only be resolved through a combination of job redesign, automation, reduced working hours and a changed industrial relations climate.

British trade unions have failed to make job design an issue of collective bargaining in the way that continental unions have. Scandinavian legislation, by contrast, gives unions the rights and resources to approve new plant layout *before* it is used. Job design includes both job rotation and job enrichment. Rotation has generated great scepticism. Once a new job is learnt, it is as boring as the last. Many workers may prefer to stay doing the same job, which they can do without much thought and where they can work with friends. Job enrichment is more promising. On-line quality control does away with the need for inspectors. It can encourage better quality levels, because operators will have less rectification work. But job design must work within the pressure to achieve output targets. Volvo's Kalmar plant, which has experimented with longer cycle times, group working and an expanded range of tasks, has had to cope with this pressure. Advanced work measurement techniques enable each supervisor to manage teams of 20 workers. Since 1977, working hours per car have been cut by 40 per cent, making it Volvo's most labour-efficient plant in Sweden. Quality has also improved: 39 per cent fewer defects now escape detection. But it is easy to over-estimate what this means for the quality of working life. At a Volvo engine plant, semi-skilled women have opted for traditional methods rather than continuing with the new system.

## Conclusions

We have put forward the following propositions: that strategic planning must inform key company decisions if industrial recovery is to succeed; that these decisions can only be influenced through packages of support which provide effective commercial leverage, so that financial assistance to industry should — wherever possible — be conditional; that broader objectives, in particular the promotion of sexual equality, should be integral to business plans to which public assistance is linked; that strategic planning cannot succeed, in the British context at least, unless it is linked to greater industrial democracy, and that the latter can only be achieved through an extension of collective bargaining; and that tripartism is unlikely to offer an adequate basis for strategic planning — instead a process of 'tripartite bargaining', which encompasses *both* bipartite and tripartite negotiations, will be required.

Trade unions, however, are unlikely to find the transition from a tactical concern with wages and conditions, to a strategic concern with issues of sectoral modernisation and corporate behaviour, an easy one to make. This poses a major challenge for a strategy of recovery which sees industrial democracy as integral to its success. Few unions are likely to be in a position to ensure that working people can and do make use of the new rights which are outlined. In such circumstances, it is vital that the power of national government be used both to promote recovery *and* to extend social control.

CHAPTER 6

# Extending Democracy In Industry: Socialist Enterprise

## Introduction

In this chapter we describe how the power of major companies can be challenged, so that long-term, democratically decided priorities can guide economic decision making in Britain. In the previous chapter we argued that private economic power can only be influenced, in the short-term at least, through the exercise of commercial leverage. Such leverage arises from the numerous forms of financial assistance given to private companies (tax relief, grants for innovation, sectoral aid, regional support and so on) and from their commercial dealings with the public sector. This chapter sets out the policy and institutional framework needed to make use of this leverage, and thereby to make strategic planning a reality.

In the first years of a Labour Government public intervention may tend to have a somewhat 'negative' character, akin to the influence private banks have over the companies to which they lend. But among the more positive elements of this industrial strategy are the following: the development of a long-term strategy for British industries, against which progress in negotiations with private companies will be judged; the extension of public enterprise, in particular through the creation of new, publicly controlled and owned companies in key sectors and processes; the building up of management skills and personnel committed to greater accountability as well as productive efficiency; and the gradual extension of industrial and local democracy as a countervailing power both to the rationale of private corporations and to the bureaucratic unresponsiveness of state institutions.

Together, these elements can help establish a *socialist enterprise culture*, creating the possibility for an active and progressive alternative to private sector management. As our discussion on extending collective bargaining concluded, the process of creating such a new 'culture' will take a long time. It will require not only a very different role for unions and working people, but also a recognition of the rights of people in their communities and as consumers. This in turn requires the use of government power to give *enabling* rights, coupled with a greater role for local government in industrial policy. Power cannot be devolved or made more democratic simply by law: it must be built from the bottom up, as well as stimulated from the top down. Nor do we favour a major programme of outright nationalisation, the result of which would often be little different from private sector ownership. We argue, rather, that our longer-term goals must be built into policy from the very beginning.

**The institutional framework**
Our key institutional proposals are as follows:
• The creation of a *National Planning Council* (as discussed in Chapter 5), to provide a forum for the development, in outline at least, of long-term plans for major industrial sectors and processes.
• *The Department of Trade and Industry* to act as the basis of ministerial co-ordination of industrial policy with enhanced status and powers to resist the influence of the Treasury in this area.
• The establishment of *British Enterprise*, to act as a state holding company — enabling public control to be extended in private industry, new public companies to be established and the leverage of existing public companies to be fully harnessed.
• The creation of a *National Investment Bank*, to manage the major capital inflows resulting from exchange controls, and to extend public ownership in the financial sector.
• The creation of a network of *enterprise boards* and *development agencies*, to promote industrial recovery at local and regional level.
• A greater role for the *Monopolies and Mergers Commission*.
The central objective of the institutional framework we propose is to implement policies of strategic planning — and, in so doing, to establish the long-term basis of a socialist enterprise culture.

## SOCIAL CONTROL AND OWNERSHIP
The policy of making public aid conditional, by giving it in the form of equity and/or loan capital, lies at the heart of our approach to extending social control and ownership. The main elements of our strategy for public enterprise are: establishing a new state holding company, British Enterprise, backed by local enterprise boards; bringing BT, British Gas (if privatised) and

other key utilities and companies back into the public sector; harnessing the economic power of existing and new publicly owned companies; and creating new publicly owned companies, both through British Enterprise and by giving greater freedom to major public corporations. In addition, we outline policies for a major extension of co-operative enterprise.

While we are not arguing for a major programme of outright nationalisation, it should be clear that we are arguing for a far greater role for public enterprise. We also want to stress the need to rethink the *forms* public enterprise can take. There are many possibilities, varying according to the following criteria.

First, *ownership*: public ownership may be 100 per cent; a majority stake; a controlling stake; or a minority stake (which may in itself give control). Moreover, companies may be wholly or partly owned by those who work in them. Companies may also be owned by consumers. Private shareholdings may or may not carry voting rights.

Second, the *level of intervention*: public intervention can be achieved at a national, regional and local level. National level intervention would, for example, be appropriate for multinationals or industries with substantial economies of scale; a regional response for regionally dominant industries, such as foundries or clothing; and a local response for smaller firms and co-ops. In order to achieve the devolution of economic power, the *minimum* necessary level of intervention may need to be pursued.

Third, *management structure*: strategic decisions should be distinguished from day to day 'operational' decisions. In the case of mainly privately owned companies, social control can be extended by a combination of commercial leverage and the extension of collective bargaining. In the case of publicly owned companies, strategic decisions may be taken by a board which includes one or more of: representatives from national government; the workforce through their unions; consumers; and local government. This can also apply to companies which combine public and common ownership.

Fourth, *industrial activity*: production technologies vary from industry to industry — as do economies of scale, the need to provide a national service and the level of development costs. In the case of the utilities — gas, water and electricity — operations must be organised nationally: similarly industries such as steel and telecommunications. Devolution of economic power is still possible through changes in *internal* structure, by encouraging operating divisions (as BSC does) or area boards (as do British Rail and British Gas). In the case of manufacturing and service industries, a national strategy (eg: for motors) can be achieved through individual companies in public ownership (eg: BL) or in mainly privately owned companies through commercial leverage.

Different approaches, varying according to these four factors, could give rise to an exciting diversity in social ownership which could help change the popular conception of it (created by past nationalisation) as unresponsive, inefficient and loss making. Above all, public and common enterprise must be able to meet people's needs as consumers — "private it's theirs" hasn't meant "public it's ours". This means, in turn, that social ownership must form part of a strategy for challenging private corporate power; it is all too easy to start with a policy of diversity and end with a rather ineffective combination of local enterprise and co-ops.

**British Enterprise**
*British Enterprise* (BE), a new national state holding company, is the most important institution we propose for making strategic planning a reality. BE would work alongside a network of local enterprise boards, building on the initiatives of local Labour authorities (Chapter 3). BE would play a leading role in increasing the public accountability of major companies, alongside direct negotiations with multinationals (Chapter 6). Local boards would work with BE to implement sector process strategies drawn up in the National Planning Council. These local boards would concentrate on medium sized companies in regionally based industries.

BE could take two basic forms. It could be established on the model of the Industrial Re-organisation Corporation (IRC) of the 1960's. Unlike the NEB its activities need not be dominated by companies facing major problems, such as BL, which could be the responsibility of the Department of Trade and Industry. Although the IRC mainly served to encourage rationalisations and mergers, a company of this kind could also be empowered to establish *new* public companies, to take public stakes and to enter into joint ventures with private companies. Where existing publicly owned companies dominate particular sectors, it could be argued that they should form holding companies independent of BE. This could, however lead to substantial problems of co-ordination for the implementation of the industrial strategy as a whole.

Alternatively, British Enterprise could, in effect, be made up of a number of holding companies. Each would be responsible for the overall operations of vertically integrated trading companies, wholly or partly publicly owned. They would therefore become the central institutions of industrial recovery across a number of sectors and processes. These holding companies could include, for example: *BE-Communications*, bringing together BT, the Post Office and Mercury; *BE-Engineering*, covering BSC, BL and other engineering companies; *BE-Aerospace*; and *BE-Information Technologies*. Such holding companies would be financed by (a) the profits generated by their companies; (b) the NIB; (c) money raised from the private sector; (d) securities issued by BE or BE holding companies.

In either form, British Enterprise could use a number of instruments to help further our broader industrial objectives. These include not only taking equity stakes but also the use of purchasing power, undertaking research and development, promoting exports, negotiating with multinationals and the direct promotion of public enterprise.

The main advantage of BE taking the first model is flexibility. BE would have substantial autonomy in identifying and following up on investment opportunities. This is important, given the unwieldy nature of many public companies. It could, however, reduce BE's impact, since it might lack the industrial muscle needed to negotiate effectively with major private — or even public — corporations.

The second, holding company, model offers the greater prospect of challenging private corporate power, by enabling the maximum use to be made of companies which are *already* publicly controlled. The leverage they offer includes (first) their size, which enables them to enter into effective negotiations with major companies, including multinationals; to be more equal partners in joint ventures; and to raise finance. Second, they play a strategic role in many key sectors, in which we wish to establish a stronger presence. Third, they possess managerial skills — both knowledge of key industries in general and of specific private sector suppliers: this expertise would be invaluable in negotiations with private companies. Fourth, their massive purchasing power could provide leverage with suppliers, be used to support firms and to encourage joint product development. Finally, their profitability could help finance joint ventures and to set up new public companies.

BE sector holding companies would have the task of co-ordinating the activities of key industrial firms — private and public — at a sector/process level. For example, BE Engineering, aware of BL's plans to retool for the launch of a new model, could establish a machine tool/robotics company. Tripartite bargaining could, as a result of this approach, become far more productive: for example, BE Communications would be a key participant in any sector planning committee on information technology. In this way, the sector holding company structure could therefore resolve the main challenge for strategic planning, by ensuring that broad strategies are reflected in company decision making. Such a structure would also provide a British counterpart to the vertically integrated holding companies that dominate the Japanese economy: these companies permit *both* competition, within and between individual trading companies, *and* substantial co-ordination of their strategic decisions.

The advantages of the holding company model could, in theory, be emulated in the first model of BE through extensive ministerial co-ordination, both within and between government departments, and also between government departments, major public companies and British Enterprise. Such co-ordination would, however, be a massive task. It would require substantial reorganisation of the Civil Service and would, in any case, have to be largely *imposed*. The advantage of the holding company model is that the means of such co-ordination would be built into its structure — it would not be dependent on ministerial will, but would come about as a result of the commercial decisions each holding company would *have* to take in order to grow.

The holding company model also offers major *financial* benefits. Bonds could be issued either by the individual trading company (eg, BT), the holding company (eg, BE-Communications) or BE itself. This would provide greater flexibility in funding public enterprise: individual companies unable to finance the issue of bonds necessary to pay for their nationalisation could still be brought into the public sector.

BE will only be effective, whichever form it takes, if it has sufficient powers: this is mainly a question of the relationship of BE and local enterprise boards to other institutions of planning, rather than statutory powers. Little leverage will be obtained if companies can get finance and other (non-conditional) forms of support elsewhere. Unconditional assistance from government departments (through selective aid schemes, regional assistance, public purchasing, and corporate tax relief) should be progressively or selectively reduced. Similarly, the actions of other planning institutions — such as the National Investment Bank, Price Commission and Monopolies and Mergers Commission — must be closely tied in with the actions of enterprise boards.

The criteria and methods of operation of BE must also be very different from those of the National Enterprise Board. BE's interventions should reflect the sectoral objectives established through tripartite bargaining: intervening company by company could otherwise be counterproductive. Moreover, the lessons of existing local enterprise boards should be heeded. Commercial leverage can — and should — go hand in hand with encouraging the extension of collective bargaining: support should be conditional upon a business plan negotiated by management and unions. This approach therefore differs from that of the last Labour Government, which saw planning agreements as *separate* from the NEB. The exercise of commercial leverage through BE and enterprise boards, coupled with new rights for working people, would make such agreements (as traditionally conceived) redundant. Finally, commercial leverage should be used to promote social objectives, in particular equality at work for women and ethnic minorities.

Local enterprise boards will only be able to operate effectively if regional policy is reformed (Chapter 6). Their social objectives should not be confused with other objectives, such as preserving jobs *irrespective* of the costs involved, lest the confusion of objectives which bedevilled the last Labour Government's strategy be repeated.

## Public ownership — towards a new vision

The case for public ownership is as powerful now as it has ever been — just as it has never been more urgent to rethink the priorities for public ownership, the methods of achieving it, the accountability and internal structure of publicly owned companies and, above all, their responsiveness to consumer and community needs. Publicly owned companies should be a model for socialism in practice. Unfortunately, for many people, that is just what they have become: unresponsive, often inefficient and often just as brutal in cutting jobs as private sector companies.

In many ways, this public image is, of course, grossly unfair. Nationalised industries are major investors: over the past ten years they have invested three times as much — for every worker employed — as firms in the private sector; and investment per unit of output has been twice as high. Moreover, companies such as BP, British Aerospace, BL, British Steel and Rolls Royce are among Britain's top export earners. Nationalised industries have also been highly profitable in recent years. Their productivity record has been impressive, outstripping the private sector. Without public enterprise Britain would have had no domestically owned company in sectors such as motor vehicles, aero engines, shipbuilding, microchips and computers.

The Tory Government privatisation programme, on the other hand, means that only the most vulnerable companies starved of investment finance will be left in the public sector. Profits will increasingly reflect the abuse of monopoly powers, rather than the efficiency of the company, and the Government's obsessive desire to cut public borrowing. These factors are, however, unlikely to win much sympathy for public enterprise. Popular opinion may not favour further privatisation but there is no positive desire for an extension of public ownership. This reflects a deep seated lack of confidence in publicly owned companies which predates the election of the Conservative Government in 1979.

### Public ownership — new priorities

In 1944 the TUC set out certain criteria for public ownership. First, the importance of an industry to the life and safety of the community: the sale of British Aerospace and British Shipbuilders' warship yards, and the intended sale of Royal Ordnance Factories, provide powerful examples of the Tories' determination to put short-term gain before long-term national interest. Second, the existence of a monopoly serving a wide public demand which, in private hands, could easily be exploited: essential national utilities, such as gas, electricity and telecommunications have been privatised, or are seen as candidates for privatisation. Third, the importance of the industry as a source of new investment: an argument which strongly applied to industries abandoned by the private sector, such as coal and steel after 1945, and companies such as BL in the 1970's. These interventions were the result of pragmatism as much as of principle. With no alternative other than to rescue companies such as Rolls Royce, Tory and Labour Governments, alike, took key loss makers into the public sector. The economic and social reasons for so doing were powerful, but the result has been the nationalisation of the commanding "depths" — not heights — of the economy.

The Tory legacy of a 'Third World' economy with which a future Labour Government must contend gives a new urgency to public enterprise. The private sector is abandoning new technologies such as electronics, while the command over vital national resources such as oil has been undermined by privatisation. There are also social arguments. The privatisation of BT threatens to divide Britain into the 'information rich and poor', with many denied access to the resources necessary to fully participate in society (Chapter 9). These economic and social factors, coupled with the sheer scale of the privatisation programme — valued at £17,000 million including council house sales — demands new priorities for public enterprise. These should not simply reflect what has just been sold off by the

Tories. British Rail Hotels are hardly as strategically significant as, for example, electronics.

Taking these factors together, we would argue that the main priorities for public ownership fall into the following (sometimes overlapping) categories:

- *Utilities* — eg, BT and British Gas.
- *Energy* — eg, BNOC, Britoil, British Gas, and British Coal.
- *Strategic* — eg, British Steel, British Shipbuilders.
- *Defence* — eg, British Aerospace.
- *Industrial Recovery* — eg, BT, BL (now renamed 'Rover Group').

Which of these categories demand full (100 per cent) public ownership and which only a minority stake is a separate question. The answer must, in part, be pragmatic. Full public ownership may be needed to achieve the objectives of social ownership in particular cases. For example, in the case of BT and other utilities, there is a range of social and industrial objectives which only 100 per cent ownership will guarantee can be achieved. The same is not true of many manufacturing companies, where the objectives for public ownership (in the short term at least) are often more limited. Moreover, a 'minority' stake will often confer effective control in many cases, given the normal dispersion of share ownership.

The public ownership programme of a future Labour Government must also recognise certain constraints — mainly, the parliamentary time involved. A 'general' Bill to reverse Tory privatisation would be both undesirable and impractical. Undesirable because this principle could just as easily be used to overturn future Labour legislation; impractical because many privatised assets have been broken down and sold off. It is likely that parliamentary time could only be found for two major companies, presumably BT and British Gas. A second, alleged, constraint is financial. This has been described in the following terms: is it better to spend £4,000 million to create 400,000 new jobs or to wholly renationalise BT? But this is to confuse two different kinds of expenditure. Spending £4,000 million to purchase BT shares is like investing savings in a profitable asset. That spending would earn the government a (further) half share in profits currently running at nearly £2,000 million a year. Alternatively, spending £4,000 million to create jobs in (say) child care or health services does not yield direct financial returns. It *does* bring resources — especially labour — into use whereas the purchase of BT shares would not by itself change production or employment. In addition, increasing government activity financed by borrowing increases the total amount of credit in the economy. Renationalising BT would merely change one kind of credit (government bonds) for another (BT shares). We discuss these issues further in Chapter 9.

**Public ownership — new structures**
Publicly owned companies must have a number of objectives, some of which will often be conflicting. They must be given sufficient freedom to succeed in a commercial environment; their behaviour should reflect the government's economic, industrial and social objectives; and they should be accountable, not only to Parliament but also to those who work in them. Under the Tories, broader commercial and social objectives have given way to financial controls imposed by the Treasury.

Industrial companies, partly or wholly publicly owned, would be accountable to government through British Enterprise and the local boards. Their responsiveness to consumers would be prompted on the one hand by their need to compete, often in world markets, and on the other by their access to investment finance for new product development through the enterprise board framework. Public ownership will not, however, necessarily reconcile the tension faced by trade unionists in bargaining over both strategic decisions and wages and conditions. The extension of collective bargaining therefore provides workers with the most effective method of influencing key enterprise decisions in industrial companies, privately *or* publicly owned.

The most important factor in reforming the structure of publicly owned companies is probably whether they have a national monopoly or not. In the case of the utilities — electricity, gas and telecommunications — efficiency demands a national service. It is therefore less easy to move away from the Morrisonian model. The same is true of industries such as steel and coal. In these cases, the sheer scale of their operations means that their *internal* structures will have to be reformed if they are to become responsive to consumers, workers and government.

The present statutory framework of nationalised industries is clearly inadequate. For example, most are incorporated by statutes which refer to the objective of a positive return on capital employed, and require an annual surplus. Most are also required to submit a corporate plan every year, but in practice these are often never formally approved. The process of approval is so long-winded and subject to political judgements that often the next plan is in gestation before the current plan has been approved. Under the Conservatives, plans based on the industry's needs have been sacrificed to public sector spending targets, which by convention cover nationalised industries' external borrowing.

Short-term political pressures can distort the long-term needs of the industries in other ways — for example, through arbitrary changes in prices in order to raise government revenue, and through intervention in the corporate planning process. The miners' strike of 1984-85 provided an obvious example of the decisive impact of political objectives. Conversely, steel is still suffering the legacy of BSC *management's* determination to pursue their favoured plan at all costs.

There is no simple way of reconciling short-term political and long-term industrial goals. Publicly owned industries will, and indeed should, always be open to government "interference": that is what public accountability is all about. The most realistic objective is to ensure that it has productive results. If this is to be achieved the following steps should be taken.

*First, a new framework is needed to judge the performance of public enterprise.* Decisions of one public enterprise may heavily influence the economic and financial environment of another; for example, CEGB decisions on the mix of fuel inputs to their power stations. These decisions may easily ignore the wider "resource" costs to the national economy — such as those of a switch away from domestic steel or coal, in terms of higher unemployment pay or of a tighter balance of payments constraint.

*Second, new methods of accountability are needed to the government, to those who work in the industries and, above all, to consumers.* The problem with adopting the wider framework we advocate is that pressures from political interests could outweigh arguments for industrial modernisation. For example, proposals for external monitoring of the performance of public corporations have been frustrated by an unholy triple alliance: of the workforce, fearful that the philosophy of public and national service will be given little weight; and of the government and the Civil Service, anxious to protect their own power and influence.

In order to increase public accountability, a new system of Parliamentary Select Committees has been proposed. This could cover each sector in which private industries operate. A Telecommunications Select Committee, for example, would oversee not only BT but also telecommunications in general. For such a system to have any effect, the Committees would have to be backed by far greater resources than are currently available to backbench MPs. Even then their impact would inevitably be limited, because of the sheer complexity of BT's operations, let alone those of the entire telecommunications sector.

The public accountability of publicly owned industries can be better influenced by a radical reform of corporate structure. One approach is for strategic decisions to be taken by a supervisory board which brings together government, trade union and (in the case of utilities) consumer representatives. Union representatives would be elected through their unions; forms of consumer representation are discussed in Chapter 8. Day to day decisions could then be taken by an executive board, appointed by and answerable to the supervisory board. The problem with this is that decisions may end up being taken where senior management is represented, on the executive board. The second approach, therefore, is for a single board, on which govermment, unions, consumers *and* senior management are represented.

A new board structure cannot, by itself, ensure a thorough-going increase in democracy inside public enterprises. The problems which trade unionists are likely to encounter in combining collective bargaining with new responsibilities on supervisory boards have already been discussed.

Other measures will be needed. British Gas has long been broken down into twelve areas, while British Rail has more recently established five 'sectors' and BT, before privatisation, 61 'areas'. These efforts to break down the operating structure of public companies can be built on: a renationalised BT could retain scope for local decision making, while BSC could be organised around product divisions. Executive boards should also be established at area level. These could assess whether strategic goals are being met in practice, and could have control, albeit limited, over specific decisions. They could give local government a voice: but this might isolate local government representatives, giving them little influence over strategic decisions at a national level which shape those at local level. There is also, therefore, a case for local government representation on the national board.

These measures to increase accountability will not, however, guarantee a more efficient service. Conflicts of interests may arise between consumers and those who work in the industry, as well as between consumers and government. Decentralisation may enable more responsive services to be provided but it would lead to union resistance if national bargaining rights, long fought for, were thereby threatened. The sale of phones, to take another example, improves consumer choice, but it also involves a threat to telephone maintenance jobs, at least of current BT employees. Resolving conflicts such as these will not always be easy.

The problem of promoting consumers' rights is especially acute in the case of national monopolies, as we discuss in more detail in Chapter 8. In such cases, an external assessment is needed, in the form of a 'value for money' audit. Such an audit must acknowledge *both* the economic *and* social objectives of public corporations, the aim being to assess the efficiency with which they are realised. By recognising the need for public enterprise to be seen to provide value for money, such an approach could help win popular support for its extension.

### Co-operatives: a third sector
Common ownership is an important complement to public ownership. The promotion of workers' co-ops by a socialist government forms a valid alternative to the promotion of small businesses by the Tories — provided co-ops recognise trade union rights and form part of an organised movement.

The experience of co-ops shows the importance of institutional support. Co-ops, above all else, need sympathetic technical advice and management help, tailored to their needs. Local co-operative development agencies have shown themselves adept at promoting co-ops by making this available. By lifting the spending limit allowed under section 137 of the 1972 Local Authority Act, this support could be extended. Local agencies derive their stength from close ties with local communities and their independence from the state, being companies limited by guarantee and controlled by a management board in which existing co-operatives have a majority vote. There is a strong case for regional agencies to help the larger co-ops.

These agencies should seek to ensure that co-ops are not left isolated. It is strongly argued within the co-operative movement that a federal body is essential, building on ICOM. This raises the role of the national Co-operative Development Agency. The Agency has come under criticism from the co-operative movement for supporting management buy-outs, but argues that it has done so only when asked to by the employees. This, in turn, raises the general issue of the relationship between the state and voluntary organisations, which should be free to determine their own priorities. The approach adopted by the GLC offers a possible solution — inviting bids for public money which give priority to the objectives of the elected body.

Financial help for co-ops will also be needed. The West Midlands County Council has set up a revolving loan fund with the Industrial Common Ownership Fund (ICOF), so that once loans are repaid the money can be used to support other co-ops. The ICOF could be expanded if it were allowed by the Bank of England to take deposits. A Co-operative Investment Bank could also be established, helped by an initial capital grant from the government. However, it may make more sense to build on existing institutions, such as ICOF, rather than setting up yet another new one. Legal and tax changes would also encourage the development of co-ops, as proposed in Labour's *Charter for Co-ops*. Capital gains tax and capital transfer tax on conversions of private firms to co-ops should in certain cases be waived. Co-ops should be able to establish an 'indivisible statutory reserve' which could be treated as equity capital by lending institutions, thereby allowing an increase in the finance available. Money put into such reserves should then be offset against corporation tax.

There is considerable scope for further innovation. The growth of co-ops is often constrained by the lack of internal finance on the one hand, and the inability of co-ops to finance substantial loan repayments on the other. Some local authorities have attempted to resolve this by setting up a new kind of co-op (an 'Equity Participation Co-op'), which gives outside investors both a return and (non-voting) shares. Conversions could also be encouraged, by adapting the American model of an 'ESOP'. Employee Stock Ownership Plans now cover seven per cent of the US workforce. Companies which give shares to their employees can offset the cost against corporate profits for tax purposes. Provided ESOPs are set up with trade union approval and are run on a one-member/one-vote basis, they can play a valid role in a socialist strategy for extending employee share ownership.

The Labour Party has proposed a statutory right for workers in private firms to convert their enterprise into a workers' co-op by acquiring the assets of the firm, and public money to help this. While desirable in principle, it is extremely hard to see how it could work in practice. Serious objections have come from the co-operative movement itself — some fear that conversion would give co-ops a poor reputation because 'forced' conversion would meet with the opposition of former owners and with failure. It has also been suggested that some owners might take the money and run, dumping their failed business on the workforce.

Experience of co-ops (Chapter 3) emphasises the importance of enabling them to develop their own demands and self-confidence in their own time, and to provide the resources and support to facilitate this. The development of a significant third sector, distinct from private and public ownership, must be a gradual process.

Forming a co-op should be one of a series of *options* available to working people, in the course of extending collective bargaining. Workforces could be given first refusal to buy their company (and establish a co-op) in the event of its failure, closure or sale. The relevant assets of the enterprise could then be frozen during negotiations. The co-operators would be able to take out a 'mortgage' to finance the purchase of the business. In order to secure the mortgage, the co-operators would have to demonstrate the viability of the business. They should be given help to do this by a body independent of the lending institution.

The success of newly established large co-ops, especially in the case of rescues, depends in part on resolving the potential conflict of interest facing stewards as managers and representatives, as the lessons of Kirkby confirm. A clear and coherent internal structure is needed to prevent this conflict, and to enable co-operators to learn management skills. One solution is for stewards to be elected on to a Co-operative Board which determines strategic objectives. Management could be appointed by and accountable to the Board, whether they come from the existing workforce or were hired from outside. The relationship of stewards carrying out traditional bargaining functions to those on the Board would be akin to the relationship between stewards and safety representatives. Steward structures in well organised workplaces have adapted so that safety representatives can develop their own skills and avoid being compromised. This is achieved by safety representatives developing some distance from the daily concerns of shop stewards.

## PLANNING AND FINANCE

The financial system — the banks, pensions funds, insurance companies and other institutions that make up the 'City' — exercises substantial power over capital flows, barring the way of particular ventures and speeding the passage of others. In addition, the City institutions now own the majority of company shares.

Any attempt to move towards a more democratic economy must therefore come to grips with the financial sector: first, because public control over the flow of funds can be a powerful instrument of planning, and a way of exercising leverage over private companies. Second, a more democratic economy would involve greater accountability over the exercise of rights of ownership. And, third (as we have already discussed in Chapter 4) the City has a powerful hold on the direction of the economy: the government relies heavily on the City to fund its debt, and important variables such as exchange and interest rates are powerfully influenced by the City.

### Financial power

Since the Conservatives lifted exchange controls in 1979, over

£60,000 million has left Britain which could have been invested in British industry. The loss of capital also represents a loss of *power*. Britain has become more dependent on, and more integrated into, the web of international capitalism.

The concept of the 'power' of financial institutions is, however, not straightforward. People who run financial institutions would claim they have very little power. They are often simply directed by clients as to where money should be invested. Interest rates are simply guided by the market. Investment decisions are made after an objective analysis of risks and returns. Their job is to use money to make money, and they do so within parameters largely beyond their control. If the extreme version of this argument were true, the pursuit of democratic control would be irrelevant: a 'socialist' bank manager will not behave differently to a capitalist one. But this argument cannot be sustained.

*First*, the numberless variety of investment decisions in identical circumstances proves the existence of choice. Whether investment is made at home or overseas, into speculative ventures or long-term projects; all these choices have a political content.

*Second*, there is room for the representation of different interests. For example, the interests of mineworkers might lie in having their savings invested in the domestic industry. It does make sense to talk about the 'power' of the City and about the need for democracy.

*Third*, the outcome of so-called 'market mechanisms' can be modified. Pension fund managers, for example, explain their decision to invest overseas by their need to maximise returns. But their choices are themselves shaped by the structure of tax and fiscal incentives in Britain. Withdrawing these 'fiscal privileges' — if say, a specified proportion of pension fund investment were not invested through the National Investment Bank (as the Labour Party proposes) — would lead to a different outcome. The market is not a black box, and it is possible to introduce broader criteria into its operations.

**Finance for investment**
An effective industrial strategy must go hand in hand with a strategy for finance. Britain lacks the institutions and structures to enable this to happen. The City, moreover, has failed to provide industry with the long-term finance it needs on the right terms and conditions; City institutions often lack the technical expertise to evaluate proposals from industry, and they often prefer 'safe' companies with large assets, rather than those with growth potential but no proven track record. Industry, for its

part, has become conditioned to accept the judgements about acceptable risk, and the time horizons, of the banks. However, an intervention in the City to make more long-term funds available would almost certainly have very little effect on its own: it must therefore be *coupled* with strategic planning of industry.

### The City's international role
The British financial system has failed to meet the needs of domestic industry because historically it has been geared to financing trade, in particular within the British Empire. When capital was raised in London it was more often than not for foreign investment, such as the US railroads. The City is now an international centre for managing foreign currencies — 'Eurocurrencies'. Banks operating in the UK lend vast amounts of money overseas, many of them foreign banks.

This international role has had far-reaching results. British investors divert more of the national income to overseas investment than any major nation. For example, the two largest insurance companies, the Commercial Union and the Royal, do 70 per cent of their insurance business overseas. Since the removal of exchange controls, 60 per cent of unit trust investment has gone abroad.

In Germany and Japan, by contrast, industrial reorganisation has been closely linked with the provision of long-term finance tailored to the needs of domestic industry. Financial institutions have accepted responsibility for industrial performance, and so developed a detailed understanding of the problems facing industry, both technical and managerial. This tradition of industrial banking laid the basis for special credit institutions. In West Germany, the Kreditanstalt fur Wiederaufbau — owned by the federal and regional governments — concentrated on regional policies, with the banks focusing on industrial financing. The Japanese economy is dominated by large holding companies, which include both industrial and financial companies: these have worked closely with MITI, the main government department responsible for industrial policy.

### The National Investment Bank
Both the TUC and the Labour Party have proposed that a new institution should be established — the *National Investment Bank* (NIB) — to provide finance for industry as part of a planning system. The Bank would, it is suggested, work alongside local authority enterprise boards lending them money for investment in local companies. The result would be a valuable link between the savings institutions and local investment projects with a high degree of democratic control.

The relationship of the NIB with other planning institutions, such as British Enterprise, has not yet been clarified in Labour Party or TUC policy. Co-ordination between financial and industrial policies may not be easy, especially as the NIB will be responsible for managing the large capital inflows which will result from the new scheme of exchange controls. It is vital that public confidence in the management of these funds is maintained. The most appropriate role for the NIB would therefore be primarily that of extending public ownership in the *financial* sector. This implies that the role of the Bank of England would also thereby be curtailed.

The NIB would carry through a strategy of financial reconstruction to mirror that promoted by British Enterprise in the industrial and retail sectors. In this way, many of the problems of voluntary regulation and public supervision could be overcome. For example, at present the Bank of England can establish lending guidelines, but these are not legally binding. The Bank's main powers are limited to the approval of new banks, and in cajoling others (but only where it has relevant information). This is a perfect example of the weakness of a basically voluntary system of regulation. Nor would a public supervisory body increase *detailed* control or accountability.

The argument that access to public finance should be conditional reflects similar procedures which have been used for many years in France, where the long-term credit agency, the Credit Nationale, requires the sanction of the planning ministry before making loans. These loans in turn provide a passport for companies to raise funds from other private and public banks.

The NIB would be a source of industrial finance — through packages negotiated by British Enterprise and local enterprise boards — in the form of both loan and equity capital. The terms of NIB loans would reflect the long-term needs of British industry. Most loans would be for up to 20 years, with repayments lower in the early years when investment is generating less return. Loans could be made at favourable rates of interest when appropriate. The criteria for loans should, in part, reflect wider social costs and gains. Assisted firms would be expected to promote racial and sexual equality, and health and safety at work. In addition, both the Bank and the boards could provide advice on technology and management techniques. Finance should be tied to the provision — and acceptance — of these services.

**Public ownership and the financial institutions**
The banking system remains overwhelmingly the most important source of external funds for companies. The banking

system in Britain is highly concentrated, highly profitable, and almost entirely free of public accountability. This is indefensible. The power to create the credit on which the economy functions is conferred by society and should be under social control. There has been a long debate in the Labour movement over the nationalisation of the banks. More recent policy has emphasised that public ownership is only one route, and by no means a guaranteed route, to social control. An alternative would be to require banks to negotiate with the planning agencies on their allocation of credit to different activities. Public ownership through the NIB would be a reserve sanction if banks did not stick to their agreement.

It has been argued by Richard Minns in *Take over the City* that public ownership of the merchant banks would be the most effective way of controlling industry. Financial institutions as a whole now own 55 per cent of company shares: the largest shareholders are the pension funds (20 per cent), followed by the insurance companies (15 per cent), investment trusts, merchant banks and other bodies. The distribution of *control* is rather different. Many smaller pension funds hand over control to merchant banks and stockbrokers. Just 10 pension funds account for over 70 per cent of all funds managed 'in-house', while just 20 institutions deal with 75 per cent of externally managed funds.

The problem with Minns' argument is that share owners may not allow their funds to be managed by the government, particularly if the government were using the ownership rights conferred to pursue active intervention in industry. As long as shareholders' rights exist they must be taken into account, along with the rights of workers, consumers, tax payers, and local communities. On the other hand, many financial institutions, particularly pension funds, are in principle subject to democratic control. By giving workers a say in the way their savings in these funds are invested, and ownership rights exercised, it may be possible to develop a new dimension of democratic accountability over companies.

The criteria which govern pension fund investment could also be broadened. In the US, the concept of 'socially responsible' investment is much more widely accepted than in Britain. Pennsylvania State, for example, has created a special $100 million investment fund to channel pension fund money to local business. Social responsibility does not, however, preclude conflicts of interest. Worker shareholders representing workers from outside an industry may have very different views about how it should develop to the worker directors elected within the industry, or representatives of elected bodies at local or national level. Such conflicts may be resolved by involving unions and local government representatives in developing sector strategies.

## PLANNING, MARKET POWER AND MARKETS

Control over market power should be central to any strategy for industrial recovery. Yet the possibility of planning *through* markets is usually ignored in the Left's discussion of economic policy. The association of planning with bureaucratic control is the main reason for this. But we have argued that markets do have a legitimate role in a socialist strategy. This section discusses four ways in which market power can be directed to progressive ends, through: bargaining with multinationals over access to British markets; changes in competition policy; giving small producers greater access to markets and, thereby, the ability to challenge the power of major retailers; and 'contract compliance'.

Access to markets is the most important theme running through this section. In the past, industrial policy has tended to concentrate on production, thereby ignoring whether the product meets needs or can be sold. Analysing market trends; moving 'up market' to produce more profitable products with a higher value-added; developing effective methods of distribution; exploiting the opportunities offered by advertising to win support for socialist values — all these are of growing significance. A strategy for production, without a strategy for markets, cannot succeed. Markets are becoming increasingly closed, dominated by specific institutional arrangements: for example, the British car market is shaped by fleet car sales and the British clothing market by the control of retailers. These institutional factors present real opportunities for extending democratic control, as we go on to describe.

### Multinationals' access to the British market

Multinational producers have had a major impact in the decline of British industries such as motors (Chapter 10) and textiles and clothing (Chapter 11). Their economic power is rooted in technological know-how which a Labour Government, faced with a 'Thirld World' economy, will need access to. But this power is not without limits. Multinationals have to be able to sell to make profits. Governments can and are bargaining with multinational producers, trading off access to the domestic market against investment in domestic design and manufacturing technologies. The ability to exert leverage in turn depends on the degree of particular multinationals' domination of their industry. In motors, no single multinational is dominant, enabling governments to play them off against each other. In computers, however, IBM dominates the global market, severely constraining even international action to limit IBM's power.

The possibility of bargaining with multinationals has been denied recently by some theorists. According to the 'product cycle' explanation of multinational location, world production will become increasingly concentrated in the developing countries because of low labour costs, which are ensured by a ready supply of a cheap labour without any tradition of trade union organisation. This explanation rests on a number of crucial assumptions. First, that the product market is becoming increasingly mature and undifferentiated. Second, that production will be increasingly dominated by a few giant multinationals exploiting growing economies of scale. Third, that production work is becomingly increasingly 'deskilled' and can be easily done by workers without experience of industrial work. As a result, multinationals will be able to dominate the most important markets, producing standard products which can be sold throughout the world at low cost. However, it is unlikely that the shift in production away from the developed countries will be so dramatic. The role of government support and the question of access to key markets will be critical. The ease with which disinvestment can occur can be overstated. And differences in labour costs between countries, although important, must be placed in context. For example, Ford's decision to build a new Escort assembly plant in Valencia rather than Halewood, Bordeaux or Saarlouis, reflected a desire for access to the closed Spanish market — the last major market in Europe that had not yet developed comparable levels of demand for cars — as well as an export subsidy of 13 per cent. The importance of labour costs varies with the type of decision under consideration:

• *Major mechanicals*, such as engines and transmissions, require heavy initial investment and little direct labour. Efficient production depends on a technically skilled labour force. Reliable production is essential because of size of the investment and nature of component. Few developing countries are seen as sufficiently stable to ensure continuity of production. Ford's decision to build an engine plant in Mexico, rather than Japan or the USA, was influenced by government subsidies that reduced the cost of construction; export incentives; rights to increase imports into Mexico; and tax reductions linked to export volume.

• *Finished items* include seats and dashboard mountings. Remote location creates problems of quality control and makes stock reduction difficult to achieve. These parts are also bulky and expensive to transport.

• *Minor mechanicals* include starters and radiators, for which the advantages of low-wage country sourcing are greatest. Such components are both relatively labour intensive and easy to ship.

The increasing importance of product led growth, coupled with future developments in production organisation, may further lessen the advantages of production in low-wage countries. Flexibility in manufacturing techniques is lowering scale economies, as we discuss for motors (Chapter 10). This especially applies to assembly, where an increasing number of model derivatives can be produced on the same line. Flexibility in manufacturing may enable nationally based medium-sized producers to survive. Moreover, increasing automation will lessen the significance of labour costs. Finally, the skills, commitment and experience of the workforce are essential to maintaining product quality as well as output. Harnessing these is an important factor in Japan's success. They presuppose a tradition of industrial work which often does not exist in developing countries.

The assumption that multinational production will shift to developing countries can be turned on its head. Instead it can be argued that multinationals will only shift production if this is necessary to secure regional growth markets. Despite the success of Ford in Europe, VW in Brazil and Mitsubishi in Australia, other manufacturers have had limited success in locating overseas — for example, VW and Renault in North America. The incentive to locate in regional growth markets is limited by a number of factors. First, despite saturation of markets in Europe, Japan and America by the end of the century, it is unlikely that the markets for many products in developing countries will be any greater. Second, it is improbable that indigenous producers will become established in developing growth markets. Domestic producers in North Korea, the Soviet Union and China have become established by selling at a low price in isolated markets, and have sought help from established manufacturers in developing new models. Third, American multinationals often do not have great capital resources for rapid expansion in risky fledgling markets. These factors suggest that any growth of new facilities in developing countries will be gradual.

Within established regional markets such as Europe, similar factors will apply, as the Ford example above showed. A company like Ford would have to balance the loss of 'goodwill' and poor publicity which would result from pulling out of Britain against any short-term advantage from lower production costs.

Decisions are also constrained to some extent by trade union bargaining over sourcing in established markets.

Governments can therefore be in a strong position to bargain with multinationals, using access to markets as the lever. Multinationals' bargaining power is, however, considerably greater if they dominate particular markets. France, for example, has tried to bridge the technological gap by developing national champions, and closing off the French market to competitors. The Mitterrand Government launched a £4 billion plan to cable France using optic fibre technology. Foreign telecommunication equipment makers were barred from the French market. The French computer company, Bull, was supported through public purchasing: Bull now supplies over 40 per cent of central government orders, while IBM's share has fallen from 55 per cent in 1970 to 20 per cent; in the case of public sector companies, over which the government has less control, IBM's share is 40 per cent compared to Bull's 16 per cent. But IBM's technological lead forced the Mitterrand Government to reconsider, and it began to open up the market to IBM in return for continuing investment in France. IBM has been given an experimental contract for an electronic telephone directory assistance system in the Paris area. Meanwhile Bull has been forced into collaboration with foreign manufacturers, as have other state enterprises in tele-communications, integrated circuits, biotechnology, medical equipment and energy.

British industry will also be forced to collaborate with foreign manufacturers, whether in the form of licensing agreements, original equipment deals or joint ventures. Thorn/EMI, (as well as Telefunken and Thomson) has built plants in Europe to produce JVC video cassette recorders — plants described by Philips as "little more than screwdriver factories". Collaboration with the Japanese carries the real danger of the European company being abandoned once the Japanese company has used its partner's distribution networks to test the market, establish its own credibility, and build up the sales volume it needs to set up its own plant. For example, its partner Sweda, the European electronic cash register company, came to rely on Omron, a Japanese firm, which then pulled out in 1980. Ricoh, the Japanese copier manufacturer, similarily decided to go it alone in 1978-79: Savin, its US partner, unsuccessfully invested $100 million in designing its own copier and has since been taken over because of financial problems. These dangers have arisen because western firms have taken a short-term view. They have failed to ensure that design work is shared or that the competitive value of their distributive networks is maintained. These dangers can only be avoided if joint ventures are between equal partners and if the western firms can use them to improve marketing strengths and technological expertise. But this will be difficult for many British firms, which start from such a weak position.

These problems can only be overcome by government support through long-term industrial planning and public purchasing. In many cases, Britain will not be able to go it alone. European collaboration will be needed, giving a new urgency to initiatives to permit greater industrial planning within the EEC. The scale of Europe's technological gap is already forcing a rethink. However, the problems in forging collaboration among competing companies in anything beyond pre-competitive research should not be underestimated. Moreover, there are also major constraints on exercising any effective trade sanction in the EEC given EEC law — constraints which must be overcome.

**Competition policy**
One of the factors which has contributed to Britain's poor industrial performance is that it is easier for companies to grow through acquisitions and mergers than through investment and product development. Companies can do this because of the way the Stock Market works, allowing companies to print their own money — shares — to buy up other companies. Government policy has also encouraged 'merger booms'. Mergers can be investigated by the Monopolies and Mergers Commission, but there is a presumption that mergers should go ahead. The Secretary of State for Trade and Industry must decide whether merger bids should be referred to the Commission: mergers are not referred as a matter of course. Since the merger boom of the late 1950's, only two to five mergers a year have been referred to the Commission and only half of these have been found to be against the public interest.

The evidence suggests that mergers have not improved industrial performance. Studies of the performance of companies which merged between 1948 and 1964 conclude that they were less profitable in a seven year period after merger than they were before. Mergers have not, moreover, involved highly profitable firms taking over unprofitable firms: the profitability of acquired firms was comparable with that of others in the industry, and the average profitability of acquiring firms was only a quarter above it. Instead, it appears that mergers have, in general, created unmanageable companies in which production facilities were merely lumped together: one study of 38 merged firms concluded that 30 shut down little or none of their plants.

This experience suggests that competition policy should

change, although more recent evidence is needed. The companies concerned should have a duty in *every* case to prove that mergers are in the public interest. It may be argued that mergers are necessary to enable companies to survive on the international market: this may indeed be true but it must be demonstrated. The definition of the public interest must also be broadened, so that the decisions of the Commission reflect the sector strategies of the National Planning Council and do not conflict with the actions of the national and local enterprise boards. The Commission must be integrated with the other agencies of planning.

### Small firms and major retailers

The growing power of major retailers is one of the most significant developments in the structure of economic power in Britain. The retail giants are able to dominate access to the market, especially of smaller producers. Textiles and clothing provides one example of an industry where this has taken place. Major retailers are able to regulate the production of smaller firms. On the one hand, this may help these firms by providing them with a secure market and enabling market opportunities to be identified. It may also help the industry by raising product quality. On the other hand, it can leave smaller firms vulnerable if the retailers fail to develop long-term relationships with them. The result may be to weaken the industry — as in the case of shipbuilding — with firms not having the confidence to invest and being unable to move from low wage/poor quality to high wage/good quality production. This has harmful effects not only on the industry but also those employed in it, as well as on co-ops and other forms of smaller firms which should be encouraged.

Tackling the economic power of giant retailers raises complex issues. The most successful retailers have considerable knowledge of the details of production, far greater than a Labour Government is likely to have at its disposal. Successful retailers, moreover, need neither a Labour Government's markets nor money. Retailers sell to individual consumers: their profits do not depend on the recovery of industry in Britain — provided there is sufficient purchasing power they can make money by selling British made *or* foreign goods. A Labour Government would therefore have little effective commercial leverage. Punitive taxes are likely to be either unenforceable or else extremely unpopular with consumers. A Labour Government could, however, make more extensive use of controls over land needed for development in being far more supportive of local councils in bargaining over new sites. Finally, the sad decline of the 'Co-op' should caution socialists who claim that they can make a better job of retailing. Indirect means are likely to be more effective in influencing retailers. By building up the collective power of small producers to gain access to the market, a countervailing force could be introduced to the big retailer. Fashion centres sponsored by Labour councils, providing a central resource that local clothing firms cannot provide for themselves, are an example.

Agricultural marketing boards have long played a similar role. The Agricultural Marketing Acts of 1931 and 1933 provided a statutory basis for agricultural marketing schemes and for producers' Boards to administer them. For example, the Milk Marketing Boards for England, Wales and Scotland were set up in 1933, following various unsuccessful attempts by farmers to obtain a fair price for their produce through forms of voluntary co-operation. The Boards consist of representatives of farmers and the Ministry of Agriculture. Each producer has at present one vote for every ten cows, although this is under review. The Boards are a kind of compulsory farmers' co-operative. All 66,000 farmers offering milk for sale are registered with the Board for their area, and, with the exception of a small number of registered producer retailers, are required to sell their milk solely to the Boards. Producers pay for the costs of the collection service. The Boards sell the milk to private dairies.

The key control exercised is the maximum price for liquid milk sold to dairies and the price paid to farmers for their milk. This enables the Boards — provided they are not subject to impossible pressures from the EEC — to regulate production. They were able to do this without direct quotas until 1984. Indeed, the introduction of quotas has proved administratively chaotic and had a disastrous impact on the farmers. Quotas proved highly inflexible in the face of the subsequent drought.

The Milk Marketing Boards have become increasingly important in the post-war period, developing to the point where they represent a major section of butter and cheese manufacture and much of the bulk transport of milk between farms and dairies. They also provide services to dairy farmers ranging from artificial insemination (for the cows) to economic and technical advice. The democratic structure ensures a certain level of producer control over strategic decisions but considerably less over day-to-day decisions. The Boards' importance to small producers grew when the guarantee price structure, and with it the regular milk cheque upon which many relied, was ended in 1977. The Boards' income is now wholly derived from the market place. The government until recently retained control over the liquid market by determining the retail price and the maximum price at which the Boards could sell raw milk to the dairies.

The operation of the Milk Marketing Boards reflects the way policy changes affect production. Fresh liquid milk is treated as the premium product with butter making as residual. This means that butter takes up all the fluctuation in production. Other countries have different priorities. In the Netherlands, for example, butter is the premium product. The control exercised through the Board structure also provides a means by which a government could reduce the country's dependence on dairy products.

These Marketing Boards illustrate two different ways in which industry can be planned and modernised, without direct state ownership or a large state bureaucracy, and in a very decentralised industry. There is scope for improvements, but many of these — in for example democracy or conditions of employment — are possible within the existing framework. For many farm products an extension of the marketing board system could cover not only purchase of farm gate produce and its distribution but also the provision of technical advice. Marketing boards could enable democratic control to be extended through the representation of farmers, farm workers (through their trade unions), consumers, technical experts and Ministry appointees.

**Contract compliance**

The market power of the public sector has already been discussed in Chapter 2: contract compliance can help to harness this power and extend the equality of women and ethnic groups working in private firms.

In the United States some 300,000 commercial and manufacturing companies are covered by the Federal Government's contract compliance requirements. Between them these companies employ around 41 million people, or approximately one-third of the total workforce. The policy had its origins in the black civil rights struggles of the late 1950's and was embodied in the Civil Rights Act of 1964. Leading black and feminist activists have few doubts that this has made a significant contribution to countering discrimination in the employment market. Empirical evidence supports these claims.

The way contract compliance works is very simple: the Federal Government requires companies, as a contractual term, not to discriminate in their employment practices. The firms must therefore be able to demonstrate that they are not discriminating in relation to pay; and be able to demonstrate that they are employing, at every level and in all areas of activity within the company, a workforce which broadly reflects the sexual and racial composition of the available workforce in the area. Where a company cannot show that it is doing this, it is required to agree a written affirmative action programme with the Office of Federal Contract Compliance. The programme must include goals linked to timetables, and the Office monitors its implementation. Failure to keep to it — or at least to show good faith in efforts to do so — could result in the company losing its current contract, and/or being disqualified from tendering for further contracts. Financial penalties specified in the contract can also be invoked.

The GLC's initiatives in contract compliance had to recognise two important differences from the American situation. First, 'quotas' are unlawful in the UK. Second, the UK does not have anything like the same highly developed database on the employment and skills profiles, by geographical localities, of the different ethnic minority communities. The GLC therefore made adherence to the Sex Discrimination Act, 1975, and the Race Relations Act, 1976, the central features. Firms wishing to remain on the Approved List, together with new applicants, had to show that they were complying with those Acts.

An extension by a Labour Government of what is legally required of companies could greatly enhance the impact of contract compliance. If spending by central government and the public corporations were added it is likely that practically every sizeable firm in the country would be brought within the scope of this policy.

Nevertheless, the practical problems involved must be recognised. To begin with, all public bodies would first have to pursue a comprehensive equal opportunities policy within their own organization. It would be morally and legally unsafe for any public body to seek to impose conditions on a private supplier or contractor which it did not meet itself. This would be a massive exercise. Second, all the public bodies concerned would need to adopt common criteria and possibly even common documentation, or else establish a central organization of some kind to handle it all on their collective behalf. It would be absurd and unreasonable to expect companies to meet different criteria set by up to a hundred or more councils and other bodies. In the USA the different contract compliance agencies use broadly similar documentation and have a working rule that the first public agency to come into contact with a firm carries out a review for all the others. Once passed by one public agency the firm is effectively cleared for them all. For both these reasons there would be advantages in the policy being administered through, or at any rate jointly with, a central government-supported agency. This could be inside an existing Whitehall department or quango, or it could be a new body. The Americans went through three major reorganizations before settling on their present model: a single, free-standing agency at federal level, exclusively concerned with contract compliance.

# PLANNING THE REGIONS

Regional policy is in need of a major overhaul. Based on the limited assumptions of post-war growth, regional policies are only partly suited to current needs. The aim of the policy was to attract mobile firms to areas of high unemployment; the result has been the establishment of highly vulnerable 'branch-plant' economies. A new approach is needed, based on enterprise boards, aimed at fostering the regions' *own* capacity for growth, alongside the more traditional aim of redistributing employment towards areas of high unemployment. Regional policy must also recognise the inner city dimension to imbalances in employment and economic growth — a dimension which is gaining rapidly in political importance.

## The legacy of post-war regional policy

Post-war regional policy *has* created new jobs: between 1960 and 1976, some 385,000 additional manufacturing jobs were created in the assisted areas because of regional assistance. According to one study by Cambridge economists, the total comes to 540,000 if jobs in related industries are included. But continual changes in policy mean that it is impossible to make precise estimates. Moreover, other studies make certain qualifications necessary. For example, studies of the South East and Scotland show that Industrial Development Certificates (IDC) have had little impact. Employment generated in projects which needed certificates was smaller compared with the gross increase in industrial employment: over 80 per cent of gross employment growth in the South East, and 55 per cent in Scotland, occurred without reference to IDC procedures. Another study, this time of the fall in manufacturing employment in Greater London between 1966 and 1974, has concluded that only 16 per cent could be attributed to businesses moving to assisted areas and overspill towns. Finally, regional policy has failed to encourage the growth of many industries: for some industries regional policy led to *fewer* jobs being created than would otherwise have been the case. Only five industries — vehicles, clothing, instrument engineering, drink and telegraphic equipment — were responsible for 40 per cent of jobs created by regional policy. This points both to the need for a regional dimension to policies aimed at specific industries, *and* for a recognition that subsidies to industry may not guarantee new jobs.

Regional policy has sought to attract mobile investment projects. The result is that assisted areas are highly vulnerable to decisions made elsewhere. In the North, for example, over 80 per cent of manufacturing employment is in firms which are externally owned. Their branch plants are weakly integrated into the local economy. High level research, marketing and corporate decision making is concentrated in the South East, so branch plants only create work for unskilled and semi-skilled workers and fail to provide secure long-term employment. Production is concentrated on low-value added goods and services, perpetuating the cycle of low wages and purchasing power. The lack of integration of branch plants with local manufacturing leads to falling investment, a low capacity for innovation, and an industrial structure which depends too heavily on large firms which cannot adapt. Product and process innovations are concentrated in the South East: firms in the North which employ research staff employ on average only half the number employed in the South East; the North, moreover, has a poorer record on the adoption of new technology than any other region on the British mainland except Wales.

Moreover, the significance of branch plant economies is increasing. Production is being concentrated in multi-plant, multi-locational enterprises and integrated within a global multinational network. Particular plants only carry out a limited range of tasks, reducing the intra-regional integration of local economies. These plants are subject to rapid technological change with the result that they are opened and closed in a short period. The growth of these branch plant economies is closely linked to the decline of inner cities. The shift of economic activity from urban conurbations to rural areas and small towns cannot be explained simply by industrial structure: studies have increasingly emphasised the lack of suitable low cost floor space in conurbations.

The emphasis in regional policy on capital subsidies has compounded the problem of 'branch-plant' economies, while providing an expensive means of job creation. Indeed, the cost per job has often been enormous. Industries which receive most regional aid — especially chemicals and metal manufacture — create very few jobs and sometimes none at all. Capital investment in manufacturing often now involves rationalisation — and job *losses* — rather than increased output. Large grants have been paid to firms for investments which would have taken place anyway: the most notorious example is the £93 million regional development grant given to a BP-led consortium for the Sullom Voe oil processing plant. The emphasis on manufacturing has meant that the opportunity to influence the substantial growth of jobs in services in the South East in the 1960's and 1970's was largely missed. Indeed the interdependence of manufacturing and services has paradoxically meant that the South East now benefits from a 'virtuous circle': multinationals' headquarters; an increasingly skilled workforce; research activities; encouragement for high-tech small businesses; and access to finance — all these now interact to attract firms to London and the South East's 'M4 axis'.

Conservative Government "reforms" have made regional policy even more ineffective. The coverage of assisted areas has been progressively reduced from 44 per cent of the country's population to less than 25 per cent, with regional aid ended in large parts of West and South Yorkshire, Lancashire, the Borders and North East, Scotland and Mid Wales. Cost effectiveness in terms of job creation has fallen considerably. Regional selective assistance — the main instrument for job creation — has been cut in half. Development grants — a capital subsidy — equal some three-quarters of regional spending. Spending on urban policy has risen six-fold under the Tories: but this money has effectively acted as another subsidy on property, site development and construction. Enterprise zones similarly offer a massive property subsidy in the form of complete rate relief for a 10-year period together with other benefits, such as freedom from many planning regulations. One report estimates that each job created in the first 11 enterprise zones cost £16,500. Moreover, the zones have only succeeded in redistributing employment around the country, not in creating new jobs. Recent government reforms have, above all, been a cover for cost-cutting. Increasing aid to services, while laudable, is rendered absurd by ratecapping given that two-thirds of the growth in service employment in the 1970's was in the *public* sector. The reforms have, moreover, done nothing to reduce the vulnerability of branch-plant economies.

**Experiments in regional planning**
The 1964 National Plan prepared by the Department of Economic Affairs included a regional element. The regional offices of the Department were given the responsibility for preparing regional plans, in association with the newly formed Regional Economic Planning Councils. These were bodies comprised of representatives of local government, industry and the unions, appointed by the government. In the early 1970's the Councils became little more than sounding boards for regional opinion.

Although the plans were then produced in association with local authorities and government departments, the lack of support from Whitehall meant that they continued to have little impact. By the late 1970's the role of the Councils had become utterly discredited and the Tories were able to abandon the system without any adverse reaction.

Even in their heyday under Labour, the government had no responsibility for drawing up, and felt no commitment to, the regional plans. Local authorities, moreover, objected to plans which overrode their own planning functions. The lack of democratic representation on the Councils meant that initiatives were not rooted in local experience and could not be implemented. Above all, regional planning foundered on the hostility of the Civil Service. There was no co-ordination, individual plans being submitted in different formats and at different times. Critically, regional plans were not linked to the national expenditure plans nor to decision making by government departments, so they could easily be ignored. Physical planning was the responsibility of the Ministry for Housing and Local Government. Economic planning was the responsibility of the Department of Economic Affairs. Executive powers in the economic sphere remained with the Department of Industry. Financial planning remained the responsibility of the Treasury.

**Promoting the regions' own capacity for growth**
The basic assumptions of post-war regional policy must now be revised. We should, however, be wary of throwing out the proverbial baby with the bathwater. There is still a case for a redistributive element in regional policy, provided it is targeted specifically at job creation. We would propose an *employment* subsidy, the costs of which should, of course, be offset against the costs of keeping people unemployed. In the long-term, DHSS spending on unemployment should be fully integrated with DTI finance for industry and DE expenditure on employment subsidies: otherwise, one government department will continue passively subsidising unemployment without any pressure to put that money to more positive use.

The emphasis of regional policy should, however, change, with the regions' own capacity for growth being built up as part of a *national* industrial strategy. This can only succeed if economic power is devolved, the regional impact of national planning recognised and political accountability extended.

In Scotland and Wales, the existing Development Agencies should clearly play a leading role, though within a framework which extends their accountability. More generally, the economic role of local authorities should be greatly increased. Enterprise boards provide a framework for intervening in local economies, the boards being able to call on local rate income, pension funds and the National Investment Bank. There is scope for institutional flexibility: local authorities may prefer to promote growth through employment committees, while the precise role of enterprise boards already varies greatly from area to area (Chapter 3). Local authorities are also best placed to help sponsor co-ops through co-operative development agencies. Similarily, they can play a far greater role in training and in developing new technologies and products, giving new opportunities to working people facing redundancy and to firms in declining markets. By giving local authorities the power to trade, municipal activity could expand in areas which are profitable and job-creating: in this way, the privatisation of local authority services could not only be reversed but also turned on its head.

Regions cannot build up their capacity for local enterprise in isolation. The plants of national and multinational firms must be integrated into regional economies if these economies are to have access to new technologies. The key decisions of such firms cannot, however, be influenced effectively at a regional level: attempts to do so only lead to escalating attempts to 'bribe' companies, such as Nissan, to locate in their region. As we have argued throughout this chapter, commercial leverage must be exercised. Given that Britain's main attraction to multinationals lies in the excellence of its scientific skills, this approach is unlikely to drive multinational investment away: even in these terms it makes more sense to phase out financial incentives and use this money to sponsor training and research within the regions. In pharmaceuticals, for example, Britain until recently accounted for 11.5 per cent of world wide research compared with 5 per cent of world wide drug production, a ratio bettered only by Switzerland. The attraction of a region's innovative capacity is, however, unlikely to be enough on its own. Negotiations with multinationals must take place at a national level, backed by the sanction of access to the market (Chapter 6).

Regional and industrial planning must be integrated by building a regional dimension into the national and sectoral framework. Faced with the urgent need for industrial recovery, however, regional considerations cannot be given priority. Regional decline is rooted in the decisions of major national and multinational companies as well as public corporations, and regional recovery can, in turn, only come about through an industrial planning framework which challenges those decisions.

Within this framework however, there is considerable scope for local action, especially for eliminating inequality *within* regions, such as between inner cities and rural areas. This scope is demonstrated in public spending plans. Central government must decide priorities for the allocation of public spending to different regions but local government must prepare detailed plans for public investment and carry them out.

This framework raises the issue of political accountability. Who should represent regional demands and draw up regional plans? Past experience of regional planning suggests that it will only be effective if it is rooted in democratic accountability. A plethora of agencies has grown up in the regions, to the extent that a *de facto* tier of regional government already exists — but it is one which has little democratic basis. These agencies fall into four categories. First, there are the development associations and other local and regional bodies, such as the Scottish and Welsh Development Agencies or the London Docklands Development Corporation. Although partly funded by local authorities, they have been increasingly sponsored by government ministers keen to block the emerging role of local authorities. Second, there are central government departments with regional offices, staffed by civil servants, with the responsibility for allocating considerable capital resources within the regions — these include English Industrial Estates, BSC Industry and the British Technology Group. Third, there are the ad hoc authorities and agencies which deal with significant public undertakings, such as water and health authorities. Fourth, there are the regional boards of public corporations, such as gas and electricity, which have weak consultative arrangements and non-elected councils.

What institutional framework is needed to put this regional dimension into effect? Given the priorities facing an incoming Labour Government and the complexities of local government reform, one option would be to establish regional planning bodies which include representatives from local unions and companies but with a *majority* of members drawn from elected local government representatives. In certain cases it may be practical and desirable to re-establish directly elected strategic authorities, but these should not necessarily follow the same boundaries as the GLC and the metropolitan authorities. These bodies/authorities would be responsible for drawing up regional plans and would oversee otherwise unaccountable agencies operating within their regions, in particular enterprise boards and other bodies for industrial intervention which operate on a regional basis.

In addition, it is vital that regional initiatives are fully integrated into the national framework for industrial planning and public expenditure. This could be achieved by including representatives from these bodies/agencies on the sector committees of the National Planning Council, and by appointing a junior minister responsible for pressing the claims of the English regions in both industrial and public spending decisions. Public spending plans (Chapter 7) must include a clear statement of their regional implications. Priorities for the allocation of public spending should reflect a broader range of criteria than unemployment alone, including housing, health care, access to child care and other indicators of deprivation. This could also ensure that objectives are not confused: in particular, that the priority of reducing unemployment does not frustrate measures to promote industrial growth by providing indefinite subsidies in a frozen regional industrial structure.

**Conclusions**
Two themes have run throughout this chapter. First, that industrial recovery depends on responding to new forms of product-led, innovation-based, competition: this requires policies of strategic planning which integrate key enterprise decisions with sector-wide strategies. Second, this can only be achieved if democratic control challenges private centres of corporate power. In the long-term this depends on developing a culture for socialist enterprise, with working people able to take increasing reponsibility for key decisions through extending the scope of collective bargaining. In the short-term, however, the exercise of government power must play the major role. The process by which collective bargaining can be extended will inevitably be uncertain and gradual. Corporate decisions must therefore be influenced primarily through the exercise of commercial leverage, linking public control over access to finance and markets at a national and local level. The use of government power in this way cannot succeed in isolation from the longer-term process of empowering working people. Rather government power must be used in an enabling capacity, devolving economic power and giving people themselves an ever larger role.

This analysis points to the overwhelming importance of establishing *priorities* for action. Given that industrial recovery will depend on achieving an effective challenge to the current structure of economic power, progress will inevitably be limited during the lifetime of a single parliament. For example, the lack of technical and managerial skills, or even institutions to develop and teach them, will act as a powerful constraint. Similarly, the experience of establishing enterprise boards shows the time that we will need to set up an effective interventionist framework. But equally, it underlines the scope of what could be achieved given the resources of national government.

CHAPTER 7

# Democratic Control And The State

From the housing department that takes months to fix a leaking drain, through a telephone service that for years supplied only one type of phone, to a nationalised car firm that became a byword in inefficiency, the image of the state is not good. Socialists criticise the state for its lack of democracy, its secrecy and exclusiveness. State agencies, such as the Civil Service, are usually staffed at a senior level by people whose ideology is deeply conservative. And they operate in ways which leave users of state services feeling isolated and confused. So anyone who argues — as we do — that the public sector should be expanded, and that central and local government can play a big part in making the economy more democratic, has to find solutions to these problems — not all of which will disappear with higher public spending.

Discussions of the role of the state often treat it as something existing outside the economy — 'intervening', using levers such as taxation and public spending. In fact the state in its various forms makes up a large part of the economy itself. It employs a third of the workforce and owns two-fifths of the capital stock. Central and local government alone directly buy one-eighth of the output of the manufacturing sector and order two-fifths of all construction. Indirect purchases through transfer payments such as social security benefits are even higher. So the state does not just intervene in the economy — it *is* a large part of the economy already.

In this chapter we look in detail at two aspects of the economic role of the state — planning the huge budget for public spending, and making decisions on large investment projects — to test how real the problems are and how they might be tackled. We conclude by discussing experiments in getting people involved in decisions that affect them, through 'popular planning'.

### Planning public spending
In some ways, public spending represents the clearest example of

resources being devoted to social need. The community collectively contributes through tax towards spending to meet collective needs. But in practice decision making about public spending is one of the most confused, secretive, and bureaucratic of processes. There are undoubtedly real difficulties in managing the deployment of resources representing one-third of national income. But the present procedures appear to involve little attempt to match spending plans to the priorities of the community.

**Present procedures**
The procedures used by central government to plan public spending have evolved rapidly in the last few years. Describing this history helps us to understand the present system. In 1961 the Plowden Committee recommended a new system of planning public spending — the Public Expenditure Survey Committee system (PESC). The government was urged to set out spending plans for a period five years ahead and to publish these plans each year.

But how were these plans to be measured? One possibility was to plan in physical terms — for example, the number of houses to be built or nurses to be employed. But this would make it impossible to compare the cost of different services and decide priorities between them. Even with a comparatively simple element like labour it is necessary to allow for the difference in skill and training between, say, basic trainee soldiers and research chemists. When it comes to the goods bought in, the variety involved makes it impossible to measure in anything else but money. However, inflation means that simple cash figures are not enough for sensible planning. Allowance must at least be made for general inflation. This is known as presenting spending in 'cost' terms — spending in cash adjusted using a general indicator of the value of money.

The PESC system tried to go beyond this to allow for the fact that some things change price more rapidly than others. During the 1960's, for example, it was generally expected that wages would rise faster than prices. This would mean that a service which employed a relatively large number of people would also get relatively more expensive over time. The PESC system used different price projections for different cost items. Changes in the figure for projected spending on a service would therefore indicate a change in the use of resources.

However, this still did not provide a true measure of the level of service, for two reasons. First, a change in volume may reflect a change in the coverage of a service. For example, an increase in the number of pensioners will give rise to an increase in the volume of spending on pensions without any change in the level of pension. And second, any improvement in the efficiency with which a service is delivered may actually show up as a reduction in the volume of spending.

The system was augmented in the late 1960's by procedures known as 'Programme Analysis and Review' (PAR). This involved a more intensive look at particular programmes to see how well their objectives were being achieved. Wider issues were examined, in order take account of some of the factors identified: but PAR remained unsystematic both in scope and timing and by the early 1970's was no longer being used.

Despite its limitations the great merit of the system set up in the 1960's was that it tried to enable the government to plan the real level of service. The first shift away from this came when cash limits — placing a fixed ceiling on the *cash* spent on particular services — were introduced in 1972. Cash limits were gradually extended in subsequent years, until in 1982 the Tory Government started expressing the spending plans themselves in cash terms. Since then a single 'cost terms' table has been published for the past and current year only.

Partly because governments tend to be optimistic about inflation, the use of cash limits tends to 'squeeze' spending *below* planned levels. In addition chronic underspending is caused by managers' fear of exceeding their limit. The introduction of cash limits has therefore made its own contribution to cuts in the real level of public services, as well as undermining effective planning of spending. Since 1982 the five-year public spending plans published by the government have told us very little except in the broadest terms about what was actually going to happen to particular services.

However spending is measured, the planning system has always been highly secretive. The planning cycle begins over 12 months before the financial year starts in April, when the Treasury issues guidelines to 'spending' departments (those with significant budgets, such as the DHSS and Ministry of Defence). Ministers who want to defend their empires take their case to the Public Expenditure Survey Committee, and disputes which cannot be resolved there are thrashed out in the Cabinet, usually in August or September. The first outline of the plans is normally published in a November statement, and the full details finally emerge in March when the Public Spending White Paper is published on Budget day.

The procedure is dominated by the Treasury, which effectively sets the terms of debate and controls the Public Expenditure

Survey Committee. Participation in planning is limited to 'spending' Ministers and senior civil servants. The procedure is secret — apart from carefully orchestrated leaks — until the plans are fixed and presented to Parliament for rubber stamping. There is no public debate about priorities. There is often little co-ordination between departments with overlapping responsibilities. And there is certainly no systematic consultation with interested parties.

One segment of public spending has, until recently, partly escaped the reach of this machine. Local councils account for some 25 per cent of public spending. Although the government publishes indicative plans for local services like education and social services, local authorities are, in principle, free to set their own spending plans other than for capital projects. Local councils have in recent years given far more opportunities for people to be involved in planning spending — for example, by consulting people over the drawing up of manifestos, encouraging attendance at committees at which plans are debated, and giving people better access to council papers. This is one important reason why the Tory Government has gone to great lengths to invent complex and confusing controls on council spending. These have involved fines and penalties on 'overspenders', imposed by clawing back the government grant which funds about half of all local spending. The latest step is 'rate capping' which effectively gives central government the power to fix a ceiling on the spending of selected councils. The next stage will no doubt be central control over what the money is spent on — already hinted at in the field of education.

### Towards a democratic public spending system

In order to move towards a more open and democratic planning system, we need to reassess the categories of public spending, the way in which it is measured, the way in which it is controlled and the way in which services are delivered. But the sheer scale and range of activities funded by public spending add two further dimensions to the planning problem. One is that the resources made available to the public sector must take into account the total resources available in the economy and the demands made by other areas. The second is that regulating public spending is the main way of ensuring that all available resources in the economy, and especially labour, are employed. As such it is a major determinant of private sector production. The scale and economic composition of public spending must therefore be integrated with a plan for the economy as a whole.

The planning process ought to be guided by the ultimate

objectives of public policy, such as the levels of health or the attainments in education to be achieved in different parts of the country. It should have at its disposal information about the way in which public spending decisions and other factors affect these standards. (Health, for example, is not determined only by the level of spending on the NHS, but also by levels of income, by spending on energy, pollution control, health and safety regulations, health education, and so on.) Since the basis of the approach would be meeting people's needs, the issues involved ought to be relatively easily understood — an important requirement for extending democratic involvement. It would mean an end to the current obsession with costs, focusing instead on the *standards* of service achieved. And it would thereby bring co-ordination into the heart of the planning system: inner city and regional policy, crime prevention and environmental health — all of which currently cut across the main spending categories as they are commonly defined — could be properly integrated with other policy objectives.

One of the principal aims of planning should be to enable issues to be decided democratically. Much of the information required to implement the social audit type of approach we advocate is not available, and many of the relationships between policy and outcome will be highly uncertain and/or controversial. Nonetheless our case is that this approach should be the implicit framework in which we operate. Public spending should always be planned to some *purpose*, with some idea of the impact that spending has — both on its prime target and in terms of its side-effects. Ultimately the process is a political one. While technical and organisational reforms can help, it is most important to make the underlying choices clear and to bring decisions closer to those most affected by them.

### Large investment decisions
One of the arguments most frequently made against government invervention in the economy is that public bodies are more likely than private, commercially guided, bodies to make bad decisions. There are plenty of examples of disastrous public investment projects such as high rise housing, or the Advanced Passenger Train.

Of course, there are plenty of examples of *private* sector disasters too. The closure of such plants as the aluminium smelter at Invergordon; paper mills at Fort William; car works at Linwood and Speke; textile factories in Skelmersdale and Coleraine; oil refineries at Milford Haven — all long before the end of their technical lives — are illustrations. A particularly striking instance is a BP plant in Sardinia which never even opened. Is it true, therefore, that there are *particular* factors built into public decisions that increase the chances of bad mistakes? And, if so, can anything be done to remove them?

The scale of projects and the nature of the technology used in such areas as energy, transport and housing, necessarily involves the making of long-term projections. The bigger the decision and the longer the timescale, the greater is the scope for 'mistakes'. And because the private sector is often either reluctant or unable to enter into such long-term commitments, it is the public sector which finds itself in the most exposed position.

Mistakes are broadly of three kinds. The least blameworthy are those arising from 'unforeseeable' changes in technology, costs or needs. An oil fired power station may have looked a good bet in 1964, but a disaster in 1974 after the oil price rise. The second kind of mistake arises from technological failure — housing built to last fifty years that falls down after ten. Once again the decision makers, acting on the best advice available at the time, may perhaps be forgiven. But the mistakes which give rise to greatest concern are those which arise from decisions taken in ignorance or defiance of the interests and needs of those who depend on — or pay for — the decisions concerned.

High rise housing is an example of this third kind. Hundreds of thousands of tenants and potential tenants knew that there was something wrong with high rise housing. But both bureaucrats and politicians ignored the evidence. Housing policies have now been reversed, but this does not suggest that decision-making is more sensitive or accountable. The change in fashion is at best only partly the result of pressure from tenants. Low rise housing fits perfectly with the current architectural vogue for homely, vernacular styles of building and with bureaucratic preferences for safe and well tried building methods after the finger-burning experiences of the 1960's. There is little evidence that this represents anything more than a process of bureaucratic retrenchment. Council tenants remain powerless because of their status as tenants. Architects, bureaucrats, building companies and politicians have come together in a network which reinforces this powerlessness. At different times, their emphasis has been on the search for the 'correct' design, the greatest efficiency in meeting housing needs or the greatest cost-effectivness, depending on the prevailing expediency. Sometimes it has produced housing disasters, sometimes good housing. The process itself has remained consistently arbitrary and undemocratic.

This example highlights some of the different ways public

decisions can 'fail'. The public agency supplying a service to users who have no choice has even greater power than commercial bodies. It may also be subject to artificial financial constraints designed to provide a crude protection against 'extravagance'. At other times politicians may give priority to short-term projects designed to show easily measurable results before the next election.

But against these weaknesses must be balanced certain clear strengths. Public decisions provide an opportunity for democratic involvement in which individuals carry weight by virtue of their citizenship, not in proportion to their wealth. Public decision makers can, in principle at least, take account of the full range of social costs and benefits, and not merely profit and loss.

In short, *any* decision — public and private — may turn out to be mistaken. Public investment decisions are simply more visible in their effects. Mistakes, when they occur, are more likely to be noticed. Our problem is to find ways of minimising *avoidable* public failures. Part of the answer lies in the following measures:

• *Opening up decisions* so that all the interests involved, including those of users and workers, can be fully and fairly expressed. This is clearly no guarantee of success — even the most costly and pointless projects may be highly popular with those whose jobs depend on them. And the process of consultation may simply bring inefficiency and delays.

• *Decentralisation*: not simply because smaller decisions mean smaller mistakes, but because there is a greater chance of making the decision makers accountable to those affected. Many public projects, however, will necessarily continue to be on a large scale.

• *Decisions being cast within a more general planning framework.* The purpose of the project should be clearly defined so that it can be monitored. And there is also a need to ensure in advance that there are points at which decisions to abandon projects can be made.

### The machinery of government
One of the most difficult problems for those who believe in making the public decision making process more democratic is the relationship between elected representatives and appointed officials. It is ironic that socialists so often find themselves defending public sector agencies which are staffed by people who have no sympathy with socialism and could be expected to obstruct a Labour administration at every opportunity. In addition, the hierarchical structure of bureaucracies has the effect of vesting great power in senior managers, who use the

promotion and patronage system to ensure that they are the only channel of communication to Ministers or councillors, to filter out 'heretical' views and to ensure loyalty to the bureaucracy before any political programme or policy.

Some proponents of Thatcherism (such as Sir John Hoskyns) also believe that their progress has been impeded by what they see as the 'consensualist' ideology of the bureaucracy, and in particular of the Civil Service. And we may safely impute similar views to Mrs. Thatcher herself, given the way that she has consistently intervened to ensure that key posts have gone to those whom she describes as "one of us".

How, then, can the bureaucracies be opened up? In terms of the range of policy *advice* which Ministers and councillors receive, a Labour administration could take two key steps:

● Appoint a range of outside political advisers to keep a close scrutiny on the bureaucracy and give them the support staff and the access to internal information necessary for them to develop alternative policy advice on all the major issues.

● Pass a Freedom of Information Act which would ensure that, in the vast majority of cases, official information would automatically be published unless it could be shown that there was a clear and pressing public interest in imposing some form of restriction.

These steps would break the near monopoly of information and advice currently enjoyed by the bureaucracy. With outsiders such as politicians, pressure groups and academics all able to criticise government policy in an informed way, and able to formulate practical alternatives, a socialist government should not be able to blame the bureaucracy for not having the full range of options in front of it — or (alternatively) for not being fully informed about the practical problems of particular policies.

As well as the question of policy formulation and advice, there is also the crucial question of policy implementation. One approach which the Thatcher Governments have followed is to identify and promote supporters of particular policies within the existing bureaucracies, and to fill some established posts with sympathisers from outside. There are dangers here. Most of the public service unions would undoubtedly oppose any unjustified undermining of a career service based on 'merit' rather than political views. There might even be dangers to civil liberties if public servants were to be penalised for holding the 'wrong' political opinions.

Nonetheless, our view is that at the most senior levels of the bureaucracy, political orientation ought to be a major factor in appointment decisions. Indeed we should do our best to dispel the myth that these appointments have *ever* been on a 'non-political' basis. Civil servants should expect that advancement beyond a certain level, say Assistant Secretary in civil service terms, would be determined at least partly by reference to political views. This should be an *announced* policy, sharply distinguished from one of piecemeal or arbitrary intervention which might be construed as infringing on the liberties of individuals. Below the designated level, promotion decisions would continue to be made on their present basis, with competence in carrying out the duties of the posts as the overriding criterion. This kind of assurance would probably be a condition of support from the public service unions.

A more openly political approach might lead to more frequent exchanges of senior personnel with outside employment, coinciding roughly with the periodic change of power between political parties. It might soon be accepted that service in senior public sector administrative positions should be more like being a councillor or a Member of Parliament than being part of a permanent bureaucracy. Short spells of full-time service in the bureaucracy by people on secondment from, say, trade unions, universities or pressure groups could become the norm. The result could be that at any one time there was a mix of contrary political views among, for example, Permanent Secretaries of government departments; but provided the overall political direction and control of the government were clear, there might actually be merit in having some people with a critical perspective at these levels.

Whatever the methods used, or the time taken to make progress, the aim should be to break the collegiate ethos which currently binds senior bureaucrats together in defence of unaccountable concentrations of power — power which over the years has steadfastly been used to maintain the status quo, protect the establishment from democratic scrutiny and control, and prevent radical social and economic change.

**Popular planning in practice: the pitfalls and the potential**
Radical experiments in opening up public decision making are currently under way in Labour local authorities. Their experience shows how it may be possible to extend democratic control over the state given greater resources and legislative support.

As part of its economic strategy, the GLC financed three pilot education and information projects for popular planning. The aim of them was to help less organised groups express their needs and, where possible, produce 'people's plans for jobs' which the GLC could then support. In under two years, the project teams worked with over a hundred groups on a huge variety of needs. In this section we focus on the lessons from the project at the Clapham and Battersea Adult Education Institute, designed to extend popular planning to childcare in the London Borough of Wandsworth.

Childcare is a vital economic activity, with a major impact on the ability of women to take paid work, even though most childcare is done unpaid by mothers at home or is under-paid, and most of the economic benefits are unmeasured, unrecognised and unrewarded. In Wandsworth alone, over £3 million is spent on childcare, of which the Council accounts for half, parents about a third, and the ILEA a fifth. This is slightly more than the Council spends on leisure and amenity services, or on its economic development programme. Childcare is a major source of paid employment — directly in nurseries and elsewhere, and indirectly through the need for maintenance of buildings, the manufacture of toys and equipment, and so on.

The Wandsworth initiative vividly illustrates the enormity of the task of genuine popular planning. The resources available were extremely limited, with only two workers — putting in less then five hours a week over 18 months — faced with the task of reviving a demoralised movement. Over 1,000 people in Wandsworth are paid to look after children, from paediatricians to childminders, and in addition there are over 40,000 parents. How can all these people really be involved in planning existing childcare provision, let alone everything else which affects childcare, from shopping facilities, parks, transport and roads to legislation on paternity leave, equal pay, child benefits and so on?

The lessons from the initiative are summarised in the following 'ten steps to popular planning':

1. *Listening to people.* Popular planning must start by listening to people and respecting their definitions of the issues, even though there may be as many different definitions as there are people, and some people are more able to assert their views than others. This creates real difficulties. First, the assumptions of the full-time workers get in the way of hearing what some people say. Second, it is easy to be swept along by activists, who may have a high visibility without reaching most people. On the other hand, going beyond the activists' network arouses their suspicion or even hostility. In the Wandsworth example, most activists were too busy to talk, but as soon as the workers talked with people independently, the activists wanted to know why the childcare workers were not going through them. In another case, the activists tried to close the project down entirely. The workers had

to prove their commitment in practice before they could work with the activists' networks.

2. *Identifying needs.* People usually recognise their individual needs and the common needs of others in similar circumstances, but with childcare there is a vast range of overlapping needs. Simply cataloguing these from meetings and conversations and putting them back to people for their comments is an important part of the process. But in order to turn very different, and sometimes conflicting, views about what is needed into effective action, it is also necessary to create a collective process in which different views can be recognised, assessed and reconciled.

3. *Kite flying.* Trying ideas out, and testing them in practice on a small scale, is an important part of creating a broader, collective process. There is no point in listening to people without being prepared to engage with them and, in the end, act on their suggestions. A guide to childcare facilities, a pamphlet on training in childcare and an information pack for childminders were therefore funded. Most of the long list of demands could not be acted on without closer working contact between the many agencies directly involved in childcare provision — social services, education, the health authority and the voluntary sector. A series of local meetings was organised to establish the need for inter-agency co-operation.

4. *Getting together: liaison.* Creating greater contact between workers fragmented in literally hundreds of workplaces — nurseries, playgroups and childminders' homes — is hard enough, before even beginning to take account of parents themselves. Long standing patterns of institutional inertia are an enormous obstacle, with education and social services running essentially the same kind of provision on quite different lines, and each part of the bureaucracy not knowing what the other is doing.

The level at which liaison is carried out also depends very much on the circumstances: in Wandsworth, there was a widespread feeling that it must take place at all levels, from workers and users up to senior management and the political level. The industrial model, of a union combine committee, is not appropriate for childcare. Committed and effective individuals within or at the top of an established bureaucracy can make a dramatic difference, by creating obstacles and absorbing information without passing it on, or by moving things along and giving others space to act. Good contacts within different institutions make all the difference in overcoming rivalries between them and challenging established structures.

Another essential condition for effective liaison is good

administration, so that discussions are recorded, communicated to everyone involved, and decisions acted on promptly. Previous attempts at local level liaison had failed because there was no one to service the groups.

5.*Getting in touch: consultation.* An effective liaison body can involve the key people concerned with a particular issue, providing both legitimacy and an administrative machinery for the process. But it is also a potential trap, where action can be seized up in endless discussion or those hostile to change can attempt to stifle it. Nevertheless, the potential is there. The emergent liaison body in Wandsworth was used to conduct a postal questionnaire of childcare workers to identify priorities among the many needs raised in earlier discussions, and to distribute both the guide to childcare facilities and a broadsheet on the economics of childcare.

6. *Taking the initiative.* Someone, or some group within the childcare field, had to make a determined initiative to pull together the people and ideas necessary to assert a comprehensive approach to childcare in the borough. Such an initiative cannot come from outside. It will only occur if people feel there is a real possibility of success; otherwise people's efforts are much better directed at small, piecemeal improvements which will bring immediate benefits to at least a few families.

7. *Drawing up a plan.* A plan is neither the beginning nor the end of popular planning, and often not the best solution for every situation. Even if a plan is based on the widest participation, drawing it up requires few people. Once a plan has been produced, it is necessary to consult again and make sure that people still want what they said they did before, and that they agree with any compromises between conflicting objectives.

8. *Promoting the plan.* Generating the political will to carry out the plan must be a crucial part of producing it. Not even the GLC could give the £1 million or so needed to implement the 1978 plan, so support had to be won within *each* of the institutions involved in childcare, against competing demands on limited resources of people's time and public money. Most people concerned with childcare were also engaged in other campaigns (for example, saving the South London Hospital for Women), resisting cuts in particular services or drawing up grant applications to bodies such as the GLC and Inner Area Programme, all of which were much more urgent.

9. *Implementation* is therefore only a distant and difficult prospect. At present, every opportunity for people to talk across institutional frontiers, every small success in warding off cuts or improving facilities, every assertion of childcare's importance in

the face of institutional indifference or the hostility of market forces, is a positive step towards popular planning.
*10. Evaluation.* Any evaluation must yield the sober reflection that the only tangible benefit that has been brought to parents and children, so far, is to squeeze a little cash from the GLC for a childcare guide and childminder's pack. The fact that these took so much haggling and over a year to extract helps illustrate the lessons of the Wandsworth experience.

## Conclusions

Socialism cannot be achieved without state power. The public sector has an enormous influence, both directly as spender and employer, and indirectly on the private and unpaid sectors. This influence can most effectively be used by shifting power towards workers, consumers and the community. And it is in this context that legislative change and public ownership must be considered.

State power can only fulfil socialist objectives if the machinery of government is made more democratic and accountable, and the very structure of decision making recast to encourage and respond to popular initiatives. Planning should be a process not of producing blueprints, but of making things happen. Popular planning means that workers and users have the power to make things happen. But this is all much easier said than done.

Even in the best of worlds, people will not spend time drawing up plans for everything that affects their lives. But if plans are drawn up on their behalf, by people paid from their taxes, they have an absolute right to set guidelines from the start, to reject and change the plans proposed, and then demand efficiency in their implementation. Competent, transparent administration is probably the most important and most difficult part of empowering people. Organising a campaign or producing a plan requires administration, if not by the people, then at least at their command. The ability of socialist authorities (national or local) to *deliver*, so that people can get results when they make demands, would take us a long way towards popular power.

## CHAPTER 8

# Beyond Production: Democracy In The Unpaid Sector

In the previous three chapters we have looked at how people's needs and wants can be reflected in the decision making of companies and of central and local government. There are clear dangers, however, in concentrating upon the sphere of production, or even of paid work, alone. Democratic planning, in the sense in which we have developed this term, is equally applicable to what might be called the sphere of consumption, and to the vast areas of *unpaid* work in our society.

Discussion of democratic planning in these areas is of particular relevance to the position of women, since women are often identified (incorrectly) with the consumer sector, and because it is women who carry out the vast majority of unpaid work. The danger of the Left's traditional preoccupation with issues surrounding production and paid work is that the needs and concerns of women become devalued — along with other groups, including part-time workers, the unemployed, the disabled and retired people. In this chapter we seek to redress the balance by discussing a number of issues frequently neglected in socialist debate, starting with the politics of consumption. As we shall see, these issues raise questions of profound importance for the politics of socialism in the 1990's.

### The politics of consumption

*What is a consumer?* This may seem a strange question but a few moments thought produces several different meanings. Perhaps the most common understanding of the term 'consumer' is someone who chooses to pay for a good or service, usually where this choice is constrained by the amount of money the consumer has. Second, the era of the welfare state has brought about another form of consumer: that is, someone who can obtain goods and services on the basis of need — without payment, or with very little payment, at the point of use. Education and health are services which exemplify this kind of consumption. Third, we can be consumers of things for which we do not have a 'need' as such, nor for which we have necessarily expressed a desire. An example of this is the environment in which we live — the houses and factories, the roads and railways, the cleanliness of the air, the green spaces, and so on. Environment can become a matter of paying for something, because in theory people have the option of moving house, going on holiday or buying second homes. It differs from the first type of consumption identified above, however: not only because choice is so constrained for the majority (because of their income) that they effectively have no choice, but also because the environment is something which is collectively consumed — one form of consumption by an individual or group of individuals may detract from (or add to) the environment available to others.

### Consumer power

Economic theory tends to treat the consumer as all powerful, with many producers competing to produce and sell for a limited market. In reality production has become more and more concentrated, while consumers' power to determine what is produced, and how, is very weak. This seems to be equally true when the producer is the state, and when consumer power is not manifested through the market but through the political process. Conservative Governments have affected to diminish the role of the state and return power to consumers through the market. But, in practice, this has been limited to changing state monopolies into private ones. A socialist approach, by contrast, would suggest the need to develop more sophisticated political processes, in part made feasible by advances in technology, as methods of enhancing consumers' power. It would also involve us in developing a strategy for social equality, because the distribution of income is crucial to the distribution of consumer power — in other words, the right *to buy* as well as the right not to buy.

### Consumers and the market

The first attempt by workers to organise themselves as consumers was in the Co-operative Movement. In many countries, co-operatives play a major role in the organisation of retailing and production. In Britain, the Co-op remains an important but steadily declining force. Its weakness derives from its failure to invest in equipment, training and management skills, at a time when retailing in the economy generally has become very capital intensive: but higher investment by the Co-op would have put greater pressure on its democratic institutions. In the event the Co-op has ceased to be either democratic or efficient.

With the growing complexity and variety of products, there has developed some co-ordination of consumers' views, by consumer organisations. Probably the best known is the Consumers Association, an independent non-profit organisation set up in 1957, with its monthly publication *Which*. In addition attempts have been made to improve consumers' rights through legislation and by setting up, in the mid 1970's, the National Consumers Council. The Council is an attempt to represent consumers' interests in respect of new legislation, both domestic and European. In Europe, by contrast, the consumers' movement is more sophisticated, with consumers being recognised for many decisions as the fourth side of what, in this country, would be tripartite discussions

Despite these market and non-market forms of consumer representation, however, there are still very few ways in which consumers can initiate changes in products and product design. The development of products, in particular for domestic consumption, continues to be determined mainly by the search for profitability — even at the expense, in many cases, of quality, reliability and durability.

The criterion of need remains secondary, and only *some* kinds of need have been met by the growth of the 'consumer society'. Labour-saving domestic appliances, for example, have in theory given many people additional time which is available for leisure or for caring. Often, however, this time is absorbed by paid employment, directed at earning income to support *further* consumption. Moreover, not everyone has benefited, and the needs of low income households have been largely neglected — indeed the position of such households has deteriorated, taking into account the growing gap between social expectations and their own standard of life.

It is clear, therefore, that one of our objectives must be to enhance the power of consumers, and to take it beyond the opportunities offered by market economics. This will inevitably create some conflicts of interest between consumers, workers and employers. On the other hand there will also be solutions which satisfy everyone, but which would not be arrived at unless each interest group can influence the outcome. There are a number of ways in which this combination of interests can be brought together — for example through social audits, or more futuristically through sophisticated polling techniques using cable technology. The latter has the potential for enfranchising not only a wider number of people but also (specifically) those who find it difficult to leave their homes to attend meetings.

## Socialism and consumption

The consumer society, as it has developed under capitalism, has many negative features. Not the least of these is the increasingly sharp contrast between the wealth, waste and extravagance of many developed countries, and the crisis of famine and underdevelopment in the Third World.

These negative features have, however, frequently misled socialists into believing that consumption is necessarily anti-social, capitalistic or 'bourgeois'. The Left, in particular, is often guilty of a puritanism which many people find alienating. Consumption can be, and indeed often is, a liberating activity — enlarging choice, fostering greater control by people over their own lives, and enjoyable in its own right.

This means taking consumption, and in particular the consumption of goods and services, much more seriously as a political issue. As well as seeking to enhance consumers' power broadly within the framework of the existing market, we need to examine totally new initiatives. Examples might be:

● Funding design collectives, capable of designing goods to meet needs currently neglected by the market — collectives of women or disabled people, in particular, could be a source of countless, hitherto untapped, ideas. Local authority 'innovation networks' (Chapter 3) show how this might be done.

● Funding recording facilities and giving access to a wider range of musicians, including those from ethnic minorities — thereby challenging the power of the retailing giants.

● Making use of new technologies, such as cable networks, to enable the communication of 'alternative' news and ideas — so challenging the domination of the newsprint media, in particular, by the Right.

## Consumers of state products, services and benefits

Just as worrying for socialists as the lack of consumers' rights over market commodities, is the lack of an effective consumers' voice in a broad range of products, services and benefits supplied by the state. The consumer representation which does exist varies tremendously between the different industries and services, leading to a confusion on the part of consumers as to exactly what their rights are and how to enforce them. There is no universal 'bill of rights' for consumers. As a result, isolated attempts to improve consumer information, for example through leaflets, sometimes confuse rather than clarify the position. Bodies like the Citizens Advice Bureaux and Community Law Centres expend limited resources dealing with situations arising out of confusion and fear on the part of clients and indifference (arising partly through overwork) on the part of providers or suppliers.

In the case of welfare benefits and services, the concept of state provision *for and by* the people has somehow been lost, to be replaced by provision *for* the people alone. The origin of the welfare state in collective struggle by working people has been forgotten, and welfare provision has come to be associated with people taking without giving, with 'scroungers' and charity. A comment from the *Daily Mail* is typical of this attitude: "The seaside social security offices are thick with subsidised cigarette smoke, the smell of alcohol paid for by the State ... leeches feeding off the hard working silent majority". People are expected to be grateful for what the welfare state does for, or to, them.

The Conservative Government's 'reform' of the welfare state is based on the idea that as a nation we cannot afford such 'charity' any more. Apart from the fact that money could be made available if spending priorities were changed, it is forgotten that the relative prosperity of the 1960's was a product of the labour of millions now dependent on some form of welfare provision. Moreover, the rhetoric of self-reliance masks the fact that people's inability to find jobs or earn higher wages is not the fault of individuals but a product of the present Government's own policies.

The representation we enjoy as consumers of the products of nationalised industries is much better than as consumers of welfare provision. Of course, we *pay* for gas, electricity, transport and so on, and its provision is therefore not associated with charity. Even so, we need to rethink the nature of this representation too. Popular dissatisfaction with the services provided by nationalised industries has, for example, greatly impeded campaigns to prevent their privatisation.

## The need for greater representation: the Nationalised Industry Consumer Councils

Discussion of consumer representation in state provided industries or services may be particularly alarming to those socialists who believe that the real power of the working class derives from the ability to withdraw its labour, and that attention to our needs as consumers will dilute this power because of ensuing conflicts of interest. But this view runs wholly counter to the analysis presented in this book. We see the power of working people being advanced through a diversity of routes.

Greater consumer representation is needed to *increase* support for public ownership. The widespread dissatisfaction with the goods and services provided by the state and nationalised industries can partly be explained by the present Government's ideological attack on public ownership, and on the cuts in public spending. But at least part of the dissatisfaction arises from people's own experiences over a long period. At present consumers do not identify state owned industries and services as belonging to them; they feel they cannot control what is produced on their behalf.

The need for some form of independent monitoring of state industries' activities by users is especially acute in the case of 'natural' monopolies. Utilities such as gas, electricity and telecommunications must, for reasons of effective provision and the need for a national service, inevitably be organised as monopolies. Competition can play little role in encouraging responsiveness to consumers: only far-reaching reforms of the *internal* structure of these companies can guarantee this.

The importance of consumer involvement was recognised when they were set up, and was given legislative backing in the 1940's. Since then, a number of legislative changes have been made creating provisions for specific industries. The effect is a hotchpotch of consultative structures, headed by dozens of Nationalised Industry Consumer Councils (NICCs), little known and with little power.

The Councils deal with the provision of gas, electricity, coal, rail and ferry transport, and posts and communications. Local authorities have their own arrangements for bus services which are mainly locally run. Gas and electricity have very similar structures, with one national and two regional councils. The latter in turn are responsible for in excess of 60 local committees. The Gas Council structure was set up by the 1972 Gas Act. The Electricity Council structure, by contrast, has no statutory basis but was created by Ministerial Minute in 1977.

Rail and ferry transport has a Central Transport Consumer Council and 11 area Transport Users Consumer Councils. Posts and communications is served by one National Council with subordinate councils for Scotland and Wales. The National Council does have contact with local advisory committees but there is no formal link and only a few of the local committees receive any form of government finance. Coal has just a single national council.

All appointments to the Councils are by the Minister responsible. Until recently a specified proportion of the local committees have been local authority appointments. These appointments, along with the local committees themselves, are being abolished by the current Government. So decisions made in the 1970's to make Councils geographically closer and more locally accountable to consumers are now being reversed.

The most staggering feature of the NICCs' structures is how under-resourced they are. This has meant that the Councils have been increasingly concerned solely with handling complaints. They have few resources for initiating research either into consumer preferences or general policy. Moreover, while part of the Councils' formal remit is to provide information and advice to the public, few consumers are even aware of their existence. Some efforts have recently been made by the Councils themselves and their associated industries to raise public awareness of their role but, again, resources are limited.

Lack of finance is, however, only one factor in explaining their ineffectiveness. They are not wholly independent of their sponsoring agencies and have no yardsticks against which to assess performance. All but a handful of NICC members are unpaid volunteers. Many regional appointees have no experience or training in consumer affairs. One survey of the electricity district/local committees showed that almost 90 per cent of the membership was aged over 45 years.

The present Government's policies will reduce the effectiveness of the NICCs yet further. The Government regards handling complaints, analysing them and drawing conclusions, as the Councils' main function, and is proposing to reduce the number of Councils — for example, by having a single consumer structure for all the utilities. These proposals are dominated by the Government's desire to cut costs and reduce spending on consumer representation even further. The Government's assertion that its proposals to cut the Councils will increase their political clout is very suspect.

The NICCs' already limited role will be further reduced if they concentrate on handling complaints. At present, the Councils' formal remits vary. The Post Office and Communications National Council has traditionally focused on the quality of service and prices, and there have been plans to conduct a 'customer audit' to look at and explain the relative movements in price and quality of service. The Rail and Ferry Transport Councils are specifically excluded from considering charges, and there is no formal obligation to inform them of line closures.

## Towards greater consumer involvement

Greater consumer involvement will, however, require more than tinkering with the structures of the NICCs. The first step towards greater involvement must be to encourage a sense of identification with the socially owned utilities. One way to achieve this might be for all individual users to receive a 'citizen's share' which would entitle them: first, to greater information (for example, through a newsletter); and second, to direct influence, at local and national level, over the decisions of the utility.

This, in turn, raises the question: can individual consumers have a *collective* voice? Direct elections for consumer bodies might be a distant ideal: but, as we have already argued, most people will want to fulfill their needs as consumers by buying what they want, not going to meetings. An effective structure for consumer involvement could, instead, build on existing methods of collective representation, in much the same way as (for example) community based bodies to oversee the decentralisation of council services are appointed. On this basis, user groups could be established at local level, and be given rights of consultation over the provision of utility services. These groups could also include members elected at community meetings and councillors.

At national level, a new body — building on the NICCs — is needed to give consumers a collective voice in monitoring public monopolies. This body would involve members of the local user groups. To be effective, such a body would require trained, independent staff; be given powers to act for consumers and have access to information; and be notified of price changes well in advance.

## Consumers' rights

While the opportunity for greater involvement is desirable, the most pressing demand is for an effective framework of consumers' rights in the field of state industries and services. These rights should apply to all consumers whether the product is electricity, housing, health or welfare benefits. Clearly the procedures for exercising these rights will vary somewhat according to the industry or service, but listed here are six main elements which could form the basis of extended rights for consumers. These principles can also be applied to the private sector.

*1. A clear framework of rights.* Consumers are often uncertain of their rights. It appears the providers of the goods and services decide what is best for their clients. The Gas and Electricity Councils have published Codes of Practice (albeit with inadequate publicity) and other industries should be encouraged to do likewise. Instead, minimum service standards and procedures for redress should be clearly set out in a contract given to each consumer. Similarly, local authorities should be required to examine the services they can offer and, in turn, make it clear to clients what they can expect.

2. *Clearly defined and easily accessible remedies.* It is important that people should know what to do about any failure of provision. For the nationalised industries the first step in the procedure is to take the complaint to the industry itself.

After that any determined consumer can take the issue up with the industry consumer council. In fact many go to better known institutions such as the Citizens Advice Centres. These Centres should be expanded, with high street facilities and professional staff able to handle complaints. Similarly, if a local authority fails to meet its obligations, individuals can go through the internal complaints procedure of the relevant department or seek the help of a more independent assessor in the form of their local councillor. In either case, however, final recourse is normally through the law courts — a fairly daunting and potentially costly procedure. In general there should be procedures for taking up complaints which provide for an independent judgement, are reasonably informal and minimise costs to the consumer.

3. *Performance targets.* Standards for the various goods and services should be developed and continuously monitored. Codes of practice should be issued and internal systems for maintaining and standardising quality improved. For example, there could be a maximum time that local authorities were allowed to leave properties vacant. This would both give the consumer an indication of the standard of service to be expected and also identify matters for further investigation by councillors and officers. Similarly, an average time for domestic telephone installations or fault repairs to be carried out could guide both the consumer and the industry. In order to be of use to the consumer, these performance indicators would have to be publicised widely.

4. *Freedom of information.* This follows on from the use of targets but involves more than the information the industries and service departments themselves choose to publish. Independent consumers' representatives, such as local councillors, Consumer Councils, and Citizens Advice Bureaux, should be given specified rights to investigate the internal working of local authority departments and the nationalised industries. In addition, any individual should have access to files in which they personally feature.

5. *Market research.* Local authorities, Consumer Councils and the nationalised industries themselves, should be actively seeking opinions on quality of service both to maintain standards

and to determine new forms of provision.

6. *Involvement of the providers.* Any new form of provision will have implications for the structure and nature of employment of those providing the goods and services. Although democracy in the workplace has been discussed in many places in this book, it is worth underlining its importance in the context of consumer rights. Involvement of workplace representatives is not only a matter of principle but essential for any successful change in procedures. Early involvement will not guarantee the avoidance of conflict, but its absence may ensure failure.

## When a consumer is not a consumer

Economists often speak as though consumption is simply the obverse of paid work, referring to the time we spend outside of the factory or office as 'leisure time'. Yet much of this is spent doing what many would call work, both in the sense that it is often onerous, and also in the sense that goods and services are produced which are useful, and in some cases vital, to our existence. Gardening and dressmaking, home maintenance and improvement, all require work and can result in useful products. Producing meals for ourselves, and otherwise caring for the young, old and mentally infirm, are all vital to existence. The common feature of this work done in 'leisure time' is that it is not paid work and its products are not sold. Yet much of the work done in leisure time can be, and in some cases is, done by paid labour. The dividing line for economists between production and consumption is not determined by the nature of the activity, but by whether it is done for money.

Taking this a step further, we need to look at decision making within the area of unpaid production, just as we have done for companies and the state sector. We should aim for a distribution of power and resources which is equitable and which adequately satisfies individual needs. Our main objective in this should be to redress the inequality between the sexes in the amount of unpaid work done — which of course is simply one example of male domination in our society. Even though women now constitute nearly half of the paid workforce, they also retain the main responsibility for unpaid production . It has been estimated that the time spent on domestic work each day amounts to almost as much as the time spent working in the formal economy.

There is, however, an important difference between the paid and unpaid sectors of production, which lies in the extent to which society can intervene to ensure a greater equality of power and resources. Direct state intervention would generally be seen as an intrusion into the 'privacy' of the home, and as a consequence there are very few policy instruments available for doing so. Of course, society *does* intervene on occasions — for example to ensure the physical protection of young children. But these are the exception rather than the rule, and apart from critical or emergency cases we can expect widespread public resistance to outside interference in domestic relationships — however inequitable we may feel them to be. What we can do, though, is to influence these relationships by making changes within paid employment, and within the state sector.

### Redressing the inequalities
Apart from women as individuals changing the sexual division of work in the home, the only other means of redressing inequalities is through public policies aimed at changing the sexual division of work within the paid sector.

First, legislation should be used to institute a minimum wage. There is already fairly widespread, although not yet overwhelming, support for such legislation among trade unions; poverty wages have certainly become an increasingly critical issue. A minimum wage would, apart from anything else, help women to achieve an independent living wage, not negotiated or set on the assumption that they should be dependent on a male breadwinner.

A second objective should be a more equitable division of work, based on a shorter working week and year for men and women alike. Although the shorter working time campaign has focused on *basic* hours, it is well recognised that one of the barriers to equality of hours is the large amount of overtime undertaken by male workers. This, in turn, is linked to low basic rates of pay which make such hours a necessity. The campaign for shorter working time and a minimum wage are thus linked.

The ultimate aim should be to reduce hours for all, and to equalise them between men and women, both in the paid sector and the unpaid sector. This is not to say that one necessarily follows the other. Indeed, many comparative studies of work done at home, with differing arrangements for paid employment among wives and husbands, have indicated that it may take considerably longer than one generation to achieve a widespread change in the domestic division of work. Nonetheless equality in hours and pay are vital preconditions for such a change.

Similarly, if people are to be persuaded that a part-time job is a 'real' job, and not simply a female activity to boost family income, the rights and status of part-time workers should be improved. The proportion of married women who work part-time has increased from 50 per cent in 1971 to over 60 per cent now, thus increasing the divide between people with 'real' jobs and women with quasi-jobs. An improvement can be achieved not only through employment legislation (which currently gives few rights to people employed for less than 16 hours a week): greater power should also be given to women through sex discrimination legislation designed to challenge conditions and practices which discriminate against part-time, and hence female, workers.

Finally, another major area for direct action on women's inequality is taxation and the welfare state. This is an enormous subject, complicated by the various forms discrimination against women takes, but as a general principle women should be treated as independent human beings — so that, for example, an unemployed woman should be treated as no less worthy of receiving child or invalidity benefit than an unemployed man. In addition certain benefits should be reassessed for possible indirect discrimination towards women — for example, earnings-related benefits. The most striking area of discrimination, however, is the persistence of the married man's tax allowance. The recent Tory government proposals for transferable tax allowances, while superficially progressive, would in practice weaken the position of women further.

All these issues are already the subject of campaigns, and there have been gradual but noticeable changes. In many trade unions and workplaces, some changes have occurred — largely through women's own activity. This activity itself, as much as the results of the campaigns, is helping to change the image of women in society — and to question the boundaries, which so often form the basis of economic and social policy, between the paid and unpaid sectors.

## Accounting for the unpaid sector

The success of policies for economic expansion is typically judged not only by their impact on unemployment levels but also by various measures of economic growth — national income, output and expenditure. Such measures are, however, flawed as measures of progress in achieving many of the objectives we have outlined. For example, increasing industrial activity will count as an addition to national output and wealth: but the pollution with which it may be associated will generate new demands, for example, in the manufacture and installation of pollution control devices, which themselves add to national output — in practice, those two forms of output may merely serve to cancel each other out, whereas the national accounts will record *two* sources of growth. Similarly the "value" added by knocking down dilapidated housing and then replacing it by new low-quality homes should, rationally, often be less than the "value" added by the conservation and maintenance of that housing stock, which can often make a greater contribution to the environment.

The limitation of traditional forms of national accounting is even more marked in the case of the unpaid sector. For example, the growth in the use of consumer durables has reduced the time women need to spend working in the home, and been associated with an increase in women's part-time employment. The national accounts would record growth from two sources — the production of durables and the increase in part-time work. A *production account* for the unpaid sector might come to rather different conclusions. Such an account would measure both the "inputs" and "outputs" of bringing up children and caring for dependants. Consumer durables are one of the major inputs — their increasing use over the past decade is reflected in Table 1:

**Table 1: Percentage of households with certain consumer durables**

|  | 1972 | 1982 | Change |
|---|---|---|---|
| Central heating | 37 | 60 | +23 |
| TV | 93 | 97 | + 4 |
| Vacuum cleaner | 87 | 95 | + 8 |
| Refrigerator | 73 | 93 | +20 |
| Deep freeze | — | 51 | +51 |
| Washing machine | 66 | 79 | +13 |
| Telephone | 42 | 76 | +34 |
| Car or van | 52 | 59 | + 7 |

Source: General Household Survey.

As the table shows, there have been notable increases in the ownership of fridges and deep freezes, central heating and washing machines. It might be thought that these indicate reductions in unpaid labour time. However, several studies indicate otherwise. An Australian study found, for example, that women who used labour saving devices made up the time saved by working longer on another job or cleaning more often; the devices also required additional time for cleaning and servicing, ringing up for repairs and buying spare parts — the total time saved was negligible. Another survey, conducted in America, showed that the time spent on laundering has actually increased, because those with washing machines are now expected to wash daily rather than weekly. Pre-prepared foods have similarly changed the nature of the food production process, rather than reduced the time involved: much more time is now spent on shopping for food than on its preparation. (According to the American study quoted above, shopping takes one full day a week compared with two hours in the 1920's). Instead of housewives being praised for their ability to produce goods from basic raw materials in the home, they are now judged by their ability to shop wisely. The problem seems to be that women's unpaid work is seen as a direct expression of their emotional commitment to husband and children: doing more in the home is therefore seen as a necessary emotional input to the household sector.

A full production account for the unpaid sector could therefore measure the extent to which women are burdened with a "double shift". They have to stuggle to maintain the "value" of household production — measured subjectively in terms of emotional input and physically in terms of factors such as unpaid time, "entrepreneurship", the value of the durables and other goods used. But they are also increasingly expected to take paid work — to provide part of the income needed to purchase the goods necessary for domestic production. The total value of women's work, if measured in this way, would be shown to be immense. It has recently been estimated that the amount of time spent on domestic work each day adds up to 7.5 billion minutes, in comparison to 7.8 billion minutes spent working in the formal economy by the 23 million people still employed or self-employed. If domestic work were charged for it would account for some *two-fifths* of the value of the formal economy. The factors which would be reflected in the accounts of the household sector are shown in Table 2.

We have already discussed the production account. An *income and expenditure* account would bring out relationships between different forms of income and unpaid time on the one hand, and public services on the other. For example, the recent decline in nursery provision is almost certainly associated both with an increase in unpaid work and a decrease in wages; the decrease in wages results both from the loss of jobs of previously paid providers of those services and also from the need by the recipients of those services to take lower paid, part-time jobs or to leave employment altogether. In addition, the decline in nurseries may be associated with an increase in paid labour in the production account as households seek the services of private child minders.

Although little can be done through direct public intervention to change the division of labour in household production, there

## Table 2: Household sector national accounts

*Production account*

| Outputs | Inputs |
|---|---|
| Care of dependants | Unpaid work |
| Food preparation | Entrepreneurship |
| Cleaning | Consumer durables |
| Shelter & Warmth | Current consumer goods |
| Transport | |
| Recreation | |

*Income and expenditure account*

| Income | Expenditure |
|---|---|
| Wages | Taxes |
| Social security | Current household spending |
| Child benefit | Interest on debt |
| Other benefits | Personal spending by "breadwinner" |
| Unearned income | Saving |

*Capital account*

| Assets | Liabilities |
|---|---|
| Housing | Mortgages |
| Durables | HP debt |
| Financial assets | Other debt |

are a number of instruments which can have a significant indirect impact. These are listed in the *capital* account, as well as the income and expenditure account — for example the social security system, taxation, policies on interest rates, housing tenure, and policies affecting wages, such as minimum wage legislation. In constructing a comprehensive set of accounts the government would, for the first time, be able to fully assess the impact of its policies on women. Such a step seems a small price to pay to begin to meet the needs of the majority of the population.

### Conclusions

People's lives are increasingly shaped by their activity in the unpaid sector, not only as consumers of products of the paid sectors but also, of couse, in shaping the quality of their lives far more generally. As working hours fall, the significance of the unpaid sector will grow still further. And for women, the division of labour in the unpaid sector has even more profound implications. For all these reasons, socialists can no longer afford to concentrate on the workplace. To do so would be to make socialism irrelevant to many people for much of their lives.

CHAPTER 9

# Case Study: Telecommunications

Developments in the telecommunications industry will have a profound impact on Britain's future, in both economic and social terms. At the heart of the UK industry is British Telecom(BT) — the largest single object of the Conservative Government's privatisation programme. Privatisation has put telecommunications in the political limelight, mainly through the efforts of the BT workers' campaign against privatisation. The structure that has been set up will pose severe problems for consumers and for competition policy by the late 1980's. There will be a growing conflict of interest between the new shareholders, on the one hand, and the workers and consumers on the other. For all these reasons it is an industry where planning is urgently needed.

Privatisation of BT could considerably weaken Britain's industrial strength, with loss of control over tomorrow's technology also threatening control over tomorrow's wealth. This danger was highlighted by the proposed joint venture between BT and IBM in 1984. Because of IBM's domination of the market worldwide, major commercial centres in the UK are increasingly using IBM systems. While this may be commercially logical, such developments could be dangerous to our national interest, especially if BT followed suit: IBM systems "might then become a central influence on how we communicate technologically. Changes of mind in IBM in Armonk (IBM's headquarters) could have a national impact on Britain" (Peter Large, *The Guardian*, 22 August 1984). The UK would be dependent on systems which would be very costly and difficult to replace, but which would only be compatible with IBM equipment.

Although there are these specific reasons for looking at BT, there are also several more general issues involved. In particular there is the problem for a future Labour government of regaining control of the recently denationalised industries. The current spate of privatisation is a challenge — and perhaps an opportunity — to re-think forms of social control and economic efficiency. Should we return to complete state ownership through re-nationalisation or are there other more effective forms of democratic control? How can control be devolved to consumers if the consumers who are in the greatest need are not those with the greatest power in the market? How can decision making be devolved to workers in the industry in a way which is also sensitive to the needs of consumers? To what extent and how should a company like BT, which has a strategic economic role, seek to influence investment and production in its supplying industries through policies such as selective purchasing, acting as a research and development resource, or through direct investment?

This case study does not set out to give definitive answers to these questions, but it does outline some of the issues specific to BT and suggests three alternative forms of social control for the company: stricter regulation of what would be a largely privately owned industry; renationalisation; and municipalisation.

**Background**
BT's 1984-85 turnover of £7,700 million, net investment in plant and equipment of £1,600 million and pre-tax profits of £1,480 million put it among the five largest industrial companies in the UK, only rivalled in the private sector by the oil companies, BP and Shell. Like the products of the similarly sized motor industry, telecommunications has a major effect on people's lives. There are about 20 million exchange connections and 78 per cent of British homes have a telephone.

BT also has a major role as an employer, with about 230,000 people working for the company. The workforce is highly unionised, with men and women doing very different jobs. About 155,000 belong to the largest union, the National Communications Union (NCU formerly POEU) — mainly male engineers. There are around 35,000 operators — mainly women — who belong to the Union of Communication Workers (UCW). A further 33,000 — mostly male technicians and managers — are members of the Society of Telecom Executives (STE, formerly SPOE). Finally, some 5,500 belong to the Communication Managers' Association (CMA). Despite recent rationalisation, this fragmented union structure may have prevented the unions from responding quickly to the threat of privatisation.

Telecommunications is undergoing a technological revolution which will have major implications for BT's workforce and its traditional suppliers — STC, GEC and Plessey. All three main parts of the telecommunications networks — local lines, exchanges and trunk (long distance) communications — are affected.

*Local lines*, at least in the short term, are the least affected because there is currently no economically viable substitute for the wires that join subscribers to the exchange and for the labour intensive process of making the connections. But over time, entire local networks may be replaced with wideband cable systems, as used in cable television.

*Exchanges*, in contrast, are already being gradually changed. About 60 per cent of exchange equipment is still of the older electro-mechanical type that requires skilled maintenance by BT engineers. This older equipment is being replaced by digital exchanges, which are cheaper, perform more services and need less maintenance. The skills required to install and maintain digital exchanges are very different, and more akin to computer programming than hardware engineering. Not only will there be fewer jobs, therefore, but they will require different skills.

*Trunk lines* currently consist of the traditional, unwieldy metallic coaxial cables. These are just beginning to be replaced by optic fibres and satellites, which are now becoming more competitive forms of transmission.

As a result of the 1984 Telecommunications Act, BT has been transformed from a nationalised corporation into a "public" limited company, with the government taking 49 per cent of the shares. The Act explictly restricts any increase in this share. Moreover, the government is required to exercise its shareholding only in a very passive way, with reserve powers of intervention only for certain special cases such as to prevent excessive foreign shareholdings.

Since BT effectively has a monopoly in most of the market there are regulatory arrangements to protect the consumer. The Act established the Office of Telecommunications, modelled on the Office of Fair Trading, to regulate the telecommunications market. Its most important job is to prevent monopoly abuse by BT and see that the company adheres to the terms of its licence. The latter essentially represents an unenforceable attempt to ensure that the company meets certain service obligations, such as a reasonable uniformity of service; the maintenance of emergency services; and the provision of rural services and call boxes. The most important licence condition restricts BT's annual tariff increases, in monopoly areas, to the increase in the retail price index, less 3 per cent.

BT will still dominate telecommunications in the late 1980's but there will be competition in five areas:

- Services to big business users — especially from Mercury

Communications, run by Cable and Wireless.

• Local services — especially from wideband cable networks installed primarily for cable television.

• Mobile services — from cellular radio technology.

• Attachments — not just Mickey Mouse phones, but also important business equipment such as automatic branch exchanges.

• Services — probably the fastest growing area. These include answering and message handling, alarm calls and information such as weather forecasts. In the future, more sophisticated consumer services based on PRESTEL, like teleshopping and telebanking, will become increasingly important. There is also a huge market for business communications, in text and data transmission between computers.

**The impact of privatisation**
The increase in competition will hardly touch the individual residential subscriber — beyond giving them a choice of telephone instruments, which is one of the less costly parts of providing a telephone service.

The desire by shareholders to see costs cut will bring to an end the steady, socially desirable increase in residential use — which has doubled in the last ten years. The bulk of new customers are likely to make few calls and little contribution to fixed costs, because those who are likely to be frequent users of phones will probably already have one. This will mean either higher connection charges, so fewer people will be able to afford connections; or that charges will stay down for political reasons, making BT more and more reluctant to connect unless it is reasonably sure that new connections will be frequently used.

The old, the sick and those living alone — precisely those who are in greatest need of a telephone — will have the greatest difficulty in getting one. BT will certainly not be under any statutory obligation to provide them with one. For the same reasons, there will be even greater resistance to extending the network in rural areas, especially now that the basic network required by business and agriculture is largely in place. BT has already found one loophole in its operating licence and is ending free repairs for emergency services.

The pressure to cut direct costs is also likely to lead to massive redundancies among BT workers. The unplanned adoption of new equipment will take place at a rate which will displace workers much faster than they can get new jobs. And, because of cuts in in-house training and retraining, the general level of skills in the economy will suffer.

This skill loss may compound and justify another tendency arising from privatisation: that of turning to overseas suppliers for equipment. 45,000 jobs are at risk because of this. BT has traditionally bought around 95 per cent of its requirements from UK suppliers. Doing this has meant accepting prices above the world level, because the UK telecommunications equipment supply industry is uncompetitive in world markets, apart from STC in submarine cables.

Many regions may suffer because of these developments. BT's capacity to generate the revenue needed to provide a national telecommunications service will be undermined by two factors. First, the loss of business revenues to Mercury. Second, because the Government is actively encouraging cable companies to provide (wideband) telecommunications services on a marginal cost basis, as well as entertainment programmes. BT could be reduced to providing marginal services of marginal profitability in regions where cable companies are not operating. It will not be able to afford to service the unprofitable regions. The consequences would be devastating, akin to a region emerging from the industrial revolution without a railway network.

The provision of wideband cable services by private operators threatens to divide Britain into two nations: the 'information rich and poor'. One nation would have cable TV, telecommunications and a whole range of services vital to daily life, such as shopping and banking — all available as a package from one company. This package would only be provided in wealthy areas of high population density. The other nation, of information poor, would be forced to rely on telecommunications operators alone for the provision of services, because of where they live or their income. These dangers are increased by the fact that one-third of BT's turnover comes from just 300 customers. If its charges have to be reduced to keep its custom, in the face of 'cream-skimming' competitors, then it will become impossible to cross-subsidise less profitable operations.

**Objectives**
A socialist strategy must have three objectives. First, to ensure that telecommunications supply takes proper account of social need and not just the needs of business. Second, to ensure that the telecommunications infrastructure is developed in ways that assist the UK economy as a whole, including the development of the information technology based service industries and BT's suppliers. And third, to ensure that BT's activities dovetail with national objectives. This might mean, for example, a massive increase in investment in optic fibres; involvement of more

women in electronic engineering; or the supply of software-skilled workers to other sectors of the economy.

The question of ownership is crucial but logically distinct. It is both a means and an objective. One means of seeking to achieve the three objectives listed above would be re-nationalisation. But this or some other form of public ownership is quite properly an objective in its own right. It should be part of a programme to ensure that profits — of £1,500 million for BT last year — are used for the public good. However, the whole economy will not be placed under public ownership immediately on the return of a Labour Government. It is therefore partly a question of priorities as to whether BT should become a prime candidate for re-nationalisation or some other form of public ownership, or whether the control needed to achieve the other objectives might be more easily achieved in other ways.

**Strategies**

The three strategies we consider are called *stricter regulation, renationalisation* and *municipalisation*. They are clearly not the only possibilities since there are many intermediate positions, but they present the choices available in their starkest form.

*Stricter regulation* would attempt to solve the problems that are developing and to achieve the objectives piecemeal, without changing the basic structure of BT as a public limited company or altering the regulatory system. This would be achieved through specific intervention in BT pricing policies — for example by altering the licence to achieve social objectives such as lower standing charges and a wider availability of the basic service. BT would be able to recoup the losses from business customers after its monopoly had been restored.

Legislation would also be needed to guarantee adequate standards of service in all areas, with specific provisions for the less economically attractive areas of low population density and for those who need telecommunications services but cannot afford them. The cable franchise system would have to be amended to ensure that franchises in prosperous areas were only made available to those who also provided services in less profitable ones. General labour legislation could strengthen the position of BT workers against redundancy. Import controls and restrictions on public procurement might ensure that BT had to buy from UK suppliers. And a business plan approved by the government could be used to control and increase BT's investment.

The danger of these measures is that of course they would very much reduce the attractiveness of BT to private shareholders. A determined management could evade much of the effect of these measures. A slight variant of this approach, which would require legislation, would be to increase the government stake sufficiently to ensure managerial control. But this could create considerable problems with minority shareholders. Further, as we shall argue below, it is unlikely that 51 per cent ownership would allow the government to pursue the full range of social objectives, 75 per cent being needed to change the company's articles of association. Finally, the American experience of a regulatory body — the Federal Communications Commission — does not augur well for Britain: the Commission has become dominated by the interests of corporate bodies.

*Renationalisation* could be defined as a return to the pre-1981 position except that the separation from the Post Office might be maintained. This would involve nationalising Mercury and a number of other concerns, including the new cable networks. A renationalised BT should certainly be able to carry out the policies outlined for stricter regulation. But a more realistic and political approach will also be needed when making appointments to the Board.

If the nationalised BT were responsive to political will, it could go further than a regulated private company. It could be used more easily and explicitly as an instrument of national economic policy, with its overall tariff levels, borrowing and rate of investment closely tied to general government aims. BT's purchasing power could be used to effect qualitative changes in supplying industries, for example by supporting worker co-ops, or by exerting leverage over companies like Plessey in order to help enforce business plans. BT could also enter manufacturing itself, building upon its research and development strengths, and creating a significant UK force in the world telecommunications industry. This might include a merger or closer links with ICL, INMOS and parts of existing telecommunications manufacturers.

A renationalised BT, with a public monopoly, would be better able to cross-subsidise operations and to meet social, as well as economic, objectives. In this way, public enterprise could build social goals into key decisions. BT could also be used as a test case for a radical extension of industrial democracy. The recent devolution of some managerial power to the BT areas might be built upon to construct area Boards. BT could lead a national effort to get genuine equality of opportunity for men and women in electronic engineering, because of the leading role it plays in training in this field. Finally, the switch from electro-mechanical exchanges might be delayed as part of a national manpower policy: the rapid switch to digital exchanges will result in critical shortages of people with software skills who are needed elsewhere in the economy, while making many of those with traditional skills redundant. BT could go further, and develop training for software engineers on the specific understanding that these people would move to other sectors of the economy.

Although it should certainly be possible to achieve a host of desirable objectives through renationalisation, it should be remembered that Britain's nationalised industries were founded on just such desires and beliefs. But the outcome has been barely recognisable in comparision. A renationalised BT of the 1990's could face many of the criticisms levelled at the public sector monoliths of the 1960's and 1970's. It could be charged with being remote, uncontrollable and undemocratic, with its own workforce having little say, and the general public and business interests accusing it of abusing its monopoly position and being inefficient.

*Municipalisation* could avoid some of these problems. Under this option, local services would be run municipally, as already happens — by a quirk of history — in the Hull area. The local service could set its own local call charges and terms and conditions of service within national minimum standards. Each locality could decide, for example, whether to have cheap but unsightly overhead lines or more costly buried lines; whether to offer a cheaper but shared line exchange service; what controls should be placed on programmes sent over the local cable TV network. It could, within the general policy for local authority investment, decide upon its own investment and borrowing. This system could be run directly by councillors, or by a board of councillors, workers and consumers.

A 'going local' policy would affect about 80 per cent of BT workers, but could not be applied across the whole of its services. Many services would still be run on a centralised basis. This would include the international services, trunk networks, competitive services for big business customers, research and development, manufacturing, training and some form of central procurement.

The main attractions of such a devolved system are that it would be easier to make it democratic and responsive to customer pressure. Even though it would not create competition, it could at least create some diversity, so that consumers can compare what is on offer in different parts of the country. And it could reduce the power that BT has through being the sole buyer in the telecommunications market.

There are several disadvantages, however. Municipalisation

would require further massive changes for an industry that has only recently gone through the traumas of privatisation. This would be exacerbated because the UK network is highly integrated and its management highly centralised, unlike in the United States where 'local' private telephone companies are the norm. Moreover, a decentralised management will still require some form of system for allocating investment funds.

Centralised management also produces uniformity of service for consumers and terms and conditions for employees. A municipalised BT would present problems of ensuring a uniformity of service — in the United States this is dealt with through statutory minimum standards, and specific penalties for failure to meet the standards. For employees, municipalisation could mean the end of national collective bargaining with its associated benefits.

Municipalisation would allow a fairly flexible approach to the question of ownership. It would be possible to adopt different approaches for different areas and different parts of the service. Indeed, the counterposing of 'centralised' nationalisation and 'decentralised' municipalisation could be overtaken by events. Management has been progressively decentralised to local levels in recent years. This process has been seen as a possible first step towards the eventual breaking up of BT into discrete companies, not necessarily all owned by the same group of shareholders.

Municipalisation would allow greater consumer and employee democracy, on top of any choice offered through the market. Nonetheless, it would be a mistake automatically to equate decentralisation with democracy. If municipalisation were to be adopted as a policy for telecommunications or any other service, far more thought would need to be given to the nature of local democracy and the exact mechanism for the expression of choice. To argue that councillors should be responsible for local telecommunications — and that their surgeries should be used to deal with installation problems — is impractical, to say the least.

The limitations of municipalisation suggest that it is more appropriate to think of some form of 'going local' as being part of the renationalisation of BT, and not as a distinct alternative: decision making should, where possible, be decentralised in a renationalised corporation.

The establishment of area boards need not, and should not, threaten national collective bargaining. The rights of BT's workers should be expanded, building up from the shopfloor as discussed in Chapter 5. The problems of simultaneously bargaining over long-term strategic issues and short-term issues underline the importance of board level representation being firmly rooted in existing methods of trade union representation, if union members on the board are not to be isolated.

### Meeting consumer needs

The extension of industrial democracy does not guarantee, however, that consumers will get a better service. There is a genuine conflict of interest. For example, within ten years the sale of telephones, together with the widespread adoption of the plug and socket, will mean that traditional telephone installation will have largely disappeared. It is self-evident that customers will want it, and workers will not because of the threat to jobs.

Meeting the needs of consumers must be the primary objective of BT once it is back in the public sector. Any failure to demonstrate that this objective is being achieved would critically undermine the case for a further extension of public enterprise. In the case of a 'national' monopoly such as BT, a range of measures will be needed which enable consumers to influence the service that is provided. The sheer scale of BT's operations and number of BT users suggest that these measures can only have a practical impact if they focus on the provision of *local* services: most users are more likely to be concerned with getting the local pay phone fixed or getting through to directory enquiries (now more difficult since privatisation) than BT's overall investment policy. Such measures could include:

• A 'charter' for consumers to establish the level of service to which consumers are entitled. This should be drawn up in consultation with a reformed consumer council for the industry and the area boards.

• Newly established area boards would, as discussed above, bring together consumers and other community groups with local authority representatives. They would consider issues decided at a local level and provide opinions on issues decided centrally. Such bodies could have high street advice shops and hold area or regional annual meetings and publish a regular newsletter for local users. There would probably have to be a statutory requirement on local authorities to help establish them.

• To ensure that services are efficiently provided, a 'social audit' commission should monitor performance. The audit should explicitly recognise, where possible, the costs of achieving social objectives such as rural phone boxes. Such a body would have to be independent of BT and would require extensive access to information.

• In addition, a Commons Select Committee for tele-communications could, if properly resourced, help extend public scrutiny. In particular, it could usefully be involved in discussions of BT's corporate plan and important one-off decisions, such as on pricing.

These measures are logically separate from the question of whether BT shareholders should continue to hold their shares: we would argue that share ownership does not, and should not, entitle owners to a greater say, while recognising the Tories' success in equating share ownership with involvement — such that many people now equate public ownership with holding shares. Rather than taking shares away from existing shareholders, all BT subscribers should be entitled to 'citizen shares', giving them full rights of participation through the structures we have proposed.

## Capital structure

By providing rights for both workers *and* consumers, BT could become a model of socialist enterprise in action, able to respond to local needs through a decentralised structure, and national needs through a coherent organisation.

This discussion of objectives and company structure does not resolve, however, the issue of BT's capital structure — who, in other words, should *own* BT? Under the present structure the government would require at least 75 per cent of BT shares to change the company's 'articles of association', which set out the objectives it should pursue: only then could BT be required to pursue the social objectives we have set out, or such industrial policy goals as 'buying British'. But buying additional shares on the open market (the government currently has 49 per cent) would be extremely expensive, and could mean diverting government investment away from other areas such as housing and hospital building. And even a 75 per cent stake would leave a substantial minority holding, with considerable scope for interference by the Courts in defence of "minority interests" against majority decisions.

Both the Labour Party and the TUC are currently committed to the principle of 'no speculative gain' — which, in BT's case, would mean buying shares back at the original offer price of 130 pence. This would certainly reduce the overall cost of the exercise — but there are major problems with it. Those who made a speculative gain because of the original undervaluation have in many cases already sold out. Moreover, such an approach could well be open to legal challenge: previous renationalisations have rested on the principles of 'fair' compensation and/or an assessment of the company's assets and prospects. Further, many BT shareholders now include pension funds: 'no speculative gain' would raise the spectre of 'robbing' pensions,

190    *Socialist Enterprise*

including those of trade union members. The principle of 'no speculative gain' is therefore unlikely to be tenable.

How then could the ownership issue be resolved without prohibitive cost ? The main options appear to be:

(a)Retaining the existing equity capital structure, but with all existing shareholdings 'bought out' with interest-bearing Treasury bonds.

(b)Reconverting BT to a public corporation, with all existing shareholdings converted to either non-voting, interest bearing securities issued by BT or non-voting shares issued by British Enterprise.

Under both options, interest payments would continue to be financed, directly or indirectly, out of BT's profits. The advantage of the second option, however, is that the issue of BT securities need not be underwritten by the Treasury. The possibility of a clash between financing other public borrowing commitments and BT's re-nationalisation should not therefore arise. Moreover, if British Enterprise were to issue equity, this could enable companies which would otherwise have difficulties in financing the cost of interest payments (etc) still to be brought into public ownership — these costs would in effect be borne by more than one publicly-owned company.

**Conclusions — a two-stage strategy**

The legislation needed for full re-nationalisation would, of course, take time. Before it is introduced, the government should make full use of its existing shareholding to alter BT's behaviour decisively. If this were to be met with opposition, the case for a further extension of public ownership would be underlined.

CHAPTER 10

# Case Study: Motors

The UK motor industry stands at a crossroads. There is a real danger that it will become little more than an offshore assembly plant of foreign multinationals. This danger is increased by the threat to sell off BL. But alternatively, the industry could retain and build up its capacity to design and manufacture, to the benefit of the entire economy.

Motors provides a useful case study of how economic planning can revitalise manufacturing industry in the UK. The problems that will have to be overcome in motors are typical of much of UK industry: the legacy of inefficient private enterprise; the partial success of state intervention in the past; the impact of rapidly changing technology and the UK's growing technological inferiority; and the need to cope with conflicting objectives. The motor industry is both unusual and of particular interest because it is dominated by a few multinationals. This means, on the one hand, that the motor companies are in a powerful position in their relationship with governments. And, on the other hand, unlike most UK industries, it means that only a small number of decision makers need to be influenced in order to influence key decisions. In many other industries those seeking to implement strategic planning have greater power but more difficulty in exercising it.

The UK motor industry, moreover, remains vitally important in terms of both employment and the use of new technologies. The four main manufacturers together employ some 200,000, and the components sector employs an estimated 500,000. About 85 per cent of these are men. In Europe, motors accounts for 20 per cent of European steel and machine tool production and 15 per cent of rubber production. The industry is also a major user of many new technologies, incorporating innovations in robotics, electronics and new materials. Thus the industry vividly demonstrates the links between new and traditional industries, and the dangers in believing Tory propaganda that there is a 'high tech' solution to Britain's problems.

Indeed, motors is one of a small group of "pivotal" industries in terms of industrial structure. Whereas most industries supply a relatively narrow range of customers and purchase from a narrow range of suppliers, and some — such as energy supply — are of major importance to a very large industry, motors is one of the few industries which is of major significance to a wide range of industries. According to the latest (1979) Input-Output tables, these pivotal industries include steel, metal castings, paper and printing, construction, hotel and catering and retailing, as well as motors. Such pivotal industries have a twofold significance. First, they represent centres of economic power which could form the basis for reorganising their client industries. Second, the major suppliers and customers of a pivotal industry cannot be planned without some knowledge of its prospects.

**Background**
Motors is dominated by four manufacturers: BL, Ford, Vauxhall and Talbot. BL is the only national and non-private company. Ford and Vauxhall (General Motors) are both owned by American multinationals, while Talbot is part of the French based Peugeot group. Together, these three multinationals account for about 50 per cent of UK car output. This multinational domination is high by international standards: the equivalent figures for Germany, the United States and France are 31, 3 and 1 per cent. Production in Italy, Japan and Sweden is undertaken by domestically owned producers only.

The 1970's witnessed a spectacular decline in the fortunes of the industry:

• *Employment* fell by 40 per cent between 1974 and 1985. UK employment in BL fell from 172,000 to 68,000 between 1977 and 1985.

• *Production* has more than halved over the past 13 years from 1.9 million cars in 1972 to 0.9 million in 1984.

• *Import penetration* has risen from 14 per cent in 1970 to a peak of 58 per cent in 1985. Japanese imports have been sucesssfully restricted to 11 per cent by 'voluntary agreements'. The most spectacular increase has occurred in *tied imports*. This has been caused by the decisions of Ford and General Motors to import cars and their parts, mainly from their plants in West Germany: indeed, car imports from Germany alone account for *half* of Britain's total manufactured trade deficit.

**Objectives**
The industry's continuing importance suggests that a manufacturing capacity in motor vehicles must be retained. This

objective should be fulfilled within the context of an integrated policy for private and public transport, with support for the industry being matched by increased support for public transport. Such a transport policy must reconcile the mobility, flexibility and load carrying capacity of the car with the need to reduce the damage imposed on the environment by private transport, the loss to human life through accidents, and the sometimes prohibitive financial cost of using the car, especially for the poor.

Transport policy has concentrated on the public role in transport — railways, buses and road building — and ignored the private car itself. This is wrong, because the car is such an important element of transport. A policy for the motor industry should seek to get cars designed which not only serve the needs of car owners more effectively, but also fit the general objectives of transport policy: cars should, for example, have good acceleration at low speeds to make effective use of road space, have far more safety features, be easier to maintain and repair, and be less polluting. At present, however, transport policy has little or no influence on the motor industry. Its one foray into vehicle design — the standard bus grant of the late 1960's — was a disaster. The enthusiasm for driver-only buses considered only narrow cost factors to the exclusion of more general transport considerations or technical design problems: the result was a major blow to the bus industry. These experiences highlight some of the practical problems which will be encountered in developing an integrated transport policy.

The objective of improving product design should, therefore, be given far greater priority, not only in the context of a strategy for motors but also as part of an overall policy for transport. In the past, minor changes in styling, leading to a rapid succession of different models and to built-in obsolescence, have typically been the means by which profits have been stimulated within the industry. But product innovation now amounts to more than adding a tailfin or a voice synthesiser. Model changes can incorporate major advances in fuel efficiency, as well as allowing the use of lead free petrol. Product durability could also be improved, and the car made easier to repair, through the use of new materials such as plastics. Innovation could, moreover, recognise the specific needs of users such as the disabled, while new models could be designed to reduce the risks of serious accidents to passengers and pedestrians.

The benefits of advances in process technology should similarly accrue to those who work in the industry as well as users. On the one hand, advances in process technology have made cars cheaper, so that many working class consumers can afford to drive. (Even so, car ownership has increased more slowly than the ownership of other consumer durables.) On the other, the intensity of work could be reduced through a shorter working week, planned automation and job design, such that the most degrading of jobs need not be done by human beings.

For those who work in the industry, however, the most important objectives are still security of employment and earnings. While employment in the industry will continue to fall, it need not do so at the rate of recent years — provided the UK industry can capture a larger share of a growing market, and hours are reduced. This will present a major challenge to a Labour Government that seeks to promote recovery through the extension of collective bargaining — how to reconcile conflicting objectives without the safety valve of new jobs. As we show in Chapter 5, the history of the last Labour Government underlines these difficulties.

### The failure of private ownership

The long-term decline of the industry poses problems that our strategy must confront. The reasons for this decline are deep rooted. One factor has been that changes in demand have not been related to planned capacity. For example, Barber's 'dash for growth' showed that reflation works: but it also led to a large increase in imports. However, reflation linked to planned capacity would not be enough to ensure recovery. For too long, the industry failed to produce cars that people wanted to buy.

The strategies of the UK owned manufacturers ignored the long-term needs of the industry. BL, formerly the British Leyland Motor Corporation, was formed in 1968. It was the product of a series of post-war rationalisations and mergers, which brought together a complex and fragmented heritage of products, facilities and markets. The Corporation appeared obsessed with capacity expansion and not renewal. A huge range of models was produced until the late 1970's, while updating of plant or equipment was neglected, and a strategy of under-pricing was pursued. Heavy reliance was placed on safe, protected, post-Empire markets. Marketing facilities were not established in many of the newly growing markets. Importers gained access to the British market because they could easily purchase dealership networks following rationalisation of the BL distribution system: by 1976 importers had 40 per cent of all dealer networks.

Given these problems it was not surprising that the industrial relations record was poor, with on average 14 per cent of its potential output lost each year as a direct result of strikes. In the boom years of the 1950's and 1960's cars were easily sold and unemployment was low. Line managers, faced with strong stewards bargaining over piece-rates, bought peace. The failure to update models and re-invest in plant, skills, and distribution networks, meant that the industry did not shift to the production of higher value vehicles. Price became the only weapon, placing intolerable strain on bargaining over wages and effort, and trapping industrial relations in a vicious circle.

By any measure the performance of UK motor manufacturers in product innovation is alarming. The proportion of expenditure on research and development in the UK in relation to value-added and gross output is lower than in the US, Japan, West Germany, France and Italy. For example, patenting by BL has collapsed from an already low level. Between 1970 and 1979, BL had only 3.5 per cent of the patents on new products taken out by motor manufacturers operating in the UK. (Ford had 21 per cent, Nissan 18 per cent and General Motors 17 per cent.)

The decline of BL enabled imports to grow and Ford to assume market dominance by renewing its model range and developing its marketing strengths. In contrast to BL, Ford and Vauxhall expanded through growth. BL virtually failed to compete in the light and medium sectors, which are vital because of fleet car sales, until the launch of the Maestro and Montego.

**Can there be a UK motor industry?**
The vulnerability of the industry raises the question, is it still credible to argue for the UK to retain a manufacturing capacity in motors? It has become fashionable to argue that there will only be a handful of viable producers by the end of the century. This *world car* perspective is supported by the argument that rising economies of scale in manufacture are essential to lower unit costs. Only the 'giants' can produce at this volume. However, this argument is circular because estimates of the minimum efficient scale of production tend to be derived from the investment decisions of a few large companies. Moreover, the world car strategy has seldom been adopted in practice: the use of common parts has been minimal and models have been redesigned for different markets. To the extent that the strategy has been adopted, it reflects an option appropriate to the specific strengths of multinationals. There is, we would argue, no one rational strategy for survival.

However, the world car perspective is also supported by the rising costs of developing, producing and marketing new models. The cost of the investment programme by US producers in new models — to reduce their size and fuel consumption —

exceeds the cost of the Apollo space programme. According to this argument, a volume of 2 million units per annum is needed to recover costs.

The *technological divergence* view provides an alternative to the world car perspective. This argues that medium-sized producers, such as BL, will be able to survive by:

• Developing sophisticated marketing techniques and exploiting national loyalties to find market niches.

• Using flexible manufacturing techniques so that several model derivatives — hatchbacks, estates and so on — can be built on the same line, bringing down economies of scale in manufacture.

• Rapid innovation to take advantage of inherently unpredictable new solutions to technical problems, which a larger manufacturer may be slower to adopt.

• Sharing development costs through cross-trading links with other companies. This especially applies to engine and gear-box (power-train) production, where development costs are enormous and probably still rising.

• Making greater use of increasingly sophisticated computer aided design and manufacturing techniques which will eventually reduce development costs.

The technological divergence view therefore suggests that a UK motor manufacturing industry *may* be able to survive and recover costs in many — though perhaps not all — areas of production. But collaboration is also needed. The *terms* of joint ventures are crucial. In the case of BL, there is a danger that much design work will be taken over by Honda and other 'partners'. This has already happened to other Western manufacturers involved in collaboration, as discussed in Chapter 6. While it is feasible that the UK motor industry will survive, it is certainly not inevitable. Many manufacturing operations may go overseas, as BL concentrates limited resources on body design, assembly and marketing. Even high value-added core components can be manufactured abroad: BL already imports VW gearboxes for the Maestro. These dangers are greatly increased by the Conservative Government's commitment to privatisation and its reluctance to support large-scale investment programmes, preventing BL from entering into joint ventures as an equal partner.

### The multinationals

Although it may be possible for a medium-sized producer to survive, the resources available to multinational producers still put BL's survival in doubt. Over half of UK car sales are met by multinationals: Ford, Vauxhall and Talbot. Nissan's new plant in the North East will increase the multinational presence still further. The future plans of these companies are therefore vital to the industry. Even Ford UK could face serious problems if Vauxhall and Nissan flood the market with imported cars.

Vauxhall has followed Talbot in running down its UK operations. Both now only assemble here. Talbot's Whitley design centre was closed by Peugeot. Productivity in Talbot plants is now high by continental standards, but their long-term future is threatened by Peugeot's plans to cut capacity.

The recent increase in Vauxhall's market share — from 8.5 to 16.6 per cent between 1981 and 1985 — has been achieved through imports of parts and cars. The foreign content of the Astra and Cavalier is 50 per cent; and 56 per cent of Vauxhall's UK sales are imported as fully assembled vehicles (Dan Jones, *The import threat to the UK car industry*, SPRU, 1985). The Nova is wholly imported from Spain. During the 1970's, the Vauxhall and Opel model ranges were fully integrated, involving the concentration of design and manufacture in Germany, the construction of a new engine plant in Austria and the building of additional assembly capacity in Spain. In a sense, Vauxhall is no longer part of a multinational, but has become the offshore assembler of General Motors' European operation.

Ford still operates as a true multinational, its production relying on a complex web of European plants. It is committed to production in the UK throughout the 1980's, having recently invested heavily in Dagenham (to produce the Escort). Despite this, Ford has downgraded the UK's capacity to produce cars, while investing in engine and commercial vehicle production.

Multinational production gives Ford the freedom to exploit national differences (in market growth, exchange and tariff rates, government grants, and the strength of labour) and to price parts differently in different countries (transfer pricing). But this freedom can be easily overstated. The future of Ford's UK plants has depended on balancing the higher cost of producing here against the profits it has been able to make. Costs have now changed in favour of the UK compared to Germany, but Ford is committed for several years to heavier investment in Germany. Ford UK has generated profits for the reorganisation of Ford's worldwide operations, by taking advantage of the relatively high car prices in the UK. While the cost of producing in the UK depends partly on productive efficiency, the recent over-valuation of sterling, especially against European currencies, is of far greater importance. This is partly offset by our low labour costs. The process of disinvestment is, moreover, not easy: to sustain productive efficiency, Ford must make further investment in existing plant and therefore increase its commitment to the UK. And future investment must be funded from current production which will be disrupted if it appears likely that Ford will pull out. Finally, the closure of a major plant would damage Ford's image as a UK producer and jeopardise its market domination.

## Strategies

A strategy for motors cannot rely on a single instrument of planning. Although there are common problems, there are important differences between planning the activities of BL and those of the other manufacturers with a UK base. These stem from the fact that BL is a medium-sized producer which is currently in public ownership, whereas the others are owned by private capital abroad, with all the resources available to multinational producers.

## Industrial democracy

Unions in the industry are not in a position to make full use of the new rights and institutions that we have outlined. Shopfloor organisation is weak in many of the major plants. At BL, the prolonged attack on stewards has left many positions vacant. In much better circumstances, BL workers were not able to develop many positive suggestions in the industrial democracy experiment of the Ryder era.

Shopfloor power is also limited in multinationals. A closer relationship between workers in plants in different countries is needed and is being developed. But this is unlikely to form the sole basis of a strategy to deal with multinationals, as is often claimed. There are few examples of solidarity action on behalf of workers in other plants. There is an important division of interest between different plants. The limited success of Vauxhall workers campaigning against Nova imports shows the difficulty of forcing a multinational to change investment plans through shopfloor action alone.

Despite this, there *are* areas of leverage. The power of production workers at Ford is an important influence over the company's sourcing decisions — where different components are produced and operations carried out. By blacking work they can have some say on, for example, the extent to which pressings are produced in the UK or Germany. But such leverage could not have much impact on the sourcing of a new plant. Paradoxically, this leverage depends on Ford's success in the UK market: there is little point in blacking work on a product that no one will buy.

Given an expansionary climate, shopfloor influence could be rebuilt. The exercise of new rights could generate increased confidence. Workers' knowledge of, and commitment to, their industry should not be underestimated, but nor should it be forgotten that this is partial and fragmented, and that exercising positive rights is very different from rebuilding defensive strengths. The limits of shopfloor power must therefore be recognised. The extension of collective bargaining will have to cope with powerful tensions: how to manage change without being able to guarantee that no jobs will be lost; severe international competition; and the legacy of resentment that has built up against management in recent years.

**Public ownership**
BL is a stark reminder of the fact that public ownership does not constitute an industrial policy, but is often a *substitute* for one. Nevertheless, there would be an overwhelming case for bringing BL back into public ownership, were it to be sold off. Private ownership could mean that BL would be reduced to the status of an offshore assembler, a Trojan horse through which foreign multinationals export to the EEC. And BL still requires considerable funding to survive. Jaguar also needs to be part of a larger operation, its recent success depending considerably on changes in the value of sterling against the dollar which could easily be reversed. Only public funding backed by a government strategy for motors will enable BL, with Jaguar, to survive as a medium-sized producer.

Nationalisation is not the most appropriate measure for coping with multinationals. They have both a freedom from and vulnerability to national boundaries. Single plants are vital aspects of multinationals' production plans, and the loss of them — through nationalisation — would be very disruptive. But on the other hand, nationalising Vauxhall's plants would simply give us assembly facilities alone, without the parts needed to make the cars. It makes more sense to force General Motors to increase the UK production content of cars they sell here, and to offset imports with exports.

However, there may be circumstances in which the *threat* of nationalisation is needed. It may deter a company from reneging on the terms of agreements with the government — provided the government actually wants to take over the plants concerned. The Chrysler planning agreement effectively subsidised the restructuring of the company. Once it was clear that the company was not prepared to honour its agreement, there would have been a strong case to take its plants into public ownership. But this would have left the Labour Government with out-of-date plants of little use. Public ownership should therefore be seen as a tactical *part* of the planning process, which only makes sense when clearly defined objectives have been established.

It it sometimes suggested that the entire industry should be nationalised and amalgamated. This is partly based on the belief that only outright nationalisation of multinationals will enable their power to be checked. The creation of another public monolith is not only unnecessary but impractical. If nothing else has been learnt from BL, it must be that it is extremely difficult to manage separate companies as one entity. Different companies contest their autonomy. When the British Steel Corporation was established, for example, the management of the Yorkshire companies — the 'Yorkshire mafia' — held on to their information and control. This does not mean, however, that a closer relationship between manufacturers should not be established, provided BL can be an equal partner — with full access to designs and manufacturing technologies — in any such joint venture.

**Beyond planning agreements**
In their negotiations with multinationals, British Governments have used a combination of investment incentives and exhortation. 'Codes of conduct' have also been proposed to regulate their behaviour. Ford received substantial public aid from the Labour Government to build its engine plant in Bridgend in 1978 in return for an understanding on Ford UK's overall balance of trade, which lasted for a number of years.

This experience suggests that effective leverage can be obtained. We have argued that public aid should be conditional, in the form of equity or loan capital if possible. But this may not be appropriate in the case of multinational motor producers. The UK will often be forced to compete with other countries for their investment, many of which will not impose conditions on the granting of aid. More to the point, it is doubtful whether a Labour Government would want a stake in four or more multinationals' UK operations. The size of the market would not justify it. Public aid can only therefore be used as part of a package.

The most effective leverage which a government can apply against a multinational is control over access to the national market. Denied access, the company will not be able to sell cars and make profits. This leverage should be used to make sure that multinationals balance their exports and imports. Such a policy must be adopted within the context of a trade policy for the industry as a whole. If this is not done, there will be an incentive

for companies to export into the UK without producing here.
If multinationals balance their trade, this preserves employment and can dovetail with macro-economic trade objectives. Such agreements should also encompass the purchasing decisions of steel and components. In this way the identification and fulfilment of a key objective also enables other objectives to be met.

The problems created by such negotiations must be anticipated. Ford management explain their need to import by the inability of UK plants to meet production schedules. A devalued pound and the low labour costs of UK operations can only offset such inefficiency in the short-term, given that we hope to move to a high wage strategy. Instead we must recognise that there are fundamental problems of efficiency which our strategy cannot ignore — Ford undeniably exaggerates these problems but it would be foolish to deny they exist. Similarly, Ford would claim that the quality of UK steel is not good enough. If this were not rectified, the strategy would result in cars with a shorter product life.

'Business plans' drawn up with major motor companies could be monitored in two ways. First, by the workers themselves: most stewards have access to information on production levels in different plants. Second, the Vehicles Department of the Department of Trade and Industry already monitors the trade flows of multinationals. This role could be expanded, backed by powers of information disclosure, within the new institutional structure that we have proposed.

**Trade policy**
Trade policy must be consistent with the objectives of industrial recovery and economic expansion. Its purpose should neither be to shut out imports nor to ban multinationals from the UK market. The policy should also recognise the needs of other countries for their own motor manufacturing industries.

BL needs a volume of around 650,000 vehicles a year to survive as a manufacturer. It would be unrealistic to forecast any increase in the UK market, given that it is already at record levels. There is scope for a limited increase in exports, but not in areas where Japanese manufacturers are already dominant. BL therefore needs a market share of around 25 per cent.

The import share should therefore be cut back to the levels of other European producers, of around 45 per cent. Imports could then *grow* in line with any growth in the domestic market. This would enable both the UK and other countries to retain their motor manufacturing capacity. It should not, therefore, cause retaliation. Indeed, both the General Agreement on Tariffs and Trade and the EEC allow countries to introduce temporary import controls if a full employment level of demand means a balance of payments crisis. Labour Governments introduced a 15 per cent surcharge in 1964 and an import deposit scheme in 1968 within the framework of the Agreement. This policy should be backed by the renewal of the voluntary agreement with Japan.

Within this framework, multinationals must be required to balance their trade. Given the limited size of the market, it may not be possible to support four multinational producers. Vauxhall, in particular, should be given the choice between increasing investment or being shut out of the UK market. Those that will invest here should be allowed to stay.

Trade controls could take a number of forms — volume quotas, prescribed levels of labour content or value-added. Such controls are, however, associated with a number of difficulties. For example, requiring 70 per cent of value-added to be produced in the UK could be side-stepped by accounting devices such as declaring that a high proportion of value-added is made up by advertising and distribution. Without the appropriate safeguards, content controls could encourage multinationals to set up assembly plants in the UK, threatening the viability of firms already here. This would further reduce the skills of the domestic industry, since core components would undoubtedly be produced overseas. Recognising these difficulties, the possibilities of more limited trade controls linking content specifically to fleet car sales should be explored. Such a measure could effectively increase the UK market by 400,000 cars.

Such a policy could more easily be implemented through planning at a European level. The threat of growing over-capacity — of two million cars by 1990 — points both to likely tensions and possibilities for their resolution. European Governments will be forced to subsidise their industries as over capacity increases. Unless agreement is reached on capacity levels, a trade war could begin, of the kind that threatened European steel before the EEC's 'D'Avignon' plan on capacity levels was agreed. The experience of such EEC initiatives has, however, been mixed — in aluminium and copper, as well as steel, British industries have borne the brunt of cutbacks in capacity. While this has largely been the result of the way British Governments have bargained on capacity levels, it does — at best — suggest that industrial planning through the EEC offers no easy panacea. European planning is also needed to prevent competitive bidding for multinational investment.

**Conclusions**
We have outlined a strategy for the lifetime of a Labour Government. It recognises the specific constraints and opportunities which are likely to exist. However, a strategy for the short-term must also build in options for the long-term. For example, the feasibility of developing short distance cars for use in the city could be assessed, which could be cheaply hired at railway stations: these could be publicly or privately owned; and they could use different fuels, so reducing our dependence on oil. Product life should be extended, weighing up the advantages of incorporating innovations against the costs imposed. Further advances in product technology which increase flexibility could make it easier to change model characteristics during the life of existing models.

The use of flexible manufacturing techniques, coupled with substantial retraining, may sufficiently reduce scale economies to enable smaller scale production units to be established, in which workers are responsible for a far greater range of tasks. Applying new techniques to product and job design would enable workers and consumers to have an early input into new models and the way they are built. Graphic simulations could enable different options to be considered and costed before development. Users such as the disabled, often ignored because they do not represent the typical consumer, could make specific demands to which manufacturers could respond by taking advantage of flexible tooling. There are many possibilities. We do not need an alternative blueprint. Instead, workers and consumers should be stimulated to develop their own ideas, which would then be applied according to their wider social, as well as economic, benefits.

# CHAPTER 11

# Case Study: Textiles and Clothing

Textiles and clothing is widely regared as a 'sunset industry', the decline of which is inevitable in the face of cheap imports from low wage countries. Critics point to:

• A fall in employment of almost a half between 1971 and 1985, from just over a million to just over 500,000.

• A drop in textiles output by about a third between 1977 and 1985, and a smaller but still serious drop in clothing output.

• A virtual halving of investment between 1979 and 1981 which, although it has increased in recent years, has still not recovered to 1979 levels in real terms.

• A high level of import penetration — imports now take about 45 per cent of the textiles home market and 37 per cent of the clothing market.

By all appearances, the industry is typical of British manufacturing in decline. Yet we should not accept this as inevitable. Decline has been caused by the action and inaction of governments and manufacturers, which strategic planning should seek to rectify. The industry poses particular problems for planning, however, because it consists of a complex and interdependent network of small, medium and large firms squeezed between giant suppliers and retailers.

## Background

Textiles and clothing is still a major manufacturing industry, with a gross output of over £10 billion. Its net output is larger than food and drink manufacturing, and about as large as iron and steel, coal mining and shipbuilding put together. It is still one of the largest manufacturing contributors to UK export earnings. The industry accounts for nearly one in ten of all UK manufacturing jobs and is a major employer of women. The industry is spread across a large part of the UK, and between its different branches dominates manufacturing employment in, for example, many areas of East London (clothing); Leicestershire and

Nottinghamshire (clothing, hosiery and knitwear); and West Yorkshire and Lancashire (wool textiles).

In contrast with other European countries which have seen the need to maintain the viability of their textiles and clothing industry, the UK has adopted a non-interventionist posture. In countries such as Italy, France and Belgium, substantial aid packages have been developed. No such sectoral support exists in the UK, with the result that the UK is disadvantaged against its major high cost competitors. Although the National Economic Development Council (NEDC) has produced various plans for modernisation, the industry's powerlessness has led to an over reliance on the goodwill of the multinational producers and the retail giants. This reliance has been largely misplaced. The sought-after investment has not taken place, and is unlikely to without planned intervention. UK governments have instead put their faith in the worldwide Multi-Fibre Agreement (a part of the General Agreement on Tariffs and Trade). The MFA, first negotiated in 1973 and renewed in 1983, was initially designed as a short-term measure to regulate the volume of textiles and clothing imports from the low cost, less developed countries, offering a breathing space within which the industry could restructure. In fact it has failed to check the rise in import penetration, and has, therefore, proved inadequate as a cornerstone of state policy towards the industry.

First, the decline of the UK industry is *not* mainly the result of Third World imports. In textiles, for example, less than one-sixth of job losses over the years can be attributed to this cause. Instead, a growing share of imports comes from high cost areas such as the EEC and USA. Second, the quotas did not anticipate the recession of the late 1970's, when low cost producers were able to increase their share of the stagnant UK market. Third, the quotas have been avoided both legally and illegally; for example, multinationals have (legitimately) switched capacity from low wage countries covered by the MFA to others, like Tunisia and the Philippines, which are not. Likewise, the MFA fails to confront the problem of 'outward processing', in which companies export semi-finished garments for completion overseas, and reimport them for sale in the UK. The TUC proposal for a 'social clause', ensuring that all imported goods are manufactured in plants offering reasonable pay, working conditions and trade union rights, has also been ignored. Finally, and more fundamentally, protection has been justified on the grounds that it will provide a 'breathing space' for domestic manufacturers to reinvest and regain their competitive position. But the UK industry's traditional reluctance to invest and modernise (and the reluctance of financial institutions to let them do so) belies this hope, suggesting instead that a protected environment may sustain complacency and inertia.

A UK industry can survive, but only through fairly rapid investment, specialisation, and an emphasis on quality production. This will create substantial jobs by replacing imported goods from developed countries, while at the same time securing a planned outlet for imports from less developed countries. It requires that the fragmentation of the industry be overcome through concerted intervention by government and trade unions.

### The structure of the sector

The UK industry has undergone a rapid transformation since 1945. Previously it was dominated by small and medium sized enterprises, often family owned, but this began to change after the war. Several factors contributed to this:

• A growing volume of trade together with new mass production processes (particularly for oil based synthetic fibres) which favoured the economies of scale offered by the larger units and vertical integration.

• Government policies in the UK, Europe and Japan encouraged mergers and takeovers, with the aim of increasing efficiency.

• The emerging textiles giants with better access to capital were able to absorb smaller firms in great quantities. The result was vertically integrated corporations such as Courtaulds.

• Increasingly capital intensive production processes accentuated the trend — hitherto more pronounced in the production of yarns and fabrics than of garments.

The industry is now split between the multi-plant, multi-sector firms and a myriad of small to medium sized ones. The extent to which concentration will increase further is uncertain. One significant factor is the development of capital intensive clothing technology, which since the 1970's has been catching up with that in textiles. Computer aided manufacturing and design processes, for example, will have far reaching effects on an industry which has traditionally relied on skilled labour rather than sophisticated machinery. However, it is by no means inevitable that all production will ultimately be controlled by the textiles giants; indeed in recent years the process of concentration has slowed down. While small textile firms have disappeared in great numbers, this has not been the case to the same extent in the clothing industry, thanks to simpler technology, the ability to identify specialized market niches and the role of the major retailers. Indeed, hundreds of new clothing companies have appeared in recent years in areas like London and the West Midlands. Nonetheless, the large companies have found it desirable to acquire substantial numbers of smaller clothing enterprises. Fashions move erratically and larger companies have an interest in diversification.

The dominant characteristic of garment production is, however, its fragmentation. Yarn and fabric worldwide tends to be dominated by a few multinationals: likewise, UK retailing is dominated by a few multiple chains such as Marks and Spencers and C&A. But squeezed in the middle is a vast array of fiercely competing garment manufacturers, for most of which success or failure depends on striking a fine balance between the monopolistic practices of suppliers and the exacting demands of retailers.

Significantly, the growing importance of multinationals in garment production has done little to affect this fragmentation. In a group such as Courtaulds, individual subsidiaries will compete against each other for major orders from Marks and Spencer, as well as against independent producers. This reflects a degree of retailer power which even Courtaulds seems unable or unwilling to change.

It is possible that this, and other factors, will lead to a period of relative stability in the structure of the industry. The trends towards concentration in yarns, fabrics, and knitted garments may now be complete, while in clothing, smaller firms may be able to compete with larger rivals because their flexibility compensates for an inability to benefit from economies of scale. This will all depend, however, on a range of factors such as retail policies and the introduction of new technology, the combined effects of which must remain unpredictable.

### The power of the multinationals

Worldwide, fewer than 40 multinationals dominate the textiles and clothing industry. In the UK three groupings have come to dominate major parts of the industry — Vantona, Courtaulds, and Tootal. Between them, they account for more than half the employment in the UK industry and an even greater proportion of output. While the trend towards concentration has generally been welcomed, it is clear that any analysis of the industry's decline cannot ignore its effects.

From the 1960's onwards the multinationals have been transferring production and investment between countries, products and industries in the search for maximum worldwide profits. In the 1970's as the world recession deepened, more and more plants closed down, only to reopen in other countries. As often as not, the move was from Western industrialised countries to poor Third World countries with cheap, non-unionised labour — often female — doing deskilled work. The 'international division of labour' is a term often used in connection with the industry. A decade ago a textile product would probably have been made in just one country. Now it is likely to be the product of several countries, or even continents. For example, a batch of clothing might start as a fabric imported from West Germany, to be cut out in the UK using new laser techniques. It could then be sent to the Philippines or South Korea to be sewn and finished, and finally reimported into the UK for sale in the shops.

The Meridian Group, part of Courtaulds, provides an example of this practice of so-called 'outward processing'. After a long period of consultation with the unions, the company set up two factories overseas (one in Portugal and the other in Morocco) to make up garments for the lower priced end of the European market. Meridian factories in Nottingham produce knitted fabric for the overseas plants, which make it up and ship it back to the UK for finishing, packaging and distribution. The unions have been faced with a stark choice; either to accept two-thirds of the work, or else have all the work shifted overseas. In such circumstances they had no real choice. UK manufacturers also buy complete garments abroad to supplement their garment ranges, and improve their profitability: for example, Courtaulds sell Italian made tights under well-known British brand names.

Now considered to be the largest textiles group in the world, Courtaulds illustrates well the process of concentration and its effects. With international interests in fibres, fabrics, garments, plastics, paints, packaging and speciality chemicals, Courtaulds exerts a major influence on the future of the UK industry. Courtaulds has achieved this position in progressive stages. From the 1920's onwards a great deal of its power came from capturing a major part of the man-made fibres clothing market. It was not until the 1950's that synthetic fibres developed by companies like ICI challenged its position. Courtaulds found itself virtually excluded from a rapidly expanding synthetic fibre market, and suffering serious problems. The need for a new strategy was obvious, and Courtaulds moved into new products, such as paint, packaging, and plastics. This did not improve the position, and so under a new generation of directors, led by C.F. Kearton, Courtaulds started to buy up textiles companies on a grand scale. Courtaulds needed to buy up, or to dominate, its competitors in order to develop its own synthetic fibres, and to guarantee a market for Rayon. Some £400 million was spent in acquiring 30 or more companies mainly in Lancashire. The government welcomed this and increased grants and other incentives. A further £40 million was spent on a major plan of investment and the 'streamlining' of production, resulting in the closure of 20 mills and the loss of many jobs which government grants had been meant to save.

The company was gradually increasing its interests in garment manufacture, and so gaining customers for its new synthetic fibres such as 'Celon'. In the open market Celon could never have survived competition with ICI's fabrics, but by buying up Clutsom Penn, Northgate and Kayser Bonder, Courtaulds had the market sewn up. By 1970 it was clear that Courtaulds had changed dramatically. In effect it had built up a vertically integrated company which owned everything in the textile chain from South African forests producing wood pulp for artificial fibres, through to garment manufacturers and high street shops.

However, from 1975 onwards the European textiles industry faced massive recession. Courtaulds responded to the slump in textiles demand and in European profitability with a rapid restructuring plan. The impact of this was felt throughout the UK as plant after plant, often recently opened with large government grants, closed. The strategy has been to eliminate as much of the company's operation as possible unless it produced a high return, by reducing dependence on the recession-hit textile industry, and by reinvesting in profitable new product areas such as paint and plastics. The result has been a rapid cut back in artificial fibres, leading to massive job losses. In addition, Courtaulds has transferred clothing production to cheap labour countries such as Portugal. Courtauld's subsidiaries in the Nottingham area shed some 2,000 jobs between 1978 and 1983 — around one-third of its local workforce.

### The future strategy of Courtaulds
It is clear that the Courtaulds of the future will be very different from the Courtaulds of today. Textiles, especially fibres, are destined for a much smaller role compared to paints, consumer goods, plastics and packaging. Moreover, much of the company's remaining interest in textiles may go abroad.

Courtaulds may well come to be seen as a classic industrial example of the Thatcher era. It has shown a marked lack of commitment to the UK textiles industry. The frantic pursuit of profits is taking it away from the UK and perhaps out of textiles completely. Its strategy is *draining* the industry of investment, causing the destruction of thousands of jobs. Can we believe that the decisions taken by such firms, left to themselves, hold the key to a dynamic and expanding textiles industry?

## The smaller firms

Despite the trend of the last 40 years, thousands of small and medium sized independent producers exist side by side with multinationals. There is no evidence to suggest that smaller firms will disappear. Small firms can exploit the flexibility of small batch production, utilise new production processes and computer technology, introduce more 'design content' into their products and target their ranges on particular market segments. The sweatshops will also survive — not through efficient production techniques, but by exploiting the skills of workers with few opportunities for other employment; in particular, ethnic minorities and women. The continued significance of small firms, however, poses specific problems for a planned approach to the industry.

## Is small beautiful?

Smaller production units, particularly in the fast changing 'fashion market', can provide flexibility and a level of innovation not always found in the large corporations. But they also suffer from a lack of capital investment; poor management and marketing; high gearing; inadequate training; and little forward planning. These weaknesses are exacerbated by massive import penetration and declining competitiveness.

Many smaller firms depend to a dangerous extent on one product line, or on one retailer or wholesaler. This has often proved fatal. When orders have not been renewed, firms have lacked the ability to develop alternative markets. Access to finance also proves a major stumbling block, with many firms (mostly small and privately owned) not achieving levels of profitability high enough to enable or encourage them to keep their machinery up to date. Such firms either decline as their profitability falls, or else compensate for low productivity by increasing exploitation of their workers.

## Small firms: a future?

It is open to question whether the increasing control of the industry by a small number of multinationals is inevitable. Some evidence suggests that the level of concentration in clothing will not necessarily reach the levels found in textiles. Basic textiles may well prove to be the sphere of production best suited to high levels of concentration, while the rest of the industry — notably clothing — may need greater flexibility. Evidence for this comes from several countries including Italy, the USA and France, where the industry has been evolving towards a complex, but highly flexible, system, linking small and medium sized firms with large contractors and distribution chains. This trend may well ultimately prevail in the UK. In Italy, however, the success of the industry has been bolstered by extensive support from both local and central government, including the provision of local resource centres for clothing manufacturers and the availability of investment finance through state-controlled banks. This must provide a lesson for future UK policies.

**A low wage industry: the effects**
The clothing industry has traditionally had a poor image, and one that has been well-deserved, with back street sweatshops, poor working conditions even in some of the larger factories, low wages and relatively low levels of unionisation (below 50 per cent for clothing workers). The textiles industry, employing more male workers (around 40 per cent as opposed to 25 per cent in the clothing trade), has fared slightly better. However, wages for both textiles and clothing workers, particularly in non-unionised smaller firms, have always been low. It is sometimes claimed that low wages are necessary for the continued survival of the UK industry — how else, it is argued, can it compete with the increasing flood of imports, or export at competitive prices?

But the largest area of import growth is now in high fashion goods from developed countries in Europe and elsewhere, where wages of clothing workers are *above* those in the UK. These imports compete on the basis of design and quality — not just price. This is the direction in which British firms must move: they certainly cannot expect to be able to survive indefinitely by increasing exploitation of their workers in order to gain a cost advantage over the less developed countries! Low wages do not therefore mean that competitiveness will be preserved, or that the UK will become an attractive manufacturing base once again. Wages are only one factor in labour unit costs, and low wages actually work against the industry in many ways. It becomes more difficult to recruit and keep skilled workers, and wage exploitation can become a *substitute* for much needed investment.

Wages Councils, unless transformed, do not offer an answer to the problems of low pay — they enshrine it. The wage rates set by Wages Councils in clothing are low — but even so well over a third of employers (small firms in particular) pay less. The number of Council Inspectors has been cut, and visits are very rare. Even this minimal protection will be weakened by the present Government's proposed "reforms" of the Wages Councils.

## Homeworking

In the clothing trade alone, in April 1982, official estimates show that about 14,500 out of 36,500 employees were homeworkers (though such figures are undoubtedly an underestimate). To the employer, homeworkers and part-time workers represent a saving in labour costs, since they seldom enjoy additions to basic pay such as overtime, sick pay and holidays. Homeworkers do not even enjoy basic rights such as redundancy pay and protection from unfair dismissal. Both part-time working and (in particular) homeworking enable employers to respond flexibly to changing demand. Predominantly female, homeworkers are rarely represented by trade unions, having little chance of collective action with other homeworkers and (because of domestic responsibilities) few opportunities for other paid work. Calls to abolish homeworking will not necessarily benefit women who need to work at home. But this need is ruthlessly exploited by many employers.

## The stranglehold of the retailers

Any analysis of the UK textiles and clothing industry must start with the retailers, whose significance has become even more marked with the continuing "high street revolution", as new outlets threaten the dominance of the traditional giants. The two factors of greatest significance are, first, the established dominance of the large store groups such as Marks and Spencer, and, second, the rise of 'new' retail multiples like Next, Principles, the revamping of Richard Shops, and the changing ownership of traditional stores such as BHS and Debenhams.

During the postwar years the handful of giant chains were able to push a large section of the British clothing industry toward long runs of standardised garments, encouraging the trend towards the concentration of production in large firms. Competition between these retailers was mainly on the basis of price, rather than design.

The concentration of buying power also made UK manufacturers very vulnerable to import competition; from the 1960's retailers managed to sharpen price competition by contracting work to low wage countries such as Hong Kong and Taiwan. From the 1970's the retailers have maintained their profits, despite periods of weakening demand, by cutting the prices and profits of their suppliers. This has been achieved both by using Third World suppliers, and through the dependence of many British clothing manufacturers, including the multinationals, on the major retailers.

The major high street retailers have combined their buying power with other forms of control over manufacturers. Two main approaches to purchasing have been adopted by retailers. On the one hand, middle range retailers such as Marks and Spencer have adopted a policy of extremely close control over their suppliers. 'M&S' is involved in every aspect of the manufacturer's business, from quality control to the type of machinery the firm invests in. With detailed knowledge of the firm's costs, M&S is in a position to determine the firm's profit mark-up. This strategy is built on the high level of dependency of many manufacturers on M&S, which often accounts for around 90 per cent of their production. On the other hand, retailers such as C&A do not concern themselves with how an article is made but only with the finished product, and most particularly with the price of that product. This strategy is associated with high levels of subcontracting of parts of the production process by suppliers, and a squeezing of prices and profits all down the line. Many subcontractors for C&A goods are offered "making prices" which do not allow them to produce the garments in legal conditions in Britain. Such multiples are therefore directly implicated in the proliferation of sweatshop conditions in the UK industry. C&A has a policy of not buying more than one quarter of any company's manufacturing output, and around one third of their suppliers are changed each year.

These different approaches to the control of production are generally linked to different approaches to design. Until recently, M&S has done most of its own design work, while retailers which take a more 'arms length' approach have tended to rely on the manufacturers to do their own designs.

Since the beginning of the 1980's, however, there has been an important change in British retailing, which is having corresponding effects on the clothing manufacturing sector. The collapse of the mass market, which has until now been dominated by the major retailers, has been paralleled by the growth of designer-led, quality fashion associated with the new wave of retail chains such as Next, Principles, and Richards. The increasing importance of these retailers has also encouraged many of the high street giants to consider raising the quality of their ranges.

This new departure in retailing in the UK has major implications for the UK clothing industry. As retailers have become more concerned with design and quality, as well as price factors, UK sourcing has expanded considerably. However, the retailers are demanding a new form of "flexible specialisation" from their suppliers, and have proved perfectly willing to look to some of the EEC countries, in particular Italy, to source their ranges. The UK clothing industry therefore faces a new opportunity but also a new threat of competition from European imports.

There are several facets to the restructuring which retailers are now demanding. Design becomes a vital stage of the production process, but whereas in the past design has been done exclusively by either the retailer or the manufacturer, an increasing proportion of manufacturers are now developing their ranges in collaboration with the buyers for retail chains, many of whom themselves have a design background. This process is particularly in evidence in the middle and upper segments of the women's market, and in leisurewear. The two-way process is seen as a vital part of increasing fashion and variety in the shops.

The change in retailing strategy also demands of manufacturers the flexibility to produce a wide range of styles and to switch production between them in response to short run trends in sales. There has been a significant move away from the traditional two-season, Spring-Autumn collections, towards as many as five or six changes a year, with correspondingly shorter production runs and shorter lead times. Many retailers have installed Electronic Point of Sale (EPOS) systems which enable them to gather precise data on each style's sales performance, and adjust orders accordingly. Lead times of six to eight weeks, or even less, have become common.

In addition to the changes outlined above, most retail chains are now looking for longer term relationships with a smaller number of suppliers. They also expect suppliers to have a reasonably diversified customer base so that they are less dependent than they have been in the past, and more in touch with a wider range of designs.

The growth of non-price competition, and the new relationship emerging between retailers and suppliers, has reduced the importance of clothing imports from low wage developing countries. However, imports from EEC countries are rising. While sourcing from the Far East is not worthwhile because lead times are too long, minimum production runs too large, quality control too difficult, and close collaboration with suppliers impossible, the same problems do not apply to some of the EEC countries, and in particular Italy.

The international success of the Italian franchise operation, Benetton, lies in its ability to produce flexibly and to supply the required goods within a very short space of time. But it is not entirely evident that British manufacturers will, in the long term, prove capable of responding to the challenge of the new fashion market. Failure to do so would be to cede the growing and profitable fashion market to well organised and well supported design-led producers in Europe and elsewhere.

## Planning for textiles and clothing

As with the motor industry, a strategy for textiles and clothing cannot rely on a single instrument of planning. The growing tendency (on the one hand) towards a complex pattern of interdependence between large producers and retailers, and (on the other) the myriad of small and medium sized firms, pose equally complex problems for a socialist strategy towards the industry. The view promoted by the NEDC that the way ahead for the industry lies solely with the concentration of production in large enterprises can be challenged, however. First, it is evident that multinationals, such as Courtaulds, have no inherent commitment to manufacture in the UK — or even to the textiles and clothing industry on a global basis. They operate essentially as investment institutions, transferring capital between companies, sectors, and countries. Only radical state intervention will reverse Courtaulds' disinvestment in UK textiles. Second, the experience of workers in such conglomerates has often been one of isolation and powerlessness. Each Courtaulds subsidiary appears to operate autonomously, often in competition with other subsidiaries. Trade union bargaining focuses on this level. Yet subsidiaries are autonomous only within the confines of a corporate strategy, which defines production targets and access to investment. This corporate level has been inadequately challenged by trade unions, fragmented as they are by competition and by the absence of links between plants. Such problems are clearly exacerbated by the need to develop links between plants in different sectors. Third, the nature of the industry is such that there is a need for small and medium sized enterprises capable of responding rapidly and flexibly to changes in fashion, often on the basis of small batch production. Many areas have been abandoned by the conglomerates because they represent too small a market, yet have been taken up enthusiastically by smaller concerns.

This is not to fall into a naive 'small is beautiful' argument. Small and medium sized firms must shoulder a large part of the responsibility for the declining competitiveness of the industry, with their underinvestment, lack of innovation, reactionary management, low pay, and poor working conditions. But since it is clear they will continue to account for a sizeable share of the industry's output, this poses a problem for socialist planning. Discussions have tended to focus on the need to plan or nationalize 'key' companies in each sector, presumably on the assumption that smaller firms are either irrelevant or could be controlled by controlling the conglomerates, yet this assumption is by no means valid. Instead, a wide variety of planning mechanisms, operating at different levels, needs to be developed within an overall strategy for the industry.

## Planning through industrial democracy

Trade union strength in the textiles and clothing industry is weak in comparison with other sectors. The unions have fought for their share of the reduced workforce, and have continually shunned collaboration. Yet large areas remain non-unionized, particularly in clothing, and many plants are unionized in name only. Women, who form a large part of the workforce, have often been doubly constrained from taking part in union activity — by domestic labour, and by intimidation from management. Union weakness is thus easily exploited, especially where the workforce in one plant can be set against another.

Overall, unions have been weakened by a continuous assault from closures, relocations, state-aided restructuring, archaic management and the consequent disillusionment of the workforce. Union organisation must be built up at all levels. For example, socialist local authorities in textiles and clothing areas could finance officers to help co-ordinate trade union recruitment and education, in particular among women and ethnic minorities. But meanwhile it would be over optimistic to expect a full response to industrial democracy proposals.

This raises crucial problems. Many large firms in the industry now have substantial interests overseas, and the growth of outward processing will continue. Even the reimposition of exchange controls would not necessarily prevent the expansion of overseas subsidiaries at the expense of domestic plants. This problem is exacerbated in the case of multi-sector firms such as Courtaulds, where planning could speed up the shift of investment away from textiles and clothing, and into the more capital intensive activities such as paint and plastics, unless business plans cover the *entire* range of the company's activities. Moreover, while such plans address many of the issues arising in the case of such companies as Courtaulds, the timing and policing of such plans will clearly raise significant problems: for example, could large firms move investment out of the industry while the planning machinery is being assembled? Furthermore, other fundamental questions need to be considered. Should the current multi-sectoral mix within existing enterprises be taken for granted, even though there may be real conflicts between corporate investment strategies and sectoral planning priorities? How can the conglomerates be broken up into smaller, more accountable units organised on the basis of function? Such restructuring could clearly be based on an extension of public ownership on the one hand, and a close relationship between sectoral plans and their execution on the other. However, simultaneous work would also be necessary at the shop floor level if the type of industrial democracy on which our strategy depends is to come about. Unions must be brought together at the sectoral level and be representative of their members if democratic planning for the conglomerates is to be meaningful.

Smaller firms must be brought into the planning system at a different level, though it should be stressed that in the textiles and clothing industry they cannot be seen as peripheral to a sectoral strategy. Even though the prospects for planning through industrial democracy in such firms seem remote at present, there appears to be increasing potential for sectoral planning at a local level. A number of local authorities, notably West Midlands County Council, Leeds and Sheffield, the Greater London Council and a number of London Boroughs have taken steps towards local sectoral planning. In Nottingham, an informal working party of members from four unions at District Officer and shop floor level is working on its own plan for the industry. Even with the limited resources available to most local authorities, local sectoral plans are beginning to achieve some success in channelling co-ordinated investment (from both public and private sectors) into their representative industries. More significantly they are beginning to open up a public area for debate on the future of key industries.

Under a Labour Government, such forms of planning could assume major importance in national industrial strategy, especially in the more fragmented industries such as clothing and textiles. Meanwhile, they have an important exemplary role to play. First, they must demonstrate their ability to mobilise participation at shop floor and district level in identifying weaknesses in the organisation and structure of the industry within particular localities. Second, they must provide a framework in which such problems can be met by appropriate investment or other intervention. No blueprint is available, and each area must experiment with its own models and develop practices appropriate to it. The task of the Labour Government will be to produce a framework sensitive enough to make a coherent national strategy. Already many Labour controlled local authorities are anticipating this, and have set up a national co-ordinating group known as "Local Action for Textiles and Clothing". In addition to providing an information exchange, LATC will promote collaboration between authorities in order to avoid wasteful competition and duplication, and will work towards a co-ordinated national strategy for the industry.

### Local initiatives
Local clothing sector studies undertaken by a number of councils have led to the development of packages of support for the industry. Notably, the London Borough of Hackney has pioneered the 'fashion centre' concept which provides a range of facilities on a collective basis for firms in the area. Collective provision retains the flexibility of smaller firms while enabling them to take advantage of economies of scale. Facilities include marketing and showroom provision to bring buyers and producers together. This bridges a major divide in the UK industry which has been responsible for a great deal of import penetration. Computer aided design and manufacture will also be provided in the centre for firms unable to bear the capital costs alone but which would benefit from its use on a shared basis. Business and production advice is also available. Discussions with the Greater London Enterprise Board have sought to bring the centre's local knowledge and contacts together with the Board's financial resources. The concept has now been taken up by other local authorities, notably in Nottingham, where a fashion centre was opened in 1984. Glasgow, Leeds and Lancashire are also exploring ways of adapting the concept to their own local needs, while the West Midlands County Council has recently done this by opening its "Clothing Resource Centre" in Birmingham. A wide range of other initiatives for the industry have also been developed across the country in response to local conditions, but increasingly informed by a national perspective on the need for planned restructuring in the sector. Some of these schemes, especially the fashion centres, have encountered considerable difficulties in their early years of operation. Objectives have often been unclear and even contradictory. Fashion centres have been criticised for supporting back street sweatshops and for providing an ineffective lever for the improvement of wages and working conditions. Their day-to-day operation is often characterised by vigorous debates and disagreements over priorities and perceptions. However, it is also clear that they have provided both valuable support for many jobs in the industry and a learning process which will

inform the future development of intervention. Policies are being continually reviewed and refined, and it is this spirit of innovation and experiment which must permeate Labour's industrial policy nationally.

## Retailing and planning

The control exercised by the big retailers derives from their dominance of the home market and, more directly, because many firms depend on them for virtually all of their output. This planning function, particularly in the case of Marks and Spencer, has evolved into an extremely sophisticated mechanism — largely determining the producer's investment, technology, management, production, sourcing, quality and pricing. Certainly in this sector it is a mechanism which cannot be ignored by a Labour Government. The challenge is to describe how, in practice, it can be harnessed.

Extending planning to the retail sector raises major problems (see Chapter 6). The successful retail giants have far greater knowledge of the market and the industry than a government department or planning institution is likely to be able to acquire; their profits are dependent neither on public finance nor public markets, nor indeed on selling goods made in the UK rather than abroad. The kind of influence which it may be possible to extend over industrial companies is therefore less easy to apply to the retail sector, given that company decisions can only be influenced through the effective use of commercial leverage (provided by, for example, equity finance and loans). In the case of the retail sector, however, land use planning and control may provide added leverage. There are, moreover, a number of options currently under examination by the Local Action for Textiles and Clothing Group in consultation with the labour movement. First, retailers could be made legally responsible for the employment practices of their suppliers — since, as we have argued, these are often dependent on the low making prices offered. Second, the significance of taxation as a lever over the retail giants is being explored. Retailers could be allowed to "choose" their tax regime through their sourcing policies, with maximum tax advantage going to firms which not only sourced their products domestically, but which also positively assisted suppliers to invest and modernise.

Other measures which might also be adopted include: first, the provision of incentives to retailers — for example, for research, product development and design — conditional on production through UK based manufacturers; next, the seconding of buyers from the large retailers into textiles and clothing firms, especially in the case of those firms assisted by enterprise boards; and third, support for a 'trade' body to promote UK textiles and clothing at home and abroad, working with local fashion centres. Such a body would place emphasis on good quality, high value-added goods. In addition, planned purchasing should include agreement on quotas to be taken from the UK industry and the Less Developed Countries, taking into account the provisions of a renegotiated Multi-Fibre Agreement.

This strategy could play a considerable role in sustaining and expanding the industry, initially through the substitution of UK-manufactured garments for imports from other developed countries. This would be more than just protectionism in a new guise. It would use the existing power of the retailers to reorganise manufacturers — small, medium, and large — to improve investment and production plans in exchange for a larger share of the market.

However, a retailing policy must go beyond the major chain stores, and producers should be encouraged to diversify their outlets both within the UK and by increasing the UK industry's share of the world market. Local fashion centres, grounded in the industry in their own areas, could play a major role in this process and their development should be encouraged. A national network of fashion centres, with one in every area where the industry is a significant employer, would help to reclaim national and international orders through a co-ordinated UK marketing strategy.

### Conclusions

While the diversity of the textiles and clothing industry's problems is bewildering, it also gives rise to exciting possibilities for planning. It clearly shows the need for both sensitivity towards the industry, and for a complex pattern of intervention at both local and central government levels. Local initiatives — building an alliance between Councils and trade unions — are a precondition of these possibilities being realized under the next Labour Government, as is a coherent labour movement strategy towards the conglomerates such as Courtaulds. What we do now in the textiles and clothing industry could be an example of how a national strategy can be built up from local effort and initiatives.

CHAPTER 12

# The Politics of Socialist Enterprise

In this concluding chapter we summarise the main themes of the book, and at the same time we outline the *politics* of an economic strategy based on socialist enterprise.

In many ways, of course, the book reflects the major shift in political debate which has taken place under the Thatcher Governments. The Tories' success in undermining the credibility of government action to create jobs partly reflects the perceived failure of the last Labour Government: certainly, reflation is unlikely to get the rehabilitation it deserves until *after* a future government has proved it works. Future generations of students may indeed look back on this period as a bizarre denial of rational economics, and wonder at policies designed to end unemployment by causing further unemployment — much as we wonder at medieval doctors who sought to end suffering by causing further suffering. But, however incompetently Tory policies have been implemented, they have had a kind of rationale to them — the brutal rationale of economic power dominated by private interest.

The Tories have sought to reverse Britain's economic decline by *strengthening* the corporate power of private industrial, retail and financial firms. The result, not surprisingly, has actually been to accelerate Britain's downward spiral alarmingly. The special combination of factors which underlies our economic and industrial weakness has been compounded under Tory policies — namely, the overseas orientation and short-term perspective of the City, and the excessive encouragement given to corporate growth by merger; the extent to which "British" industry is in reality an offshore arm of multinational producers which have no special loyalty to the long-term needs of the British economy and people; the uncertain and limited opportunities in the domestic market; and the failure of post-war government industrial policies to engage with corporate decision making.

We have argued that, in order to reverse Britain's decline, new forms of democratic, socialist enterprise will be needed, and that the power of private interest, expressed through the market, will need to be challenged. This argument may raise a further question in peoples' minds: how can such policies enable Britain to compete with more successful economies, the prosperity of which seems to derive from the freedom enjoyed by private capital? Our answer is that, in Britain's case, the major decisions of individual enterprises tend to reflect a short-term and limited perspective, one which is contrary to the country's long-term needs. In other words, the objectives of British capitalism, as a matter of historical fact, do not coincide with those of the British people.

We have gone one step further and argued that the advent of new forms of product-led competition requires us to place major enterprise decisions in the context of some overall plan for particular industries and processes. The institutional framework which underpins strategic planning varies between different countries, being built on particular national traditions. We too need an institutional framework in Britain which recognises our own constraints and opportunities — one which challenges private corporate power and lays the basis for socialist enterprise.

This approach will inevitably bring us into confrontation with the rule of market forces. Market mechanisms typically ignore the broader costs of private decision making and the needs of future generations. More profoundly, markets further strengthen private corporate power, deepening the already undemocratic nature of decision making in the British economy. For these reasons we share much of the now traditional critique of the market put forward by other socialists.

This does not mean, however, that market mechanisms will have no role to play in the kind of economy we want, or that we should continue to embrace uncritically traditional concepts of socialist planning. Nationalisation of the commanding heights and the central allocation of resources are unlikely to achieve our objectives of greater democracy and efficiency. Nationalisation is now widely associated with bureaucracy, insensitivity to need and a degree of overcentralisation which denies initiative and involvement. The very concept of "the commanding heights" has, moreover, been undermined by changes in industrial structure. The growth of multinational production is perhaps the best illustration of this. Moreover, few sectors are, in fact, dominated by monopoly producers — industrial sectors vary greatly, with the manufacturing function often now less significant than retailing or finance.

It is not only changes in industrial structure which limit the relevance of traditional approaches to planning. Equally important is the lack of scope under these approaches for working people to exercise control — either individual or collective — over the major economic decisions affecting their lives. People, in our upside down economy, have always been put in second place. The industrial policies of the last Labour Government were, sadly, little exception. It was not that radical policies were abandoned — rather that the policies were never sufficiently radical in the first place. Both left and right in the party shared the belief that the *legislative* power of government was sufficient to effect change. Hence the faith placed, by the left at least, in planning agreements. We have argued that this faith was misplaced for two main reasons. First, planning agreements — if implemented — would quite probably have *undermined* trade union involvement. They would have been negotiated over the heads of working people, and in many ways would have marked little change from the normally cosy relationship between major firms and their sponsoring departments. Perhaps as a result, there was only ever limited pressure from trade unions at the company level to conclude planning agreements. (Ironically, this has been taken to indicate the lukewarm commitment of working people to industrial democracy.) Second, as we have argued throughout this book, major corporate decisions can only be influenced through the exercise of *commercial* leverage. Legislation can, of course, have a commercial impact, but it is unlikely to be effective on its own. Even commercial leverage is likely to be rather negative in character. The power to initiate research, develop new products and processes, and to attract financial backing — the *positive* capacity for enterprise — would remain firmly in private hands.

We have therefore sought to develop a strategy for *socialist* enterprise. Our objective can only be fully realised over a number of decades, and would require far more than just formal changes in ownership. People themselves must acquire the will and the means to influence the major decisions which affect their lives. Such a "cultural" shift must go hand in hand with changes in the structure of economic decision making. Hence the emphasis we have placed on self-management and decentralisation, and on extending rights to individuals, their unions and their communities. Hence, also, the wider concept of progress we employ — one which embraces the household, in particular, as well as paid work in the orthodox sense.

This strategy for socialist enterprise cuts across the traditional boundaries between planning and the market. For example, if working people are to influence sector strategies and the decisions of individual companies, both planning and market mechanisms will be involved. Trade unions in steel and motors will have a mutual interest in, on the one hand, the quality and reliability of steel production and, on the other, the demand for steel. But this does not mean that all the decisions on co-ordinating production — much less consumption — can feasibly be planned.

In this book we have often focused on the short-term, and in particular on policies for a Labour Government elected in the late 1980's. However, our emphasis on socialist enterprise has equally important implications for longer-term strategies.

Socialist visions of the future are often somewhat hazy: nightmare images of Lang's "Metropolis" jostle with the more comforting communist Utopia portrayed by Marx, in which people — freed by technology from the need to work — will be able to fulfil their creative potential. More recently, Andre Gorz has bid "farewell to the proletariat" in his discussion of post-industrial socialism. For Gorz, technical changes affecting paid work have profoundly important *political* implications. Automation will not just make paid work increasingly unnecessary: workers will also have less and less control over their working lives. The modern production process is deliberately designed, Gorz argues, to eliminate all discretion and initiative on the part of workers. And as a result, workers will become incapable of acting as agents of social change. They will also increasingly accept the values and goals of consumer capitalism. Instead, Gorz argues, only the so-called "non-class" forces — women, blacks, environmentalists — will be able to change society. He goes on to argue that these forces will increasingly reflect individual demands for self-expression and fulfilment, as capitalism is superseded.

The first problem with Gorz's hypothesis is the implication that it is futile to challenge the existing, undemocratic, concentration of economic power. He places enormous trust in the benign development of capitalism. But no such trust is justified: capitalist development will continue to be shaped by the demands of private profitability and will not unwittingly lay the foundations for socialism. There is absolutely no reason to assume that an increasingly automated system of production will lead to the workless, leisure society at the core of so many socialist dreams of the future.

Second, the concept of non-class forces is very suspect. Many women are of course employed, often in part-time work. Moreover, while these so-called 'forces' will undoubtedly play a vital role in transforming society, their exclusion from the production process also limits the leverage which they can exert.

Gorz also fails to explain how these different groupings will be brought together. The basis of their oppression is not necessarily shared, and divisions of sex, race and age may prevent any easy identity of interests.

Our strategy for socialist enterprise therefore implies a rejection of many of the assumptions made by the prophets of post-industrial socialism. The advantages of this strategy are, we would argue, three-fold. First, it links broader political objectives with the need for economic survival and success — something which any credible strategy has to face up to. Second, it reflects the special characteristics of the British economy, and the need for shifts in the structure of power within it. Third, it involves a recognition that this can only be achieved by linking socialism firmly with greater democracy. Only in this way can we lay the basis for an irreversible shift of power — one which is rooted in people's control over their own lives, at home and at work. For only then can socialist enterprise be put into practice.

# BIBLIOGRAPHY

## Preface

CONFERENCE OF SOCIALIST ECONOMISTS LONDON WORKING
GROUP, *The Alternative Economic Strategy: A Labour Movement
Response to the Economic Crisis* (CSE Books and Labour Co-ordinating
Committee, London, 1980)
SAM AARONOVITCH, *The Road from Thatcherism: The Alternative
Economic Strategy* (Lawrence and Wishart, London, 1981)
ANNA COOTE, *The AES: a new starting point* (New Socialist, Nov/Dec,
1981)
ANDREW GLYN AND JOHN HARRISON, *The British Economic Disaster*
(Pluto Press, London, 1981)

## Chapter 1: Introduction  Chapter 2: Economic Power in Britain

KAREL WILLIAMS ET AL, *Why are the British Bad at Manufacturing?*
(Routledge and Kegan Paul, London, 1983)
KEITH SMITH, *The British Economic Crisis* (Pelican, Middlesex, 1984)
BEN FINE AND LAURENCE HARRIS, *The Peculiarities of the British
Economy* (Lawrence and Wishart, London, 1985)
WILLIAM KEEGAN, *Mrs. Thatcher's Economic Experiment* (Penguin,
London, 1985)
NICOLAS KALDOR, *The Economic Consequences of Mrs. Thatcher*
(Duckworth, London, 1983)
PETER RIDDELL, *Thatcher's Government* (Blackwell, London, 1985)
BOB ROWTHORN, *Capitalism, Conflict and Inflation* (Lawrence and
Wishart, London, 1980)

## Chapter 3: Planning Now

HILARY WAINWRIGHT AND DAVE ELLIOT, *The Lucas Plan: a New
Trade Unionism in the Making* (Allison and Busby, London, 1982)
JUDY WAJCMAN, *Women in Control: the Dilemmas of a Workers' Co-
operative* (Open University Press, Milton Keynes, 1983)
TONY ECCLES, *Under New Management* (Pan, London, 1981)
JENNY THORNLEY, *Workers' Co-operatives* (Heinemann, London, 1981)
LABOUR PARTY, *Charter for Co-operatives* and *Charter for Local Enterprise*
(Labour Party, London, 1985)

JOHN BENNINGTON, ADAM SHARPLES, *Local Economy* (London Economic Policy Unit, Issue No1, Spring 1986)
PAUL HARE, *Planning the British Economy* (Macmillan, London, 1985); reviewed in *Economics of Planning* (Feb.1986 issue)
GEOFF HODGSON, *The Democratic Economy* (Pelican, Middlesex, 1984)
ALEC NOVE, *The Economics of Feasible Socialism* (George Allen and Unwin, London, 1983)
BRUCE MCFARLANE, *Economic Planning: Past Trends and New Practices* (Contributions to Political Economy, vol 3, 1984)
JIM TOMLINSON, *The Unequal Struggle: British Socialism and the Capitalist Enterprise* (Methuen, London, 1982)
GEORGE BLAZYCA, *Planning is Good for You: the Case for Popular Control* (Pluto Press, London, 1983)

## Chapter 4: The Right to Paid Work

ANNE PHILLIPS, *Hidden Hands: Women and Economic Policies* (Pluto Press, London, 1983)
MICHAEL BEST, *The Political Economy of Socially Irrational Products* (Cambridge Journal of Economics, vol 6, 1982)
RUDOLF BAHRO, *Socialism and Survival* (Heretic Books, London, 1982)
COLLECTIVE DESIGN, *Very Nice Work If You Can Get It* (Spokesman, Nottingham, 1985)
HUGH STRETTON, *Capitalism, Socialism and the Environment* (Cambridge University Press, Cambridge, 1976)
LABOUR PARTY NATIONAL EXECUTIVE COMMITTEE, *The Socialist Alternative: Statement to 1981 Conference* (Labour Party, London, 1981)
LABOUR PARTY, *Labour's Programme 1982* (Labour Party, London, 1982)
TUC/LABOUR PARTY LIAISON COMMITTEE, *Economic Planning and Industrial Democracy* (TUC/Labour Party, London, 1982)
TUC/LABOUR PARTY LIAISON COMMITTEE, *New Partnership: New Britain* (TUC/Labour Party, London, 1982)

## Chapter 5: Extending Democracy in Industry: The Case for Strategic Planning

GREATER LONDON COUNCIL, *The London Industrial Strategy* (GLC, London, 1985)
MICHAEL BEST, *Strategic Planning and Industrial Policy* (Local Economy, Issue No1, Spring 1986)
WYN GRANT, *The Political Economy of Industrial Policy* (Butterworth, Cambridge University Press, 1982)
COVENTRY, LIVERPOOL, NEWCASTLE AND NORTH TYNESIDE TRADES COUNCILS, *State Intervention in Industry: a Workers' Inquiry* (revised edition) (Spokesman, Nottingham, 1982)
PAUL HARE, *The Preconditions for Effective Planning in the UK* (Socialist Economic Review, Merlin, London, 1983)

STUART HOLLAND, *The Socialist Challenge* (Quartet Books, London, 1975)

SAUL ESTRIN AND PETER HOLMES, *French Planning in Theory and Practice* (George Allen and Unwin, London, 1983)

DAVID MARSDEN ET AL, *The Car Industry: Labour Relations and Industrial Adjustment* (Tavistock Publications, London, 1985)

PAUL WILLIAMS AND GRAHAM WINCH, *Innovation and Management Control: Labour Relations at BL Cars* (Cambridge University Press, Cambridge, 1985)

WOLFGANG STRECK AND ANDREAS HOFF (eds), *Industrial Relations in The World Automobile Industry* (International Institute of Management, Berlin, 1982)

W.W.DANIEL AND NEIL MILLWARD, *Workplace Industrial Relations in Britain* (Heinemann Educational, London, 1983)

WILLIAM BROWN, *The Changing Contours of British Industrial Relations* (Basil Blackwell, Oxford, 1981)

## Chapter 6: Extending Democracy in Industry: Socialist Enterprise

KEN COATES ET AL, *Freedom and Fairness* (Spokesman, Nottingham, 1986)

RICHARD MINNS, *Take Over the City: the Case for Public Ownership of Financial Institutions* (Pluto Press, London, 1982)

ROBERT COHEN, *The Internationalisation of the Auto Industry* (The Society of Automotive Engineers, Technical Paper Series, 1982)

CHRISTOPHER LORENZ, *Beware Japanese Bearing 'Gifts'* (Financial Times, 16 January, 1984)

MICHAEL BRECH AND MARGARET SHARP, *Inward Investment: Policy Options for the United Kingdom* (Chatham House Papers No.21, Routledge and Kegan Paul, 1984)

PARLIAMENTARY SPOKESMANS' WORKING GROUP (John Prescott MP), *Planning for Full Employment* and *The Alternative Regional Strategy*

REGIONAL STUDIES ASSOCIATION, *Report of an Inquiry into Regional Problems in the United Kingdom* (Geo Books, Norwich, 1983)

ANDREW FRIEND AND ANDY METCALFE, *Slump City: the Politics of Mass Unemployment* (Pluto Press, London, 1981)

## Chapter 7: Democratic Control and the State

LONDON EDINBURGH WEEKEND RETURN GROUP, *In and Against the State* (Pluto Press, London, 1980)

## Chapter 8: Beyond Production: Democracy in the Unpaid Sector

MARTIN SMITH, *The Consumer Case for Socialism* (Fabian Society pamphlet, no.513)

ANNA COOTE AND BEATRIX CAMPBELL, *Sweet Freedom* (Picador, London, 1982)

## Case Studies

A. ALTSHULER ET AL, *The Future of the Automobile: the Report of MIT's International Automobile Program* (George Allen and Unwin, London, 1984)

## Chapter 12: The Politics of Socialist Enterprise

KEN COATES ET AL, *Joint Action for Jobs* (Spokesman, Nottingham, 1986)

ANDRE GORZ, *Farewell to the Working Class* (Pluto Press, London, 1982) and *Paths to Paradise* (Pluto Press, London, 1985)

RAYMOND WILLIAMS, *Towards 2000* (Chatto and Windus, London, 1983)

# CONTRIBUTORS

**Diana Gilhespy** *is a trade union research officer.*

**Ken Jones** *is a trade union research officer.*

**Tony Manwaring** *is Political Assistant to the General Secretary of the Labour Party.*

**Henry Neuburger** *is Economic Adviser to Neil Kinnock MP.*

**Adam Sharples** *is Research Officer with the National Union of Public Employees.*

*A new series of publications and meetings on the agenda:*
*21st CENTURY SOCIALISM*

# Joint Action for Jobs
# A New Internationalism

*Edited by Ken Coates, with a foreword by Stuart Weir*

Unemployment is laying Europe waste. With twenty million people out of work, the number of direct victims has become intolerable: a common scandal. But there is every reason to believe that this number is growing steadily, whilst the direct sufferers already include whole populations. Yet there is no reason to believe that unemployment is unavoidable or fore-ordained. A mere fraction of the ingenuity which has transformed our technical capacities could re-arrange our social rules in a way which would guarantee a useful role for all our people.

Of course, action by Governments can improve or worsen this condition. If all or even some of the European Governments were willing to act together in order to reject mass unemployment, there is no doubt that conditions could be radically improved. But this is not a problem which can be left to governments. Because it concerns everybody, it needs action by all of us. The work which is necessary requires us to find ways of joining needs to resources, of restructuring institutions to regain the democratic initiative in the global economy. We must find ways to replace the policies of 'beggar my neighbour' by those which seek instead to 'better my neighbour'.

*"These excellent essays show how vital it is for socialists who wish to have an impact on unemployment to broaden their horizons, and think internationally".*
**Ben Pimlott**

*"Reflecting the thought and experience of those who have already been involved in local enterprise, and building networks to transcend national boundaries, it is an important contribution not only to the debate but to the practical answer to the tens of millions of people without jobs and without the prospect of work in the industrialised world".*
**David Blunkett**

*Paper £4.95*          *ISBN 0 85124 428 9*
*Cloth £17.50*         *ISBN 0 85124 427 0*
*232pp*

**SPOKESMAN**
**Bertrand Russell House, Gamble Street, Nottingham, UK**
**Tel. 0602 708318**

*A new series of publications and meetings on the agenda:*
*21st CENTURY SOCIALISM*

# Freedom and Fairness
# Empowering People at Work

*Edited by Ken Coates, with a foreword by*
*John Prescott MP*

Trade unions in Britain have undergone a double ordeal since 1979. Mass unemployment has diminished their bargaining power in many sectors, often weakening their actual membership, and eroding their funds. At the same time, there has been an unprecedented legal assault calculated to impose many restrictions on union behaviour. These two pressures have forced unions to think and respond politically.

Naturally they hope that a new Labour Government will provide a more favourable economic and social climate. Specifically, they expect that the rights and immunities which have been taken away will be restored in a more reliable form, so they can begin to represent their members effectively again. This has been a matter of intense debate in the TUC and Labour Party. The discussions leading up to the latest documents are carefully charted and considered in *Freedom and Fairness, Empowering People at Work*.

**Contributors:**

| | | |
|---|---|---|
| Stephen Bodington | Roy Green | Jim Mortimer |
| Ken Coates | Stuart Holland MP | Andrew Wilson |
| John Edmonds | John Hughes | |
| Bob Fryer | Emma MacLennan | |

*Paper £4.95*
*Cloth £17.50*
*160pp*

*ISBN 0 85124 450 5*
*ISBN 0 85124 440 8*

**SPOKESMAN (for the Institute for Workers' Control)**
**Bertrand Russell House, Gamble Street, Nottingham, UK**
**Tel. 0602 708318**